The literary relationship of James Joyce and Wyndham Lewis has previously been described in merely biographical terms. In *The fictions of James Joyce and Wyndham Lewis* Scott W. Klein takes Wyndham Lewis's criticism of *Ulysses* in *Time and Western Man* and Joyce's implicit response to Lewis in *Finnegans Wake* as an emblematic opposition signalling significant textual relations within and between the fictions of the two authors. The seeing eye and the world, the creating mind and fiction, language and its aesthetic and political object, and the processes of history: all appear in the work of both Joyce and Lewis, as related thematic structures that raise questions about binarism, dialectic, and the reconciliation of opposites. Detailed examination of key texts by Joyce and Lewis reveals hitherto unperceived affiliations between the two writers, and offers new insight into the politics and aesthetics of modernism.

# THE FICTIONS OF JAMES JOYCE AND WYNDHAM LEWIS

MONSTERS OF NATURE AND DESIGN

# THE FICTIONS OF JAMES JOYCE AND WYNDHAM LEWIS

MONSTERS OF NATURE AND DESIGN

SCOTT W. KLEIN

*Wake Forest University, North Carolina*

Published by the Press Syndicate of the University of Cambridge
The Pitt Building, Trumpington Street, Cambridge, CB2 1RP
40 West 20th Street, New York, NY 10011-4211, USA
10 Stamford Road, Oakleigh, Melbourne 3166, Australia

© Cambridge University Press 1994

First published 1994

Printed in Great Britain at the University Press, Cambridge

*A catalogue record for this book is available from the British Library*

*Library of Congress cataloguing in publication data*
Klein, Scott W.
The fictions of James Joyce and Wyndham Lewis: monsters of nature and design / Scott W. Klein.
p.   cm.
Includes bibliographical references and index.
ISBN 0 521 43452 1 (hardback)
1. Joyce, James, 1882–1941 – Criticism and interpretation.
2. Lewis, Wyndham, 1882–1957 – Criticism and interpretation.
3. English fiction – 20th century – History and criticism.
4. Modernism (Literature) – Great Britain. 5. Influence (Literary, artistic, etc.)
6. Authorship – Collaboration. 7. Intertextuality.
I. Title.
PR6019.09Z676 1994
823'.912 – dc20    93-44793 CIP

ISBN 0 521 43452 1 hardback

*For Karen and Benjamin*

# Contents

| | |
|---|---|
| *Acknowledgements* | *page* xi |
| *List of abbreviations* | xiii |
| Introduction: opposition and representation | 1 |
| 1  The tell-tale Eye | 24 |
| 2  The mirror and the razor | 65 |
| 3  The cracked lookingglass of the master | 113 |
| 4  Minds of the anti-collaborators | 153 |
| Conclusion | 198 |
| *Notes* | 208 |
| *Bibliography* | 242 |
| *Index* | 252 |

# Acknowledgements

A critical book is a palimpsest, through whose present outlines one reads the indelible marks left by others. My most profound thanks go to Ian Duncan and Harry Segal, who read and commented upon drafts at various stages of composition. Catherine Burroughs and Jahan Ramazani brought their specialties to bear upon individual chapters, making available useful critical leads and valuably different perspectives. I owe a debt of gratitude also to Stephen Lacey, who deserves much of the credit for the collegial atmosphere in the Department of English at Cornell College, where I wrote much of the first version of this study; our discussions about Shakespeare and Freud pale only before that gift of warmth. All provided me with the sustenance of rigorous intelligence, heartfelt encouragement, and innumerable suggestions for improvement. They will recognize the impress of their signatures here.

Others helped in professional capacities. J. Hillis Miller advised the dissertation at Yale that was the basis of this book, and I owe much to his generosity and critical example. Harriet Chessman, Paul Frye, and Jennifer Wicke read that earlier manuscript, and helped me frame and refine my argument. More recently John Paul Riquelme and Derek Attridge have offered encouragement and cogent suggestions for revision. I am grateful to the College and Graduate School of Wake Forest University, which supported this project in the form of a summer research grant. Parts of the first two chapters have appeared in slightly different forms in the journals *Twentieth Century Literature* and the *James Joyce Quarterly*, and I thank the editors of both journals for permission to reprint this material. I also gratefully acknowledge Omar Pound for rights to quote from the works of Wyndham Lewis, (c) the Wyndham Lewis Memorial Trust, by permission, and the Society of Authors, the Trustees of the Estate of James Joyce, Random House, Inc., and Jonathan Cape, publisher, for permission to quote from the Gabler edition of *Ulysses*, (c) Random House, Inc., 1986, and from the other works of James Joyce.

In *Ulysses* Stephen Dedalus berates Buck Mulligan with a telegram reading "the sentimentalist is he who would enjoy without incurring the immense debtorship for a thing done." Rather than stand so accused, I must also acknowledge my immense debtorship to my parents, Norman and Sonya Klein. Their love and support over the years have provided me with fundamental opportunities without which this book could not exist; these thanks can be only meager repayment. Finally, to my wife Karen, who supported me unwaveringly through this work's prolonged creation and lent her considerable professional skills as editor and proofreader at every stage, my debtorship exceeds even the author's traditional claim of insufficient ability to acknowledge. While she shares the dedication with our son Benjamin, the whole is for her, with love.

# Abbreviations

**WORKS BY JAMES JOYCE**

*FW*    *Finnegans Wake*. New York: The Viking Press, 1939. References indicate page and line number; for section II.ii footnotes are indicated by "F" and note number; right and left side notes are indicated by "R" or "L" and order on page.

*P*    *A Portrait of the Artist as a Young Man*. New York: The Viking Press, 1975.

*U*    *Ulysses: The Corrected Text*, ed. Hans Walter Gabler. New York: Random House, 1986. References indicate chapter and line number.

**WORKS BY WYNDHAM LEWIS**

*AG*    *The Apes of God*. Santa Barbara: Black Sparrow Press, 1981.

*B*    *Blast*, ed. Wyndham Lewis. No. 1, June 1914; No.2, July 1915. Reprinted Santa Barbara: Black Sparrow Press, 1981. References to the two issues are indicated as *B*1 and *B*2 followed by page number. Obvious misprints in the original are corrected.

*MWA*    *Men Without Art*. London: Cassell and Company Ltd., 1934.

*T*    *Tarr* (1928 version). Harmondsworth, Middlesex: Penguin Books, 1982.

*TWM*    *Time and Western Man*. New York: Harcourt, Brace and Company, 1928.

*WB*    *The Complete Wild Body*, ed. Bernard Lafourcade. Santa Barbara: Black Sparrow Press, 1982.

# Introduction: *opposition and representation*

> In the struggle today between the infinite number of modes that have been successively accumulated in the practice of modern painting, an older and more permanent struggle has been forgotten. I refer to the opposition between the methods of those painters who devoured Nature to feed a restless Monster of Design within them; and those who, on the other hand, offered their talents upon the altar of the Monster Nature; which talents, after absorption into the body of this mechanism, refused to be digested, and led a precarious and sometimes glorious existence in its depths.
>
> Wyndham Lewis, "Prevalent Design"

> [S]urely to be double and to be 2 are not the same.
>
> Aristotle, *Metaphysics*, 987a

Nature and design: As Wyndham Lewis argues in his 1919 essay "Prevalent Design," the two are the poles of representational procedure. To surrender to the first is to cede control to pure content; to insist upon the other is to master nature's content within the pure figurations of form. Yet the two are not benign opposites. Within Lewis's rhetoric, nature and design are the subjects and objects of struggle, alternately predator and prey. The artist devours or is devoured, and is master or victim of a representational procedure that is figured as the division of monster against equivalent monster. Such is the vision of opposition, simultaneously Darwinian and Manichaean, that typifies Lewis's work in all of its rhetorical forms: painting, fiction, and artistic and ideological polemics. Throughout his extensive career Lewis divided and subdivided experience into patterns of opposition rooted in the painter's stance of mastery towards the perceived object. He set the ego against everything in the world that was in perceived defiance of the ego. Lewis's work develops a theory of proclaimed unity – particularly of the self and of the image – that finds its strength in the artist's ontological posture towards the world, and survives through its recognition and establishment of difference.

This adherence to opposition provided Lewis with both subject matter and a program for his position towards others. The most powerful, and surely the best known, of these oppositions was Lewis's championship of space in aesthetics against time. For Lewis form equaled spatiality, and he claimed that this philosophic fissure divided him irreconcilably from the prevalent practices of modernism, in virulent criticism of which he was matched only by Georg Lukács. The modernists were obsessed with temporality, according to Lewis, and their representational assumptions were based upon a faulty ontology that accepted flux as the source and end of being. The supreme literary representative of this obsession was James Joyce. In his famous attack on *Ulysses* in *Time and Western Man*, Lewis charged Joyce with valorizing temporality at the expense of concrete form in narrative, and of surrendering to a Bergsonian vision of reality that dangerously typified the modern intellect. The assumption of this vision, which Lewis also saw as implicit in the works of Proust, led Joyce to the "very nightmare of the naturalistic method" (*TWM*, 91). To adhere to temporality was to cling to the things of the world that were exclusive of artistic ordering: to cede control to nature rather than design. *Ulysses* presented a universe open to all sensory and psychological phenomena, and as such was the opposite of true art. Joyce left what was perceived by his characters unshaped, thereby nullifying the meaning of what they experienced. Moreover, since Joyce paid more attention to style than to the content of his representations, which Lewis considered excessive, traditional, and sentimental, the work as a whole deflected attention from the conservatism of its materials onto the extrinsic experimentation of its styles. "What stimulates him," Lewis writes, "is *ways of doing things*, and technical processes, and not *things to be done*" (*TWM*, 90). Like Picasso, Joyce fell prey to what Lewis called early in his career "the perpetual peril of virtuosity" (*B*1, 145). The combination of this lack of shaping and fetishism of style led both to the fragmentation of characters' personalities and to a false creation of the artistic self through an Eliotic delusion:

> In *Ulysses* we find on the surface the naturalist tradition of a scientific "impersonality." But the "time," the "mental," – the telling-from-the-inside-method – makes it gravitate everywhere on to the ego of the author, to the confusion of the naturalist machinery pulled out and set going for nothing. (*TWM*, 262–63)

By surrendering to the monster of Nature, according to Lewis, Joyce succeeded only in creating the modern self, fragmented and passive in the face of the perceptual world.

Lewis's critical reaction to Joyce is significant, for it signals textual relationships in both authors' work whose formal and thematic importance well exceeds the attention they have been granted hitherto. Joyce took Lewis's criticism seriously. He admitted that Lewis's was the best hostile criticism written about *Ulysses*, but complained to Frank Budgen: "Allowing that the whole of what Lewis says about my book is true, is it more than ten per cent of the truth?"[1] Joyce, in turn, sought his own revenge by parodying Lewis in *Finnegans Wake*, recasting his one-time friend as a significant component of Shaun, his "everdevoting fiend" (*FW*, 408.18). Such exchanges have served as useful footnotes to elucidations of *Finnegans Wake*, for the relationship between Joyce and Lewis has remained for critics largely a matter of biographical and literary anecdote. Yet these biographical exchanges point to a larger dynamic within both Lewis's and Joyce's writings. Ever the truculent partisan of duality, Lewis cast Joyce as his aesthetic opponent, explicitly in his criticism and implicitly in his own massive fictions, particularly *The Apes of God*. And rather than ignoring this challenge – the artist's likely response to noisome criticism – Joyce entered into the argument. Where Lewis declared his separation from the mainstream of modernism, Joyce refused to allow that separation to remain unquestioned. Lewis becomes, as literary archetype, a fundamental aspect of Joyce's last work.

Why that should be so is the express question posed by the present work, which takes Lewis's self-declared dichotomy between "space" and "time" not as the singular determining factor that sets Lewis off from Joyce, but rather as an exemplary pair of oppositions standing for the inclusive dichotomies that define both their aesthetic projects. Opposition, rather than the simply western or "logocentric" structure discovered everywhere by post-structuralist thought, is a particularly enabling figuration for Joycean and Lewisian representation. Both authors make opposition an explicit structural principle in their work, as a source of thematic conflict and as an intrinsic aspect of form. The seeing eye and the world, the creating mind and fiction, representational language and its aesthetic or political object, and the processes of history: all appear within Lewis's and Joyce's work, albeit in variable combinations and with differing emphases, as structural centers around which both authors explore fundamental questions of binarism, dialectic, and the reconciliation of opposites.

These structures are by no means unproblematic. One may see irresolution in Lewis's statement on the struggle between the artists of nature and design, written in 1919 but already demonstrating the aesthetic purview that would later take Joyce as its ideal adversary. While Lewis condemned Joyce for his unmediated apprehension of the things of the world, Lewis was best known to his admiring contemporaries as a painterly and writerly stylist *per se*. For Pound he was "one of the greatest masters of design yet born in the Occident," for Eliot "the greatest prose master of style of my generation."[2] Yet Lewis's description of the monsters of nature and design contains a representative and proleptic paradox. "Monstrousness" is by definition unnatural, a distortion of a norm. To declare nature itself to be monstrous is to emulate Lear in dramatic contradiction, eliding the context by which monstrousness itself can be known. The idea of a "monster of design" is similarly ambiguous. If the alternative to the "monster nature" is to feed a monster of design within oneself, then design becomes by definition a distortion rather than a truthful representation, a "monstrous" recasting of the unmediated nature without.

## Introduction: opposition and representation

What is external becomes organic, design subsumed within the presumably natural processes of the body.

Lewis's metaphor of opposition thus reveals in each of its halves a paradoxical aesthetic. The first artist may devour nature in order to digest it into design, but the monstrousness of form refines that original nature out of existence. The second artist sacrifices the self to an alien nature, but he imports organism into "mechanism," living rather than dying within its distorting embrace. In either case, that which is set out as oppositional is rhetorically implicated in its antithesis. In one case the artist imports nature within the bounds of the self, and organism becomes the site of design. In the other, the self is imported within the bounds of nature, but design flourishes within the nature that presumably devours it. Lewis compromises the autonomies of nature and design even as he rhetorically establishes their "struggle." One adheres within the other as a sign of its own rhetorical disfiguration or "monstrousness," organism and mechanism circling one another in restless prowl.

Lewis notes this elsewhere. In a somewhat later study he writes:

According to present arrangements, in the presence of nature the artist or writer is almost always apriorist... he tends to lose his powers of observation (which, through reliance upon external nature, in the classical ages gave him freedom) altogether... So he takes his nature, in practice, from theoretic fields, and resigns himself to see only what conforms to his syllabus of patterns. He deals with the raw life, thinks he sees arabesques in it; but in fact the arabesques that he sees more often than not emanate from his theoretic borrowing, he has put them there.[3]

What seems to be nature in mimesis may actually be design, a sign that theory has imposed upon observational practice. What is set out as a duality emerges as a problematic interrelationship between the self and what lies beyond the self: an interrelationship that Lewis implicates thematically with representation.

This is typical, as the pages that follow will show, of Lewis's aesthetic and fictional rhetoric, in which the subject's quest for unity – of the observer, of the authoritative and authoritarian voice – coexists uneasily with his recognition of the role played in potential unities by the doubleness of opposition. "I prefer *one* thing," Lewis declared to the Italian futurist Marinetti,[4] and he spent a career of painting and writing dedicated to capturing a unity that remains defined by its paradoxical internal and external doubleness. In *Time and Western Man* Lewis wrote "action is impossible without an *opposite* – 'it takes two to make a quarrel'" (*TWM*, 21). If observer and observed must struggle as indistinct opposites, so must the singular artist guarantee his strength by choosing and defining his antagonist.

Lewis's desire for both "one thing" and engagement with the problematics of multiplicity provide the rationale for exploring his relationship with Joyce. Joyce, like Lewis, was deeply concerned with the thematics of unity and multiplicity, particularly as these issues merged with theological and philosophical speculation about the nature of the reconciliation of opposites. The status of the Trinity, which obsesses Stephen throughout *Ulysses*, and the disposition of Stephen and Bloom as opposite yet substitutive characters (most comically as they become "Blephen" and "Stoom" in the "Ithaca" chapter of *Ulysses* [*U*, 17.549–51]) point to Joyce's larger fascination with issues of opposition, which are recalled philosophically in his work through the ideas of Aristotle and Giordano Bruno. Yet Stephen's contemplations, like Lewis's description of nature and design, provide a doubled source of paradox. Stephen erects irreconcilable visions of the Trinity in his consideration of the heresiarchs Arius and Sabellius. In attempting to determine the relationship between the persons of the Trinity he tries to solve the logically impossible task of choosing between a simultaneous unity and diversity, an impossibility that, as we shall see, has reverberations for *Ulysses* as a whole. Aristotle and Bruno, moreover, are themselves figures of an irreconcilable intellectual opposition. Aristotle states in the *Metaphysics* "contraries are the principles of things,"[5] but offers no overarching reconciliation of these contraries. For Bruno, on the other hand, oppositions come into being precisely to resolve themselves. As Joyce quoted from Bruno in a letter: "Every power in nature must evolve an opposite in order to realize itself and opposition brings reunion."[6] The coincidence of Aristotle and Bruno in Joyce's thought is itself irreconcilable. It marks out the importance of contraries while establishing a second-order opposition in their place. Each philosopher insists upon the existence of contraries while establishing a vision of the nature of opposition that is irreconcilable with its own opposite.

These Joycean juxtapositions, like that of "nature" with "design" for Lewis, are examples of the larger issues represented within each author's work. That such oppositions are central to both Lewis and Joyce is not a novel observation. The reconciliation of contraries is, after all, one of the things *Finnegans Wake* is famously "about," while one of Lewis's earliest critics, Hugh Porteus, noted "In all Mr. Lewis's work it is possible to trace the presence of a conflict between two opposite principles," continuing to compare Lewis's treatment of character to Joyce's separation of his own creative self into the "intellectual" Stephen and the "sensualist" Bloom.[7] The counterbalance of oppositions in both Lewis's and Joyce's work, however, suggests a concomitant and problematic reflection of their own artistic opposition. Lewis considered Joyce to be his opponent or "Enemy," while Joyce made Lewis, in *Finnegans Wake*, an idiosyncratic and archetypal figure of aesthetic conflict. The relationship of thematic and stylistic oppositions within Lewis's and Joyce's texts can thus be taken as a reflection or measure of the announced philosophical opposition of their respective aesthetic projects, an opposition that can be traced throughout their works.

The patterns of these works are in some respects parallel, although in the first instances coincidentally so. Joyce's and Lewis's earliest fictions derive from similar concerns about art and selfhood. Both *Stephen Hero* and *Blast* treat problems of mediation between the artist and the world, the championship of the Classical versus the Romantic temper, and the elevation of individual talent above the levelling mass considerations of nationalism and politics.[8] Both authors began their mature careers with collections of stories rooted in the ethos of a particular place; the Dublin of *Dubliners* finds its counterpart in the Breton that serves as setting for Lewis's *The Wild Body*. Their first significant novels, *A Portrait of the Artist as a Young Man* and *Tarr*, autobiographically based novels about young artists, were serialized in *The Egoist*, *A Portrait* appearing from February 1914 to September 1915, and *Tarr* following from April 1916 to November 1917. There coincidence ends. Lewis intentionally challenges Joyce's *Ulysses* with *The Apes of God*, a massive fiction that satirizes the artistic world of London. And as drafts of *Finnegans Wake* appeared in the 1930s, Lewis further responded in kind with *The Childermass*. In this work Lewis transforms Joyce's landscape of the dreaming mind into a different vision of a world beyond the known world, a surreal plain of the afterlife born from the embers of the First World War. Lewis's most important fictions, in other words, are in large part parodic responses to Joyce. *The Apes of God* is a kind of anti-*Ulysses*, which attempts to put into fictional practice a revisionary theory of modernist representation, satirizing Joyce's achievements and deflating the pretensions of Bloomsbury. *The Childermass* adds a share of *ad hominem* criticism to literary parody. James Pullman, its protagonist, had taught at the Berlitz in Trieste, breaks his glasses when pushed over, and "never looks at the objects of his solicitude but busies himself in the abstract."[9] He is a patent portrait of Joyce as Lewis understood him, while Lewis's gnome-like and authoritarian antagonist, the Bailiff, spouts paragraphs of pseudo-Wakean nonsense as part of his erratic rule of the other world. When Joyce satirized Lewis in *Finnegans Wake*, Lewis earned such treatment through more than his comments on *Ulysses* in *Time and Western Man*.

The importance of these parallelisms was not lost on their contemporaries, who thought of Joyce and Lewis together as the most experimental prose stylists of their time. Ezra Pound wrote in 1920 "the English prose fiction of my decade is the work of this pair of authors."[10] Such contemporary literary judgements are historically suspect – after all, John Ruskin loudly championed the poetry of Charles Kingsley over that of Pope – yet Pound's grouping of Lewis and Joyce persists in studies of modernism as a truism about antagonism, if not about their

## Introduction: opposition and representation

subjects' literary value.[11] Less well recognized is the importance of Lewis to the shape of Joycean criticism, which may be with some justice traced to Lewis's essay on *Ulysses*. Lewis's argument was not new in every aspect. While he emphasized that *Ulysses*' shapelessness was a function of its Romantic abandonment to the ravages of Time, commentators had previously complained about Joyce's lack of formal rigor. Richard Aldington, in a 1921 review of *Ulysses* in *The English Review*, bewailed *Ulysses*' chaotic presentation and its seeming lack of classical order. In "*Ulysses*, Order and Myth" (1923) T. S. Eliot explicitly countered Aldington's strictures, and by emphasizing the work's continuous parallel with the *Odyssey* stressed that the apparent formlessness masks a rigorous and new form of "classicism," in which myth provides a possible structure for the aimlessness of contemporary history.[12]

Only when Lewis published "An Analysis of the Mind of James Joyce" in *The Enemy* (1927) and reprinted it the following year in *Time and Western Man* did defense of Joyce begin in earnest and neatly chronological response. Joyce authorized the earliest books on his work, and they are as much defensive manifestoes as critical analyses. The first, *Our Exagmination Round His Factification for Incamination of Work in Progress*, a collection of essays written on behalf of the emergent *Finnegans Wake*, appeared in 1929. The abundance of its attacks against Lewis, and its appearance the year after *Time and Western Man*, suggests a more than casual relationship between Lewis's analysis – which included criticisms of the sections of *Work in Progress* then appearing in serialization – and Joyce's self-organized defense.

This exchange had lasting critical ramifications. The timing and thematic emphases of Stuart Gilbert's *James Joyce's "Ulysses"* (1930) and Frank Budgen's *James Joyce and the Making of "Ulysses"* (1934) suggest that they were further attempts to counter Lewis's aggressive voice. Concentrating on the structural elements of *Ulysses*, Gilbert's study expands Eliot's defense of "classicism" of design at book length. Joyce's unusual patience with Gilbert's interrogations and with his excessive attention to esoteric themes suggests that Joyce desired a more substantial document than Eliot's to stand testimony to the rigor of his fictional techniques against accusations of Bergsonianism. Budgen's work presents itself more directly as a response to Lewis. Lewis's name appears periodically: Joyce asks Budgen whether he knows Lewis's painting during their first meeting, and when Budgen insists during a later discussion of characterization in *Ulysses* that "Bloom is a Jew but he is no stage Jew," he is responding, without explicitly naming his predecessor, to an objection from *Time and Western Man*.[13] Budgen explicitly calls Lewis to task for describing Stephen Dedalus as priggish and objectionable. However, his unlikely rejoinder that Stephen is as sympathetic as Dostoyevsky's Stavrogin resonates fully not only within the general context of literary England, where Constance Garnett's translations had recently made Dostoyevsky available as the new measure of psychological fiction, but in the specific context of Rebecca West's review of *Tarr*. There she compared the novel to Dostoyevsky and notes, with reference to the character Kreisler, "it contains one figure of vast moral significance which is worthy to stand beside Stavrogin."[14] Budgen acts as advocate for Joyce by counterbalancing West's claims for Lewis.

These corrections are symptomatic of Budgen's general reaction to Lewis. Mixing explicit rejoinder with implicit qualification, he claims that Joyce's works live up to Lewis's aesthetic expectations rather than questioning the validity of Lewis's critical categories. This tendency to correct Lewis within his own terms provides a possible solution to the question of why Joyce's initial skepticism about Budgen's project gave way to active endorsement. Budgen, like Lewis, was a working painter and was able to marshal an advocate's case for Joyce as a literary critic could not. His technical perspective on *A Portrait* and *Ulysses* allowed him to laud their visual virtues against the implicit pressure of Lewis's painterly critique; Budgen thus attempted to establish Joyce's visual allegiances and legitimize his continuity with the continental avant-garde. According to Budgen Joyce's technical choices are based in space. Bloom stands alternatively in the "middle distance" and the "foreground plane" of *Ulysses* (65). *A Portrait* blends the conservative vision of the academy with the perspective of the newly emerged geometrician, written "across a space of time as the landscape painter paints distant hills, looking at them through a cube of air-filled space, painting, that is to say, not that which is, but that which appears to be" (60–61). Time is spatialized. The "cube" of space emerges in a conversation in which Budgen calls the "Cyclops" chapter of *Ulysses* Cubist rather than Futurist in style – associating the writing with techniques of modernist spatiality rather than modernist flux (153) – and Budgen emphasizes throughout the degree to which Joyce's characters and techniques avoid the temporal labels assigned them by Lewis. As an advertising canvasser, Budgen declares, Bloom is a "spacehound" (93), while Joyce's work is sculptural like that of Rodin (90). Most forcefully, Budgen argues that despite Joyce's valuation of music above other arts – a taste which Lewis satirizes in his 1920s drawing of Joyce "The Duc de Joyeux Sings" – Joyce concocts canvases rather than scores: "his view of life is that of a painter surveying a still scene rather than that of a musician following a development through time" (153).

These attempts to recuperate Joyce within Lewis's painterly categories are underlined by remnants of satiric rhetoric in Budgen's prose. While the initial reviewers of *Ulysses* gestured towards satire and naturalism to make generic sense of Joyce's treatment of his Dublin characters, by the early 1930s such gestures had been largely subsumed within more flexible criteria. However, when Budgen announces that Blazes Boylan is a "comic automaton" (67), notes that adultery is a "mechanical and grotesque incident in marriage" (71), and states that *Ulysses* shows the "grim, noiseless laughter which shines out through the eyes of a mask" (72), he imports the vocabulary of dehumanization into *Ulysses* through Lewis's idiosyncratic language. "Grotesque," "mask," "grim laughter," and "automaton" are compulsive terms from the worlds of *Tarr* and *The Apes of God*. One need not press the evidence too tenaciously to suggest that in defending *Ulysses* against the criticisms of his painterly forerunner, Budgen attempted to recuperate Joyce's art as satire precisely as Lewis was concurrently championing satire as the necessary corollary of realism.

Budgen's response was not idiosyncratic. Harry Levin's *James Joyce*: "*A Critical Introduction*" (1941), published over a decade after *Time and Western Man*, is similarly unable to free itself from Lewis's critical example. Levin blames Lewis's "malice" for comparing Bloom's interior monologue to the prose patterns of Mr. Jingle in Dickens's *Pickwick Papers*, and then proceeds to make the same comparison, distancing himself from Lewis while repeating his insight.[15] Levin compares Joyce with the Elizabethan writer Thomas Nashe without mentioning that Lewis had previously compared the same two unlikely figures, and when he notes that the philosopher Bergson "also held that the intellect 'spatializes'" one cannot but recognize an implicit response to Lewis's accusation that Joyce was dedicated to Bergson and that Bergson was exclusively interested by temporality.[16] When Richard M. Kain in *Fabulous Voyager: James Joyce's "Ulysses"* (1947) compares Joyce to Swift and Bloom's wanderings to those of Gulliver, Candide, and Rasselas, it does not take further references to the "cubistic arrangements" of *Ulysses* or even Kain's attempts to redirect critical attention from technique towards the book's human drama to see the persistent influence of Lewis's satiric and painterly categories upon later commentary.[17]

Lewis's haunting of the criticism of the 1930s and 1940s reaches its apotheosis in the work of Hugh Kenner. Kenner's investigations of Joyce almost invariably begin with Lewis's criticisms of Joyce. In *Dublin's Joyce* (1956), he takes seriously Lewis's essay – which he calls "the most brilliant misreading in modern criticism"[18] – in order to contest Lewis's conclusions about Joyce while building upon his insights. When he equates realism and cliché in *Dublin's Joyce* Kenner draws on Lewis as does Budgen, accepting Lewis's categories but reversing his diagnoses. *Joyce's Voices* (1978) bases one of its most noteworthy ideas upon a counter-reading of Lewis's analysis of a passage from *A Portrait of the Artist*, while the book's overarching thesis, that realism eventually becomes distortion and parody, owes much to Lewis's later formulations of the relationship between representation and satire.[19] To clinch the association, Kenner flourishes Lewis's vocabulary throughout his criticism. He calls both Aquinas and Charles Bovary the "Dumb Ox;" the Joycean artist and then Bloom and Stephen considered together are a "split man;" Richard Hand in *Exiles* is "the ape of God."[20] Kenner's career-long nods towards Lewis suggests the central power of Lewis's ironic and skeptical reading of *Ulysses*, an approach that Derek Attridge and Daniel Ferrer further singled out in the 1980s as an early non-recuperative vision of Joyce whose emphasis on the disjunctions between narrative form and content "leads directly to [the] current preoccupations" of post-structuralism.[21]

Lewis's status as negative reader of Joyce may be taken as indicative of a larger history of oppositional disagreement that has consistently shifted its valency, if not its tenacity, in the decades that separate *Time and Western Man* from the introduction of French theory to the literary academy. Our foray into Joycean metacriticism has followed out merely one strand of a complex tapestry of exegesis. *Ulysses* in particular at different times has been viewed as optimistic and as pessimistic, as naturalistic and as symbolic, as a testament to the wholeness of the world and as testament to its fragmentation (which is also to say as theological and as anti-theological), and, most recently, as a deconstructive site for the proliferation of signs and as a hyperrealist project that can only be fully understood when grounded in the social and cultural world of its production. Criticism attempting to explain the coexistence of these dichotomous schools of interpretation, in a sense opened up for analysis by Lewis's essay, has turned outside Joyce for its recuperative models.[22]

To explore Lewis's and Joyce's treatment of opposition and reconciliation is thus to establish what there is in Joyce's texts that not only invites conflicting interpretations, but actively demands them. With Lewis's work the challenge is different. The critical literature about Lewis is not so much oppositional as unfocused. The strongest modern critics of Lewis, Hugh Kenner and Fredric Jameson, have issued a challenge that has had, until recently, few takers. And as seems appropriate for a literary figure with such a constructed rhetorical persona, the figure of Lewis emerging from each critic is different, often dichotomously so. For one he is a satirist and author of fiction whose claims as novelist are slight, while for another he is a novelist first and foremost.[23] For Kenner he is the "Man from Nowhere," a figure of constructed personae whose self-contradictions are elided or subsumed under his rhetorically provisional self-creations, while for Jameson he is the political modernist *par excellence*, whose contradictions are part and parcel of his ferocious political reaction, which itself demands to be read against the grain as an unfortunate corollary of modernism's finest insight into the processes of a modern social collectivity.[24] With each Lewis comes a different canon of his work, selected to support each reconstruction. Jameson reads *The Childermass* and the remainder of *The Human Age* as the central document of Lewis's artistic achievement while dismissing *The Apes of God* and paying scant attention to the period of *Blast*. For some critics *Tarr* is a central text, while *The Revenge for Love* marks a stylistic retreat; for others *The Revenge for Love* is a central work while *Tarr* is deeply flawed. If Joyce has attracted an oppositional canon of literary criticism, Lewis has been constructed by what criticism exists as an oppositional canon himself. While excellent critical work exists, including significant treatments of Lewis's relations with Pound, seldom do scholars consider Lewis in the company of the other modernists who recognized him as one of the most compelling voices of his generation. Instead, too often Lewis emerges as an ideological or psychological case rather than as a writer of creative prose, partitioned off from his peers because of personal idiosyncrasies and disturbing political opinions.[25]

My analysis is not innocent of psychoanalysis and ideological investigation. These are essential tools for studying an author whose ideas about public life are everywhere on the surface of his writings, and whose conception of self is inseparable from the actions of his characters, who are frequently arrayed within his fictions in dizzyingly ironic *mise en abyme*. The Lewis I have constructed here (whom I hope may be justly confused with the reality of his work) is indebted to the example of Jameson, the first critic of Lewis not to minimize his self-consciously ideological identity or the contradictions of his polemical and fictional personae. Yet the Lewis I trace is particularly the writer and aesthetic thinker whose style and ideological engagement leads him into direct confrontation with Joycean practice, and as such is best represented by works outside Jameson's purview. For this reason *Tarr*, which in its 1928 version is Lewis's finest novel, remains only implicit throughout and behind my argument, while *The Childermass* lies only implicitly ahead. This study deals with the radical manifestoes of *Blast* and with *The Apes of God* as representative documents of Lewis's emergent modernism and as twin pivots for a career that shifted its emphases from aesthetics to politics as its oppositional techniques became more variegated. Not that the two are ever separate. In *Men Without Art* Lewis writes "Implicit in the serious work of art will be found politics, theology, philosophy – in brief all the great intellectual departments of the human consciousness" (*MWA*, 9). I take Lewis at his word here, keeping in mind his frequent emphasis upon the relationship of surface and depth, a distinction with political as well as aesthetic import. Implicit in all of Lewis's work is a tension between the desire to create and imagine a world made of pure surface, an aesthetic which clashes with his announced critical project "to look *behind* everything, however trivial, in the art-field" (*MWA*, 9) for its social and political content.

Political content is where my study concludes. As early as the 1920s, Lewis viewed Joyce as an artist whose work had profound ideological ramifications, and his insight has taken decades to reclaim. Much has changed since Lionel Trilling could include Joyce among modern writers for whom political issues were a matter of indifference.[26] Since that time critics have done much to restore to view the political materials of Joyce's reading and life, and have in different ways recontextualized Joyce's work within public culture, arguing for the radical potentials of Joyce's language, the complexity of its interrelations with its contemporary world, and its negotiation of aestheticism and materialist culture.[27] Scholarship has rediscovered a Joyce alive to the nationalist and political movements of his day, redefining his work as anything but the solipsistic withdrawal from public discourse perceived by its earliest critics. The political nature of Lewis's work, while always more apparent, is also more controversial. In emphasizing the ideological dimensions of others' art, sometimes despairingly so, Lewis implicitly demands that his project be evaluated in his own terms. Yet there are dangers in so doing. Lewis's aesthetic and philosophical radicalism stands uncomfortably aside from his political authoritarianism. While this paradox is exemplary rather than unique to Anglo-American modernism – one thinks of Pound, Eliot, Yeats, and Lawrence – it is nowhere more available as intellectual dilemma than in Lewis's writings. Critics are hard pressed to negotiate its difficulties. The temptation is equally pressing to elide the difficulty of the symptomology altogether, a tactic chosen by many of Lewis's early admirers, or alternately, to make the contradiction central to an analysis that puts technique at loggerheads with content. Jameson's work on Lewis, for instance, has been compared by Edward W. Said to Lukács's essays on Balzac. Said finds in both progressive critics who discover politically redemptive value, one presumes disingenuously, in qualities of style – avant-garde innovation for Lewis, naturalist social observation for Balzac – that are antithetical to the expressed political views of their subject authors.[28] One might add that in so doing, Jameson adopts Lewis's mode and turns it against its creator, for Lewis performed the same kind of ideological analysis of Joyce, separating the progressive "craftsman" of *Ulysses* against the conservatism of its content, discerning ideological ramifications in style as well as content. Critics less skillful than Jameson must be on guard to avoid falling into dichotomies shaped by Lewis but lacking his complexity, positioning style and form as purely aesthetic phenomena against political content, which is postulated as immanent in history or materiality. Those who have diagnosed and bridged the full complexity of these dichotomies have tended to evaluate Lewis's writing and art against the compelling backdrop of intellectual and political history, their emphases, however, falling strongly upon the latter.[29]

This work reverses those priorities. Although recent criticism of Joyce and Lewis properly foregrounds their enmeshment in intellectual and social history – diachronically, if one will, a method most uncongenial at least to Lewis – the two authors were not, except for Lewis in his discursive writing, firstly documentarians of their age. Their initial and abiding concern was for aesthetic problems, and their most interesting visual and prose work is rooted in investigations of representation and selfhood. This is certainly true of the period from before the First World War to around 1930, my focus for Lewis in this work, although my chronology for Joyce extends to 1939 to include *Finnegans Wake*. I seek to redress the balance of recent inquiry, which has too often divided historical and political issues from linguistic considerations, treating literature first as an object of cultural study, responding only secondarily to the formal features that distinguish literature as something other than social artifact. I contend that linguistic and philosophic criticism need not wear synchronic blinders, but can reveal affiliations between the formal and material aspects of its objects of study. While I attempt to avoid the limitations of a purely aestheticist or a purely materialist analysis, many of my presumptions derive from post-structuralism, in the belief that what is a formalist *cul de sac* to its detractors may be instead an analytic tool of considerable flexibility and weight.

There are compelling reasons for pursuing such models in the exploration of Joyce and Lewis. Their pervasive attention to binarisms and their stance as a writerly pair make them particularly fruitful subjects for post-Hegelian inquiry: their works attend to the oscillations of opposites even as the authors themselves hold one another at arm's length and utilize each other's insights in sometimes surprising ways. Both Joyce and Lewis make philosophic problems of authorship, and the relation of consciousness to the symbols it creates, central to their fictions, and they insist within their work upon the integrity of the subject, while they antithetically demonstrate its fragmentation. Most generally, post-structuralism offers a gestural vocabulary that allows purchase on modernism's most central concerns. Paul de Man has argued against reductively equating creativity and analysis, averring that the twentieth century cannot be divided into an actively modernist period followed by a reflective theoretical modernism that replaces the first as parasite.[30] Yet it does not reduce or equate the two to note that Joyce's influence upon Jacques Derrida (which will at times be a tributary subtext of my argument) and the Surrealists' influence upon Jacques Lacan are well established. To use their theories in analyzing the works whose ideas ultimately gave them birth is not to step outside of literature and impose something foreign upon it, but rather to return ideas to the grounds of their origination. The relation between abstraction and origination is central to my analyses, particularly as that relation becomes embodied and complicated in language. It is commonplace to note that language in modernist works foregrounds its own disjunction from the ultimate knowability of truth or the external word. In Conrad's *Lord Jim*, language is the last fragile cover over the Irrational, while in Lawrence's *Women in Love* it is a "dumb show," distinct from meaning but all that can stand in its place.[31] Apostrophized as salvation from the abyss of unreason, or decried as a failed approach to reason itself, the problem of symbolic referentiality is my first concern in analysis of *Blast* and *Ulysses*. Yet while I utilize some classic post-structural categories in exploring these texts – distinctions between voice and writing, the fragmentation of selfhood, and the relationship between language and desire – it is with the understanding that these potentially hermetic concerns finally open from the text into the world. In *The Apes of God* and *Finnegans Wake*, Lewis and Joyce ultimately articulate these themes with one another as literary predecessors and characters, and with politics as an analogous structure.

These mutual articulations border upon collaboration, although Joyce and Lewis were not collaborators in any literal sense. Lewis "blessed" Joyce in the first issue of *Blast*, and later promised to include Joyce's work in a planned revival of his journal *The Tyro*, but they never ultimately co-wrote, edited, or published one another's work. Yet Joyce and Lewis were pervasively present to one another as anxious competitors, and if they kept their professional distance outside the pages of their books, they were nonetheless what I call after *Finnegans Wake* "anticollaborators" (*FW*, 118.25), a neologism, coined in the charged atmosphere of the 1930s, that reverberates with chilling political connotations. To what degree is this nomenclature valid, even where collaboration is qualified by a negating prefix? In the preface to *The Playboy of the Western World* Joyce's countryman Synge claims that all art is collaboration.[32] This is commonsensically true, insofar as an author's work participates in the shared language and culture of his contemporaries. In Joyce's and Lewis's case my focus is narrower. I do not in the first instance emphasize their shared body of historical experience, nor do I concern myself exclusively with gathering intertextual references. Instead, I explore the ways in which Joyce and Lewis mined similar veins of aesthetic ideas and structural forms, separately at first but later taking one another's work as implicit and explicit subjects in their fictions. And if I use the term "fiction" to encompass the various anti-collaborative works under discussion, from *Blast*'s journal through *The Apes of God*'s picaresque satire to the generically anomalous *Ulysses* and *Finnegans Wake*, this marks my agreement with T. S. Eliot, who noted that Lewis and Joyce had written only one proper "novel" apiece, *Tarr* and *A Portrait of the Artist as a Young Man*.[33] In Joyce's and Lewis's fictions, narrative often bows in importance to language itself, and, in Lewis's case, to the polemical creation of "selves" as fictitious as any created character.

My argument deals with many overlapping matters: two authors and their works, the notion of literary modernism, representation, writing, and politics. To negotiate between these issues I have cast Lewis's and Joyce's differences as a debate over representational authority. Susan Eilenberg, in her study of the collaboration of William Wordsworth and Samuel Taylor Coleridge, argues that the poets' collaborative activity devolved upon the trope of possession – of material goods, of spiritual being, or language.[34] Possession or control of language is similarly central to the interrelations of Joyce and Lewis. The question "who controls language?" is also the question "who possesses the more powerful rhetoric?," the answer to which crosses the semantic border between aesthetics and politics. To be an author is to assert the power of representation, the ability to sanction through the word or image. To produce an image or narrative is to claim the validity of one's creation as a persuasive or intrinsically valuable object, one that has a real and powerful referent, whether that referent be the world outside or the processes of symbolization itself. That this authority (which can also be political or cultural) may be problematic, either irreducible to unitary origin or open to self-contradictory issues raised by its own claims, has been the source of much recent linguistic and social criticism, including valuable works on Joyce that have placed in the critical foreground the problematic relationships within his fiction of teller with tale, unity with multiplicity, and rebellion with submission.[35] The relevance of these issues to Lewis will be made clear in the following pages. The stance of the creator towards his creation, that creation's stance towards the reality it implicitly claims to represent, and the status of the authoritative "voice" offered by the text: all are central to my argument, which juxtaposes the variously authoritative voices within the texts of Lewis and Joyce against their nominal opposites in the works of the other.

The larger structure of this study alternates between readings of works by the two authors, in search of congruences and contingencies, points of tangency and of identification. These points are seldom found on the surface. Lewis's and Joyce's works are distinct from one another in style, tone, and subject matter. No attentive reader would mistake a page of Lewis's explosive prose for that of even Joyce's most extreme experimentation, despite Lewis's complaints that Joyce stole the Vorticist style of his play *Enemy of the Stars* for use in the "Circe" chapter of *Ulysses*.[36] While Joyce claimed that the stories of *Dubliners* were written in a style of "scrupulous meanness," readers and critics have all too often joined F. R. Leavis, seeing in Lewis's work only an unscrupulous aggressiveness that verges on brutality.[37] Joyce and Lewis further differed in their creative premises. Lewis created according to programs of aesthetic intent, first Vorticism and later satire, that he developed theoretically before creating the works that would give them substance. Joyce, in comparison, altered techniques in response to the materials at hand. His famous schemata for *Ulysses* were codified only after the fact, implying a degree of preliminary planning in an act of retrospective arrangement as pellucidly disingenuous as any Jamesian preface.

In examining Lewis's and Joyce's earlier works I thus emphasize individual philosophic structure and formal organization rather than stylistic connection or programmatic similarity of intent. Lewis proudly claimed in the 1930s that when painting he was "burying Euclid deep in the living flesh."[38] Both discovering and creating the skeleton under the body's superfices, Lewis applies his apothegm to the conceptual truths that underlie all aesthetic appearance. In my first two chapters I articulate some of these buried skeletons, in *Blast* where the bones of contention lie close to the fictional surface, and in *Ulysses*, where buried geometries clothe themselves in a dense body of stylistic embellishment. The first chapter examines the philosophy of the image that informs Vorticism. I treat *Blast* as an integral work of art, and measure its manifesto's vision of the creative self against the dramatic enactment of those ideas in the play *Enemy of the Stars*. I measure that vision and the play in turn against the concept of Romanticism that Vorticism curiously contemns yet introjects. In the second chapter I look at the philosophy of language implicit in *Ulysses*, balancing Joyce's treatment of linguistic division against the nominally "dialectical" portrayal of the creative self presented by Stephen in his lecture on Shakespeare in "Scylla and Charybdis." These chapters are autonomous, although they are similar in form. Both deal with the implications of drama as literary genre, and both measure the philosophic visions of *Blast* and *Ulysses* against narratives that appear centrally within them; *Enemy of the Stars* and Stephen's lecture emerge as inset parables with disruptive implications for the wholes that generate them.

Separately, these chapters provide the fundamental "working materials" of Joyce and Lewis on which I draw for the following chapters, where the authors' theories of representation appear in aesthetic and increasingly ideological juxtapositions. The third chapter deals with *The Apes of God*, which is no one's favorite book. Even Lewis's most committed critics wax frankly tepid towards his longest single narrative, declaring it unreadable and leaving its intricacies largely undiscussed.[39] Gestured toward rather than carefully appraised, *The Apes of God* remains a massive and inscrutable volume buried in the plains of modernism as part of a kind of literary Stonehenge, a monolith admired from afar in the company of books such as Gertrude Stein's *The Making of Americans*, works whose weight and apparent unintelligibility are seemingly more interesting in the fact of their group existence than as individual artifacts. Here I attempt to illuminate *The Apes of God* in the light cast from *Ulysses*, or, to shift metaphors, I attend to Joycean echoes in Lewis's fictional constructions, concurrently exploring the relationship between the novel's social vision and the "broadcasts" of the protagonist Horace Zagreus. *Ulysses* acts as a frame of implicit reference, a text that lies beneath the surface of Lewis's fiction as a satirized but anxiously entrapping precursor, a parodied original that cannot be negated but only ambivalently revised. The chapter begins with formal and linguistic analyses, but moves midway through into analysis of the analogies that Lewis postulates between painterly representation, fiction, and political structure. At this chapter's end synchronic structures merge into questions about the relationship between representation and history.

In the final chapter the parallel lines established in Lewis and Joyce's earlier fictions cross in the most explicit of ways, where Lewis enters *Finnegans Wake* as pervasive fictional presence. I use the term "presence" advisedly. When a voice in *Finnegans Wake* asks "How, not one Moll Pamelas?" (*FW*, 569.29), the allusions to Daniel Defoe's Moll Flanders and Samuel Richardson's fictive Pamela suggest a generalized dismay at the absence of traditional characters, at least as they are understood in the English novel at its historic source. In the void left by such traditional constructs, I explore the aesthetic and ultimately political significance of Lewis as profound contributor to *Finnegans Wake*, not simply as a biographical source or as the butt of idiosyncratic humor, but as an intellectual figure whose ideas are central to Joyce's last work. At this chapter's conclusion, politics become inseparable from Joyce's treatment of language and history, a confluence for which Lewis plays a major part. As in the first two chapters I focus upon the role of inset narrative, examining how the fables of *Finnegans Wake* operate in the linguistic and historical context of Giambattista Vico's *New Science*. Within each of the four chapters I approach issues of authority in terms of a dichotomy similar to the Russian Formalists' distinction between *fabula* and *sjuzet*, that between the "nature" of thematic materials and the "design" of narrative form, as manifested by drama in *Blast* and *Ulysses* to broadcast and fable in *The Apes of God* and *Finnegans Wake*, and by the formal ramifications of the relationship between represented creative voice and that which it creates within the text.

In all cases, the nature of oppositions – whether they can be resolved, must remain unresolved, or elude such unitary formulations entirely – holds center stage, to borrow a Lewisian theatrical metaphor, even as they take on both political and linguistic roles. They delineate a movement that will become apparent in both authors' works, from emphasis upon the nature of the individual towards emphasis upon the individual's creation of and subsumption within the public world, emphases that ultimately foreground the ideological interconnections of Lewis's and Joyce's later works. In describing the function of oppositions in Lewis and Joyce I have attempted to refamiliarize and defamiliarize a crucial artistic relationship of modernism, grounding it in the terms that were not merely chosen by its participants but which also dissemble their authentic affinities. By attending to the interrelationships between the monsters of nature and the monsters of design in Lewis's and Joyce's fiction I hope to show that what proclaims itself as oppositional in their work marks a guarded continuity both repressed and expressed by those works that most defiantly proclaim their authorial, and authoritative, difference.

CHAPTER I

# The tell-tale Eye

> Should we not say that we make a house by the art of building, and by the art of painting we make another house, a sort of man-made dream produced for those who are awake?
>
> Plato, *Sophist*

> X. – I am a machine that is constructed to provide you with answers.
>     I am alive, however. But I am beholden for life to machines that are asleep.
>
> Wyndham Lewis, "Tyronic Dialogues – X. and F."

As a defense against accusations of madness, the narrator of Edgar Allan Poe's "The Tell-Tale Heart" confesses the history of his growing obsession with and ultimate murder of the old man with whom he lives. The reason for the killing, he explains, was the man's disfigured eye, which unnerved him to the point of violence. Yet while attempting to vindicate himself, the narrator seems to suggest that he had actually chosen the eye after the fact to rationalize an inexplicable fear and hatred of the other:

> It is impossible to say how first the idea entered my brain; but once conceived, it haunted me day and night. Object there was none. Passion there was none. I loved the old man. He had never wronged me. He had never given me insult. For his gold I had no desire. I think it was his eye! yes, it was this![1]

In this passage from the tale's opening, the narrator admits that he cannot reconstruct the causes of his repulsion. Only during the act of narration does he appear to seize upon the eye as a motive, as though the desire to produce a coherent story for his questioners leads him to transform an arbitrary thought into retrospective truth.

This choice of the deformed eye is psychologically consistent with his narrative. It can be read as an emblem of the fears that lie behind both the murder and his confession. The narrator is terrified by the possibility that he is mad, and he presents his story explicitly to convince both others and himself that he has avoided the fracturing of the self that insanity implies. His fear of a disfiguration of the ego has a displaced linguistic equivalent in the old man's deformed eye – it stands as the externalized representative, that is, for his fear of a deformed "I." His fixation upon the eye is inseparable from his self-obsession, in which his growing fear of madness is diverted into hatred of the other through the mechanism of an actualized pun. The seemingly arbitrary choice of motive suggests that the narrator is disturbed less by the nominal stimulus of the cataract than by the more general implications of the old man's otherness. His hatred of the man has no other basis but that the man is part of an inaccessible external reality, irreconcilable with the narrator's desires. Yet as Poe's narrator discovers, the apparent gap between self and other conceals powerful connections. The narrator's destruction of the old man ironically predicates his own downfall. When he rids himself of the alien eye he also completes the dismantling of his own autonomy, surrendering to the internal and external imprisonments of madness and the police. The beating heart – whether supernatural reality or subjective hallucination – forces itself upon the narrator as a sign that the self is not distinct from its victim. It implicates the narrator in his own violence by revealing the destruction of the eye as a double action that destroys actor as well as object.

In the early fiction of Wyndham Lewis the man with the disturbing eye is subject to different rules. Bestre, a pivotal figure in the collection of stories *The Wild Body*, is aggressor rather than victim, and although as obsessed with the other as Poe's narrator he seems to be free from the ontological complexities that bind the characters in "The Tell-Tale

Heart." Bestre makes a game of belligerence. Although bound by his profession as an innkeeper on the Breton coast to provide refuge for others, he is anything but hospitable. Instead of minimizing the distance between himself and potential clients he subjects them to mental warfare, turning the other into an unwilling participant in a series of irrational confrontations. These combats, described by Lewis's narrator Ker-Orr as "stark stand-up fight[s] between one personality and another" (*WB*, 82) are silent and seemingly unmotivated. Ker-Orr, fascinated by Bestre's behavior, concludes they are part of an abstract struggle that Bestre wages against an external reality that he perceives as a threat to his own integrity. Bestre views the external world as "so many ambushes for his body" according to Ker-Orr (*WB*, 84), and he chooses to revenge himself upon it incorporeally, using his perception of the other as both motivation and method. Bestre plays out his attacks – against various neighbors and the wife of a painter – on the battlefield of vision, using a panoply of stares as defensive armor and offensive weaponry. "What he selected as an arm in his duels...," Ker-Orr explains simply, "was the Eye" (*WB*, 83). In these battles, Ker-Orr continues, Bestre turns his eye into the sole representative of his self, allowing it to command a military allegiance from the rest of his body, a "tyrannical appropriation" (*WB*, 85) of his expressive potential. By willfully subordinating himself to his vision Bestre makes his eye the ruling synecdoche for his "I." He sacrifices his access to the multiplicity of human response in order to confront reality, in the guise of the threatening other, with ambushes of his own.

Ker-Orr is intrigued by Bestre's strange subordination of self to vision, and he revels vicariously in Bestre's victories as triumphs of the individual over the material world, seeing Bestre as the "bester" in any confrontation. He hints that his tale of Bestre is a sort of metaphysical parable. He calls Bestre "one of my masters" (*WB*, 84), declaring that the innkeeper's visual pugnacity is the model for his own understanding of reality, which is implicitly also his understanding of narrative. The nature of that understanding is only implied in "Bestre," for Lewis explores Ker-Orr's behavior in detail in "A Soldier of

Humour" and "Beau Séjour," the stories that precede "Bestre" in *The Wild Body*. However, an earlier version of the tale, "Some Innkeepers and Bestre," published in the *English Review* in June 1909, considers its significance directly. Here the narrator suggests a more comprehensive interpretation of Bestre's symbolic importance. "Has Bestre discovered the only type of action," he muses, "compatible with artistic creation ...?" (*WB*, 231). Unlike Poe's narrator, who looks upon the other and sees nothing but destruction, Lewis's narrator looks upon the struggle between self and other and questions whether the root of that destructive force paradoxically provides the sole dialectic for creation.

Lewis withholds an affirmative answer to his narrator's speculation in either version of "Bestre," but the posing of the question suggests that Poe's and Lewis's fictions are ethically and philosophically disjunct. Bestre's comic survival alone seems to be a dismissal of the destructive interconnectedness that informs "The Tell-Tale Heart." Moreover, as Lewis was vituperatively critical of the "Romantic" in literature and art throughout his career, any relationship postulated between Lewis's fiction and the gothic world of Poe's tales may seem tenuous. Nonetheless, Lewis alludes to Poe with sufficient frequency in his early writings, despite the ambivalence of their contexts, to suggest that the earlier author held a minor but significant place in his developing conception of art. In *Blast* 2 Lewis lists Poe alongside his fellow Vorticist Pound as one of the creators of "the best art so far produced north of Mexico and south of the Pole" (*B*2, 82). In a dialogue published in *The Tyro* some years later, in turn, he uses Poe's poetry as a sardonic emblem of creativity. Here, Phillip, one of Lewis's "immense novices," explains that the artistic impulse comes upon him "like Poe's RAVEN. It says, over and over again, CREATE! CREATE! CREATE!" This allusion is a jibe at sentimental conceptions of inspiration rather than homage. Phillip's greatest artistic achievement is trivial, a design for a hat, as though his creative voice says in fact "Nevermore."[2] In Lewis's first novel, however, Poe's role as a model of the artist is unambiguous. At the end of *Mrs. Dukes' Million*, Lewis's hero Hercules Fane escapes from England to begin a career as a painter in Paris, and the name he assumes as he "feigns" a new identity is Edgar Pope – the author of "The Tell-Tale Heart" transformed by a single letter into a type of creative infallibility.[3] Frederick Tarr, the artist and eponymous hero of Lewis's second novel, seems also to be named from Poe. Poe relates in his tale "The System of Doctor Tarr and Professor Fether" how the inmates of a French madhouse take control of their asylum and create a parodic society by crazily imitating the bourgeois habits of their keepers – certainly an accurate, if metaphorical, description of the "bourgeois-bohemia" of the Parisian artists in *Tarr*.[4]

These allusions, both veiled and direct, suggest that Poe was oddly relevant to Lewis's developing modernism. One might read this homage, it is true, as an acknowledgment of Poe's peculiar stature as a literary figure rather than agreement with the content of his writings. The particularly Parisian and artistic contexts of both *Mrs. Dukes' Million* and *Tarr* suggest that Lewis associated Poe with the continental avant-garde, who iconized Poe because of Baudelaire and thus provided a valuable alternative to the Victorian taste that Lewis pilloried in *Blast*. It is equally possible and tempting, however, to suppose that Lewis saw in Poe's theories of poesy a congenial predecessor for his own developing aesthetic. Poe anticipated Lewis's insistence on eradicating temporality from art, for instance, in "The Philosophy of Composition." As Fredric Jameson has noted, Poe emphasizes brevity in this essay as a literary ideal, arguing that short forms provide the asynchrony of language with a containing structure that approximates the synchrony of the visual arts, allowing the reader to experience the work as an aesthetic unity: "surmounting time... translating a formless temporal succession into a simultaneity which we can grasp and possess."[5] Poe's concern to grant language the benefits of the visual and his insistence upon timelessness and unity as criteria for aesthetic success prefigure Lewis's Vorticist manifestoes, and even point to the later arguments of *Time and Western Man*. Yet if Poe and Lewis ultimately shared aesthetic conclusions, they arrived at them from opposed disciplines. Poe concerned himself solely with literary form, showing little interest, except by association, in theories of the visual arts. Lewis's ideas about both plastic and narrative art, on the other hand, were centrally rooted in visuality. He considered himself to be a painter first and only secondarily a writer, and his aesthetic was inseparable from his experience with canvas and brush. His expectations of both painterly and literary form, which he presented in *Blast* and other theoretical writings, were based directly on his understanding of the relationship between the visual artist and the external reality that is his perpetual subject.

To reconcile the image of successful art raised by "Bestre" with Lewis's allusions to Poe, one must turn to this discussion and to the relationship between self and other that it ultimately implies. Once the difficulties of Lewis's polemical aesthetic have become clear, we may explore how their lines of force shape and disrupt one of Lewis's most striking early literary works: his play *Enemy of the Stars*. The issues raised by Poe and Bestre translate quizzically into this emblematic narrative, which originally appeared amid the manifestoes of *Blast*. To understand the infidelities of this translation one must travel along an intricate route: through painterly metaphysics, an inquiry into the nature of the Vorticist self, exposition of the philosophical biases of *Blast*, and, finally, after analysis of *Enemy of the Stars*, an investigation into the dynamics of readerly drama. To understand the unanswered questions of "Bestre" demands that one investigate the implications of that most contemned of Lewisian conditions, Romance.

In his early manifestoes Lewis attacked the conventions of painterly realism as acts of bad faith, whose motivation contained the seeds of their inevitable failure. Following Nietzsche's *The Gay Science*, which he identified in *Rude Assignment* as one of the favorite books of his youth,[6] Lewis railed against traditional pictorial representations as being dubious attempts to translate reality directly into art without interpretative mediation. In erecting a system of signs to capture the superficies of natural objects, Lewis argued, the artist creates only shadowy replicas of the external world that necessarily pale before the things themselves. The artist acts mechanically towards an impossible and irrelevant task, for he competes with a nature that is already complete in itself. In "bowing the knee to wild Mother Nature" (*B*1, 19), the artist sacrifices his own creative potential, subordinating his invention to the random and often uninteresting forms of the perceptual world. By pedantically adhering to these externalities he ratifies their superficial shapes to the exclusion of their inner meaning. "Imitation, and inherently unselective registering of impressions, is an absurdity," Lewis wrote in *Blast* (*B*2, 45), for the result can never "give you even the feeling of the weight of the object, and certainly not the meaning... which is its spiritual weight." In searching for this significance in appearances, the naturalist mistakenly displaces the weight of artistic meaning onto the represented object itself. He assumes that his subjects, because they are authentically real in and of themselves, provide an intrinsic justification for their representations. He trusts that they validate his images by their mere presence as referents, an assumption shared even by the Cubists and Futurists, who persisted in basing their art upon the impressionist values of posed models. For Lewis, on the other hand, the assumption that art's figurations are legitimized by an intrinsic quality of the object they signify – the subject's existential presence in the perceptual world – betrays the intellectual rigor that is essential to art. It confuses art's realm of permanence and exactitude with the flux and imprecision of the everyday world of "life." By equating appearance with significance the artist limits his apprehension of both the real and art. He reduces the artistic subject's complexity to a sterile diagram of "accidental form."[7] Because programmatic naturalism and its modern descendants ignored the object's emotive and intellective reality, Lewis considered them to be forms of institutionalized "*nature morte*" that killed what they tried to vitalize. In fetishizing the intrinsic value of the signified, their various forms of stylistic rigidity only precluded the artist from reaching what was most "alive" in his subject.

For Lewis, the aesthetic conservatism of academic painting and the failure of representative abstraction were both inextricable from the artist's assumptions about the relationship between image and reality. By believing that whatever was most valuable and authentic in the object could be reached through appearance, the artist in turn assumed that the object's accidental form provided a valid link between the object's essence and his iconography. To Lewis, however, the preservation of the object's planes and colors, even in the Cubist's altered arrangement, led by its very nature to misrepresentation. The product would inevitably be related only to the closed system of the artist's developed conventions, rather than to the object under inquiry. "The essence of an object is beyond and often in contradiction to, its simple truth" (*B*2, 45) he objected in *Blast*, using the word "truth" to encompass painting's postulated mediation between the image and the real. The act of painting was incompatible with implicit equations of form with essence. Painting sought to illuminate the object's significance, but by a perpetually evolving "valuation" of the real rather than relying upon a set of static equivalences. Art searched for the "POSSIBILITIES in the object" (*B*2, 45) and was thus, as he stated in "Essay on the Objective of Plastic Art in Our Time," allied to philosophy.[8] The naturalist's implied assurance about the relationship between his signs and reality, on the other hand, was part of an absolutism that drew heavily upon the assumptions of science, which had replaced philosophy as the central approach to phenomena in modern western thought and was, therefore, invoked frequently by the realists as the justification of their craft.[9] Based on the agreement that man can approach an understanding of the real through empirical observation, science grants that for practical purposes one can assume a consistent relationship between reality and the intellectual constructs by which it can be known. The scientist claims for his symbols a direct, if provisional, relationship to the real. The naturalists, according to Lewis, assumed this relationship by analogy, but elided its provisional nature. Instead they made a "tacit assumption that truth *can* be reached, other than symbolically and indirectly" (*TWM*, 304–5) and played out a "Romance about science" (*B*1, 144), rather than science itself in their discussion and practice of representation.

This rejection of "Romance," and distaste for its multiple

ramifications, typifies Lewis's mimetic practice. For now we may construe "Romance" in a limited sense as a condemnation of the naturalist's tendency to overstate his power in adopting science's valuation of symbolic constructs, making greater claims for their relationship to the real than they can bear. The absolute, although the ultimate goal of the empiricist, hovers irretrievably beyond the reach of the naturalist image, and the artist who attempts to use his images to touch the real dooms himself to a Platonist's self-delusion. Like Picasso, whose experiments in sculpting with pieces of everyday objects aroused Lewis's wrath in *Blast*, he erects a "reality" of his own as a substitute for striking through to the nature of things, but remains crucially unaware of his failure. As Lewis warns in one of his early manifestoes, emphasizing its exaggerations with capital letters, the naturalist creates an artificial "REALITY [as] the nearest conscious and safe place to 'Reality.'" Any form of representative iconography is an illusory military or Homeric snare, its "reality" is "the Waterloo, Will o' the wisp, or siren of artistic genius" (*B*1, 139).

As a reaction against the tradition of literal valuation of the object, Lewis turned to the aesthetic potential of non-representational abstraction. Most discussions of Vorticism understandably emphasize abstraction as its salient characteristic and greatest achievement.[10] In *Blast* Lewis expressed interest in the purely non-referential painting then gaining currency among certain Expressionists and Futurists on the Continent. He included an excerpt from Kandinsky's *Inner Necessity* in the first issue, praised Balla in "Vortices and Notes" for his use of totally abstract images, and lauded Boccioni for becoming progressively more abstract in his then recent work. As a protest against the excesses of convention he rejected externality entirely, insisting that the world's appearance had little to do with the Vorticist's art. Abstraction served as both a reaction against the tyranny of the academy, and as a pedagogic service for viewers who had grown slovenly in their visual habits – "There should be a bill passed in Parliament at once," he wrote hyperbolically in *Blast*'s second issue, "FORBIDDING ANY IMAGE OR RECOGNIZABLE SHAPE TO BE STUCK UP IN ANY PUBLIC PLACE" (*B*2, 47).

Abstraction in *Blast* becomes an intrinsic good, a key not only to art but to all of one's interactions. Lewis "blesses" the seafarer, for instance, because he chooses to travel on the "vast planetary abstraction of the OCEAN," exchanging "one ELEMENT for ANOTHER. The MORE against the LESS ABSTRACT" (*B*1, 22). In a burst of Vorticist humor he similarly lauds the hairdresser, who creates abstraction by turning the "aimless and retrograde growths" of nature into "CLEAN ARCHED SHAPES and ANGULAR PLOTS" (*B*1, 25). In its concern to eradicate recognizable form from art, as Lewis would later recall, "Visual Vorticism ... was dogmatically anti-real."[11]

Yet dogma is not practice, and Lewis's recollection is only partially accurate. Even in his earliest and most radical writings he never considered the total rejection of natural form to be an unambiguous alternative to naturalism's limitations. His strictures were rooted partly in the practical, rather than philosophical, doubts of the working painter and critical viewer. He found that many completely abstract paintings, such as Kandinsky's, lacked pictorial tension in their conscientious efforts to avoid forms that might suggest definite objects. More significantly, he doubted that artists could ever truly break free from the tyranny of mimesis. Even the most assiduous abstract painter could not avoid occasionally approximating forms in the known world with his juxtapositions of line and color, and because these accidental representations were beyond conscious control they were even more "dull and insignificant" than those of the naturalist – "You cannot avoid the conclusion," Lewis added, "that [the abstractionist] would have done better to ACKNOWLEDGE that he had (by accident) reproduced a form in Nature, and have taken more trouble with it FOR ITS OWN SAKE AS A FRANKLY REPRESENTATIVE ITEM" (*B*2, 40). This quizzical infringement upon representation was the non-representational artist's fatal and unavoidable flaw. Even the most abstract shape could be interpreted as a version of a natural object, and its perceiver would inevitably connect it with the context of the world in which he lived – no matter how esoteric or unlikely, every shape had a "twi[n] in the material world" (*B*2, 43) to which it seemed to refer. The artist who was philosophically dedicated to the non-representational fought against two insurmountable barriers. His innate tendency towards representation and the natural desire of his viewers to reintegrate his images into a conventional conception of reality, undermined his attempt to create wholly new art free from reintegration into the viewer's pragmatic context. The act of putting paint on canvas made it "impossible... to avoid representation in one form or another" (*B*2, 43), even where the artist intended most thoroughly to subvert his image's dependence upon reality. The non-representational painter was trapped by the natural world as completely as the naturalist. He could no more transcend the real than the academician could wholly capture it, "always REPRESENTING" (*B*2, 42) despite himself.

The conflicting demands of naturalism and pure abstraction bound Lewis with a paradoxical apprehension of the source of the image's value, its ability either to capture – or adequately elude – the real. The represented object was itself an illusory source of iconic significance – "The 'Real Thing' is always Nothing" he warns in *Blast* (*B*1, 139) – but the image which attempted to react against the known was inevitably flooded with unwanted value associated with the world it tried to reject. Reed Way Dasenbrock has argued that Vorticism thus occupies a borderline position between abstraction and representation, putting abstraction at the service of representation, and naturalizing contradiction into a complex, but coherent, singular practice.[12] This formulation is useful, pointing the way to the geometrically informed naturalism of Lewis's later painterly style, as well as that of other Vorticist painters such as William Roberts and David Bomberg. Dasenbrock's formulation, however, tends to undervalue the degree to which the contradiction between abstraction and representation remains grindingly unresolved within Lewis's early writings, even if arguably balanced within the artworks themselves. One can see this contradiction between resolution and contradiction reflected in *Blast*'s iconography. The Vortex, Lewis's central visual metaphor, is an articulate symbol for the perceived duality of image and object. Radical emblem and organizing concept for his early work, it is a visual reification of this central enigma of modernist representation. A system of constant movement whirling about a stillness at its center, the Vortex has been understood as a vital presence that signifies the moment or locus of imaginative power. Pound, for instance, described it in terms of his own Imagism as "the point of maximum energy," an intensification of presence (*B*1, 153).[13] Yet in the context of Lewis's analysis of representation it can also be interpreted as a symbol of an insecure imagery that is centrifugal from, yet inescapably linked to, the referent that is integral to its power. Defined by an uncertain signified – the void around which the system whirls – it consists of contained instability. Its shape is a function of the constant recontainment of its energetic attempts to move outward and away from its own center. If the center itself is understood as a void that replaces the naturalist's posited noumenon, then the Vortex foregrounds the tenuous bond between image and referent in a balance that is simultaneously polar and dialectical. It is an image of energy that tries and fails to escape the uncertain reality in which it is rooted, yet which paradoxically gains its power from that struggle. Its structure depends equally upon the force of its dubious referent, and upon its attempts to escape from that referent into pure acontextuality. Only the inescapable pull of the center prevents the system from flying apart into incoherence. Only the struggle to transcend the gravitational pull of its dubious core prevents the system from collapsing, like a black hole, into pure absence. The linkage between the signified and transcendence of the signified – each of which are implicitly self-destroying – allows the Vortex to exist as an aesthetic totality that can whirl as a unity against the void. If, as the sculptor Gaudier-Brzeska wrote in his own manifesto, "THE VORTEX WAS ABSOLUTE" (*B*1, 157), Lewis was also aware of the contingency of that unity. Its "disastrous polished dance" (*B*1, 149) depends upon the successful containment of diametrically opposed forms of annihilation.

At this level of iconography the Vortex acts as a symbol of contradiction contained within a precarious larger coherence. Juxtaposing this image with the ideas in the manifestoes, nonetheless, creates an interpretive dilemma. Although the manifestoes authorize the image of the Vortex through their exposition of Vorticist philosophy, they are not entirely compatible with that image's symbolism. Like the Vortex they describe apparently conflicting positions. Unlike the Vortex, however, they stop short of reconciling oppositions within a dynamic balance. Instead Lewis uses them to foreground irresolvable statements that emphasize gaps in argumentation, rather than resolution of inconsistencies. This lack of resolution is self-reflexively clearest in *Blast*'s explicit pronouncements on reconciliation and disunity. Some of Lewis's statements openly support the Vortex's figurations of containment, positing a practical relationship between pure surface and pure content, the former a metaphor for abstraction, the latter a metaphor for "life." "The finest Art is not pure Abstraction, nor is it unorganized life" (*B*1, 134) Lewis writes when considering the failures of Futurism, and describes true art as a mediating language that would produce the true synthesis of opposites that Dasenbrock has described, a "New Living Abstraction" (*B*1, 147). Lewis stresses the artist's obligations to phenomena, noting similarities between the re-creative powers of the abstract artist and that of the natural world. "We must constantly strive to ENRICH abstraction till it is almost plain life," Lewis writes in "A Review of Contemporary Art," "or rather to get deeply enough immersed in material life to experience the shaping power amongst its vibrations, and to accentuate and perpetuate these" (*B*2, 40).

In advising the artist to co-opt this "shaping power" Lewis analogizes the Vorticist's production of geometrical structure with nature's ordering of the visible world. He suggests that the artist can learn from nature without adopting its surface manifestations, for art "finds the same stimulus as in Nature" (*B*1, 33). Yet this startlingly organicist metaphor stands paradoxically against his equally unambiguous dismissals of externality. As Lewis urges the artist to produce a second nature that is necessarily contingent upon the first, he contradictorily emphasizes that the Vorticist "want[s] to leave Nature... alone" (*B*1, 7). What the artist can imitate suitably from nature remains provocatively unclear. If Lewis calls for a Coleridgean apprehension of creativity as an organic process he also rejects organicism as art's enemy. On one hand, "the one purpose... of a work of Art... [is] Life" (*B*1, 140) but it must be a different "life" than that of nature, for a few pages earlier he states that art is "no EQUIVALENT for Life, but ANOTHER life, as NECESSARY to existence as the former" (*B*1, 130). As with the term "nature," however, the word "life" appears largely throughout *Blast* only pejoratively as part of the argument against phenomena that stand against, rather than inform, art. Lewis argues that the artist must distance himself from life as part of his creative agon – "There is... only room for ONE Life, in Existence," he writes, and art must "behave itself and struggle" within its own parameters (*B*1, 133).[14]

This shifting valency of the words "life" and "nature," like Lewis's undifferentiated use of the word "reality," to refer both to the naturalist's illusions and to the world's authentic condition, upsets the reader's expectations that the language of *Blast* can be interpreted singularly. It becomes a personal rhetoric of divisive polemic gestures. Thus, *Blast*'s language is implicated in the oppositions of its content. By juxtaposing ideas with their own rejections and pivoting his arguments upon shifting terms, Lewis props up his representational skepticism with an equally unstable linguistic scaffolding. He acknowledges through iconography the Vortex's ability to reconcile the irreconcilable, while simultaneously undermining its symbolic discourse with the manifestoes' paradoxes of logic and connotation.

Confronted by this maze of contradiction and instability, Lewis's critics can scarcely be blamed for dismissing him in the terms with which Otto Kreisler rejects Nietzsche in *Tarr*: "[he] was always *paradoxal* [sic]: he would say anything to amuse himself" (*T*, 228). Yet while *Blast*, as its name implies, shares with other radical manifestoes the desire to shock with provocative rhetoric rather than convince through coherent argumentation, Lewis's paradoxes are neither unorganized nor arbitrary. Instead he attempts to recontain his apparent doubleness under the larger rubric of the general ratification of the irreconcilable. "You must talk with two tongues, if you do not wish to cause confusion," he advises in the second issue of *Blast*, "You must be a duet in everything" (*B*2, 91). Faced by his inability either to unify or to elude art's limitations, Lewis implicitly redefines aesthetic value as the formal mirroring of art's irresolvable difficulties. The Vorticist must seek out discontinuity and make it central to his art. Creation is the intentional erection of dualities as a substitute for the thing-in-itself:

1. Beyond Action and Reaction we would establish ourselves.
2. We start from opposite statements of a chosen world. Set up violent structure of adolescent clearness between two extremes.
3. We discharge ourselves on both sides.
4. We fight first on one side, then on the other, but always for the SAME cause, which is neither side or both sides and ours. (*B*1, 30)

In this passage, which directly follows the violently Manichean list of "Blasts" and "Blesses," Lewis adjusts the Vortex's lessons. In rejecting the failed transcendence of the naturalist and abstractionist projects, he denies that art is validated either by the pure surface of the image or by the essence of the represented object. Significantly, he locates value instead in the tensions generated by oppositions. His metaphors of both violence and stasis – the erection of structures and the avoidance of action – paradoxically enact the oppositions for which they stand, reflecting the Vortex's oxymoronic "immobile rhythm" (*B*1, 149) as figures of speech. In place of art's traditional striving for transcendent unity Lewis offers the artist the new goal of manufactured doubleness. He suggests that art should turn away from reconciliation towards the compensatory frictions of intentional difference.

Even this apparently direct discourse is paradoxically double, for it contains within it a formulation for artistic coherence and singularity. While Lewis denies art's ability to reconcile difference his rhetoric simultaneously suggests that the irreconcilable is itself a kind of displaced transcendence, one centered not in the image, the object, or in the relationship between them, but in the artist himself. The artist's ability to create oppositions implies that he himself is a unitary and powerful source, even if his images are not. "Beyond Action and Reaction we would establish ourselves" is a statement of transcendental intent, transposing Nietzsche's good and evil into the painter's dialectic of physical law. Similarly Nietzschean are Lewis's implicit claims for the Vorticist's ability to control his environment. Although the "would" of his pronouncement suggests desire rather than ability, he unambiguously grants the Vorticist the power to break free from the boundaries and conditions that confine both the naturalist and the abstractionist. The artist starts from a "chosen" world rather than from the received phenomena of the naturalist. He erects "violent structures" of signification rather than working within the parameters that are typically available to the artist.

The two issues of *Blast* locate this power in the will. The new art comes from the "Will of Man" (*B*1, 39); the syntheses of Vorticism are formed in conjunction with "the combinations of the Will" (*B*2, 78). "We establish ourselves" thus equates the Vorticist's strength with the closed system of self-nomination. The artist gains his power not by public consensus or external materiality, but through his sheer desire to create himself as a conscious agent – to "invent [him]self properly" (*B*2, 91) – and to place that self against the world's oppositions. Lewis adopts the vocabulary of militarism to describe this artistic stance – "we discharge ourselves on both sides" suggesting a "fight" without singular allegiance. The artist is a "Primitive Mercenar[y]" (*B*1, 30) ideally free of personal motive, able to turn gleefully against the contradictions of the world that would otherwise limit his creativity. As the sole containing force for his own energetic paradoxes Lewis's ideal artist is a coherent agent who links the will's creative force with the violence that is its opposite. He is a self-empowered and containing vortex who is drawn towards transcendence through both absence and presence, destruction and creativity, "neither side or both sides and ours" (*B*1, 30).

The power of the self is omnipresent in *Blast*. As the artist provides the validation for his image's significance, and the will is a function of the self, selfhood is the direct source of the artist's oppositional power, integral to all aspects of aesthetic production. The Vorticist not only nominates himself into existence, but is the principal recipient of art's value. Aesthetic action is for "our" side. It is created for the artist and those who share his standards rather than for the idle perceiver. Like the mercenary's art, its value for others is a secondary function of its obvious benefits for the actor himself. Furthermore, the passage suggests that Vorticist art is a direct product *of* the self. The phrase "We discharge ourselves" positions the self as both subject and object. It defines the artist grammatically as both originator and medium of his creation, nominating the self as not only his precondition, but also his authentic, if secondary, material. True art necessarily constructs an intellective self-portrait of its creator, for it relies upon the materials of the self to delineate the world. In creating the image the artist, in a sense, creates himself. "There is Yourself: and there is the Exterior World...," Lewis explains, "You knead it into an amorphous imitation of yourself inside yourself" (*B*2, 91). The Vorticist directs his selfhood outward, even as he draws the materials of the world inward for the self's reformation. Ultimately, because he can encompass externality within selfhood, the Vorticist becomes the final arbiter of the image's significance. He provides the mechanism of the image's creation, and is its indisputable referent. His power is a trustworthy replacement for the naturalist's "science" as a validation of aesthetic significance. "There is one Truth, ourselves," Lewis writes, "and everything is permitted" (*B*1, 148).

At this point Vorticist paradoxes no longer merely strain against themselves, but threaten to buckle under their own weight. In his quest to reject the forms of nature yet imitate their processes, conjoin abstraction with an irreconcilable naturalism, and produce the truth of reality through non-representational form, Lewis apparently denies reality and lapses into an antithetical solipsism. Yet in arguing that the self is the "only truth," Lewis does not suggest that externality is either subjective or unknowable. If externality were devoid of meaning, the image could easily elude its semiotic grip. Lewis insists, rather, that the Vorticist is able to achieve a higher degree of objective insight into the real through the self, using it as a mediator that allows validity to show forth. Inventing rather than interpreting, the Vorticist patterns phenomena into geometrical shapes, recreating the real without imposing meanings upon his subjects from without. He allows the objective world to achieve its own aesthetic significance by engaging it with his consciousness, selfhood acting as a catalyst. This restructuring only reveals what the object paradoxically already contains, the significance that is hidden from consciousness before it is perceived yet is independent of the artist's mind. The self is the "only truth" not because it is the only reality, but because it provides externality with its ultimate author as well as a validating witness, both the Berkeleyean perceiver and paradoxical source of the significance that it perceives. "Intrinsic beauty," as Lewis explains, with emphasis on the locus of "intrinsicality" and the etymological connection between vision and divination, "is in the Interpreter or Seer, not in the object or content" ($B1$, 7).

The Vorticist's reality is thus Kantian, if despite itself. Reality hovers between the complementary extremes of the mind and the world, and is the product of their duality. Reified by the opposition of self and object, it is manifested by the forms that the mind creates through its patterning of externality. Without this intellective shaping the world's significance remains potential, trapped within its own materiality. Only the mind can "pla[y] its searchlight on the objective world"[15] as illumination. Vorticism finally emerges in the manifestoes as an intellective relationship between the mind and externality, as well as a version of reality itself that is independent from the created image and inextricable from the artist. "Reality," Lewis concludes, "is in the artist, the image only in life" ($B1$, 135).[16]

At this point we must step back from the Vorticist self to advance our understanding of its position within *Blast*. Objectivity, independence, and multiplicity within singularity, are only some of the contexts that are crucial to Lewis's self-presentation in the manifestoes. Thus far we have focussed on the structural elements of the philosophy of *Blast*, bracketing off its cultural pronouncements in favor of its treatment of mind and self. In *Blast* Lewis also makes large generic and historical judgements. He rejects culture's tendency to turn to the past, for instance, as both political and aesthetic gestures. England suffers from sentimentality, Lewis claims, which demands that one fall into clichéd patterns rather than demonstrate any individual response, and he defines it through a literary analogue, claiming England was built upon "Dickens' sentimental ghoul-like gloating over the death of little Nell" (*B*1, 133). Even more than the historically defined products of the Victorian age *Blast* objects to Romanticism, which Lewis understands not as a period but as a philosophical approach which led to, and included, Victorian sentimentality. Although *Blast* criticizes Keats directly (*B*1, 133), Lewis, with T. E. Hulme, associated "Romantic" art more generally with habits of thought unrelated to historical conditions. For Lewis Romanticism meant temporality as well as the host of social conditions with which he conflated it. He rejected Futurism as "Romantic" for fetishizing time, while he lauded "Classicism," which emphasized the hard-edged forms of space. That English artists should be the "great enemies of Romance" is *Blast*'s rallying cry (*B*1, 41), for Romance is the "fostering of... unactual conditions" (*B*1, 8) whether that fostering be the excessive valuation of time, or the sentimentalizing of mass culture. Modernity thus has its quotient of Romance, hiding within the modes of avant-garde that Lewis rejects: the futurist movement is no better on this score than the excesses of Victorian decadence and realism: "Wilde gushed twenty years ago about the beauty of machinery," Lewis writes, "Gissing, in his romantic delight with modern lodging houses was futurist in this sense" (*B*1, 8).

At the base of such cultural criticism remains the self. Because the coherence of the artist's mind and will are central to the creation of meaning, Lewis emphasizes even at this early stage of his career the difficulty the artist faces from the modern world, where Romantic and temporal ideologies threaten the self's integrity. Here it is helpful to view *Blast* with the hindsight offered by Lewis's non-fictional prose of the 1920s, in which he criticized explicitly those aspects of modernity that emphasized fragmentation and endangered art. For instance, in *Time and Western Man* and *The Art of Being Ruled* he bridled at the general acceptance of psychoanalytic thought as fact, for he felt that it reduced man's innate complexity to a mechanistic set of urges, subordinating the creative mind to schemata of the unconscious. He complained that the postulation of universal structures subverted man's awareness of himself as a distinct being and belittled the power of consciousness, therefore denying both of art's essential conditions: "There are no *individuals* in the Unconscious;" he wrote, "because a man is only an individual when he is *conscious*" (*TWM*, 310). He rejected socialism for similar reasons; it regarded consciousness as a servant to a larger political mass, it "systematiz[es] and vulgariz[es] the individual," as Lewis has his Tarr expound (*T*, 26), and diminishes the individual's importance both to society and to himself. The price for its order is uniformity, and, as Lewis wrote in defending his opinions as early as *Blast*, "The only person who objects to uniformity and order... is the man who knows that under these conditions his 'individuality' would not survive" (*B2*, 72). Moreover, socialism imposed an ontological fragmentation upon the artist, removing him doubly from both the source and product of his work. Where capitalism divided modes of production, socialism divided the self from its labor. It had the same destructive ramifications for the creator's integrity that Ruskin described in "The Nature of Gothic," producing a general alienation of value that followed metaphorically from economic discontinuity – "It is not, truly speaking, the labor that is divided;" Ruskin wrote, "but the men: – Divided into mere segments of men – broken into small fragments and crumbs of life."[17] For Lewis no less than Ruskin the work of art was a product of wholeness. The fragmentation of society's vision of the individual was also a fragmentation of the creative self.

In conflating Romance with temporality and modernity itself, Lewis reserved his most vituperative attacks for the philosophy of Bergson. The French philosopher's conception of reality as a product of temporal flux was the ultimate acceptance of fragmentation as man's authentic condition. Lewis's fundamental objections were typically painterly. Bergson's subordination of space to time as the determinant of the real subverted the integrity of the image. Bergson was vision's enemy because he denied that the objects of the world had a synchronous coherence in space. To Lewis the object's essence was irreducible to the sum of its temporal fragments, and Bergson's declaration that it was best understood as the totality of its perceptible alterations through time handed the palm of authenticity to the naturalists. By reducing the object to a series of sensory impressions, Bergson, according to Lewis, implies that any of them could claim equal validity as a representation. The object itself disappeared under a torrent of intangible moments. Bergson's thought and the relativist philosophies it engendered "trans[port] 'reality' away from the central object ... and be[stow] it upon its immediate sensational appearances: the succession of which, in its spatio-temporal history, it *is*" (*TWM*, 398). Moreover, because the self is material, Bergson subordinated man to the same existential asynchrony. For Lewis such subordination not only denied that the self stood apart from the world that it re-created intellectually, it also implied that the self was itself illusory. To Bergson the self was merely the mind's attempt to graft coherence upon its experience in time, a succession of sensations both unconscious and discontinuous. By declaring that both animate and inanimate matter were bound to time, Bergson conflated the self into the world and reduced both to the condition of spatial incoherence. Bergson's philosophy denied that the world and the self were divided into separate entities, while claiming that the mind was a product of temporality rather than an empowered granter of signification. Bergson's real was the opposite of Vorticism's discrete set of images that could be grasped and molded by consciousness. As Lewis's contemporary T. E. Hulme wrote in *Speculations* Bergson's reality was "a flux of interpenetrated elements unseizable by the intellect."[18]

This resistance to Bergsonian fragmentation is registered early in *Blast*, amidst the cultural and philosophic conditions against which Vorticism defines itself. Lewis lists Bergson among the "blasted" in the first issue, and derides him in the manifestoes as a "philosopher of Impressionism" (*B*1, 132). He notes gnomically that the modern world confuses the realms of ego and other, mirroring the Bergsonian doctrine of the sectionalization of reality. Individual demarcations are confused, Lewis writes, for man finds himself in an intellective world where "frontiers interpenetrate." He can no longer distinguish the boundaries of self: "We all today ... are in each other's vitals," Lewis continues, "overlap, intersect and are Siamese to any [sic] extent" (*B*1, 141). The wholeness of the self can no longer be assumed in an age that mitigates against uniqueness. "Dehumanization is the chief diagnostic of the Modern World" (*B*1, 141), he writes in "The New Egos," equating the loss of conscious individuality with a debasement of the human condition. The artist must be aware not only that the self is powerful but also that the self has to establish its primacy in a hostile environment; otherwise he, and man, loses that which makes him most human. If the artist surrenders his control of externality and the sense of his own distinctiveness he fragments into the secondary and automatic self that Bergson described approvingly as man's natural state in the sensory world, "broken to pieces ... [and] gradually los[ing] sight of the fundamental self."[19] The consciousness of self that the modern world occluded was for Lewis the artist's only protection against his own dissolution.

The imagery of Lewis's descriptions of failed art equate the self's misunderstanding of externality with Bergsonian fragmentation and incoherence. For example, when the naturalist becomes involved with the "machinery" of his constructed reality, Lewis writes, he is "soon cut in half – literally so" (*B*1, 139). Indeed his fascination with phenomena leads to other metaphorical dangers:

The Artist, like Narcissus, gets his nose nearer and nearer the surface of Life.

He will get it nipped off if he is not careful, by some Pecksniff-shark sunning its lean belly near the surface, or other lurker beneath his image, who has been feeding on its radiance. (*B*1, 134–35)

This Melvillian imagery implies that the naturalist's technique breaks him in two. Like the mythic gazer who falls in love with his reflected image, the artist confuses his selfhood with his sensory apprehension of the world. The naturalist's unwillingness to distance himself from reality endangers his art. He is in thrall to the illusion that his selfhood lies in the phenomenal world, and commits the Bergsonian error of confusing the realm of the self with the fluid materials of "life." He not only weakens the lines of his images but also dilutes the metaphysical lines of his own definition, "weaken[s] the esoteric lines of fine original being" (*B*2, 91). Lewis implies that most artists imperil themselves by accepting their "reflected" presence in the phenomenal world, their secondary Bergsonian self, as an aspect of truth. Just as Narcissus dies because he cannot reconcile his illusory dual nature, the naturalist cannot extricate himself from the dangers of his postulated real, the bite of the "Pecksniff-shark." His representation lives only parasitically upon the image's true essence or "radiance," and the Victorian hypocrisy of his aesthetic turns back upon its creator and threatens him with diminishment.[20]

The Bergsonian confusion of subject and object is a metaphoric interpenetration. "Most fine artists cannot keep themselves out of wood and iron, or printed sheets," Lewis writes, "they leave too much of themselves in their furniture" (*B*1, 134). Here Lewis conflates both visual artists and writers, those who produce "printed sheets." Both confront the easy lures of comfortable "life" as well as the inability to extricate their personalities from their work. The "sheets" of their "furniture" suggests the creature comforts of homely relaxation, but also the work of printing relevant to the mechanical production of a journal such as *Blast*. "Furniture" consists of the wooden or metal pieces – iron in the mid-nineteenth century – used to create spaces between type and the margins of printed pages.[21] The additional overtones of this double usage, conjoining eroticism and unconsciousness ("sheets" and "furniture" inevitably implying the bedroom) suggest that such artists need to undergo a "course of egotistic hardening" (B1, 134) to define the self's limits. The artist who identifies himself too closely with his images gives in to a sensual, rather than aesthetic, desire.

The metaphoric association of desire with the conditions of printing returns us to the contingencies of Romance. In *The Art of Being Ruled* Lewis quotes Julien Benda to the effect that most contemporary artists are emotional rather than intellectual in their approach to the image, "Romantic" rather than "Classical" in their apparent wish to encompass and become part of their creation. Benda notes, and Lewis quotes approvingly, that this relationship is inherently sexual. It arouses the same kinetic emotion in the viewer that "the sight of two people embracing would awaken." Benda equates the motivations of imperfect art with the more general motivations of the self:

Let us learn to recognize, also, in [the emotional artists'] will *to install themselves inside* things, a kind of thirst to sexually invade everything – to violate any intimity, and mix themselves in the most intimate recesses of the being of everything met.[22]

The improper artist's intercourse with the real is dangerously sexual, a surrender to nature's action and reaction. This surrender is implicit in Lewis's image of the artist as Narcissus. Rather than seeking the real, the artist seeks only himself, or his images, as an object of desire. Because he attempts to "install himself" in the real he seeks the opposite of art, some object outside the self with which he can intermingle. The world of "life" threatens integrity not only because its flux fragments the self, but also because its metaphoric sexuality directs the self outward and away from its own value. It leads the self to embrace, rather than oppose, the other.[23]

Defined as Classicist, autonomous, anti-Bergsonian, anti-sentimental, and rejecting the trappings of desire and its imbricated ideologies, the Vorticist emerges from the manifestoes of *Blast* as a selfhood that must transcend emotional and Romantic yearnings to achieve the full integration of a "harmonious and sane duality" (B2, 91). Like the Joycean artist, he assumes an "exile" as the basis for his strength. He sets himself apart from the materials of the world both to claim aesthetic validity from reality and to avoid the fragmenting kinesis of desire. Like an Archimedes claiming that he can move the world, the Vorticist exerts leverage over the real insofar as he can step outside of its control. His opposition to temporality and desire is integral to his self-sufficiency, for it demonstrates his unwillingness to sacrifice selfhood to the incoherence of "life." The Vorticist therefore opposes externality. Although whatever exists outside the self provides the raw material of art – "that fat mass you browse on" (*B*2, 91) – it is automatically a lure and a potential diminishment because it is not the self. The Vorticist must reject the other as a corollary of his power. Only by breaking the bonds between himself and the world can he produce his images with a free and whole intellect. To establish the self's primacy he must reject all that stands outside it.

Independence from the other is therefore Lewis's first requirement for creation. However, the manifestoes that proclaim this belief cannot prove whether Vorticist polemics translate into effective art, particularly in the creation of fiction. *Enemy of the Stars*, which is the only example of Lewis's non-polemical prose in *Blast*, thus provides the perfect test case for *Blast*'s claims. This experimental play, comparable in its extravagant unperformability to works by the Russian Futurists and Antonin Artaud, occupies a crucial position in Lewis's work. The centerpiece of *Blast* attempts to demonstrate that language can be abstracted from representation as earlier experimentation had succeeded in doing with the visual arts. In contrast to the work of its continental fellows, however, the dramatic form of *Enemy of the Stars* is a matter of Lewis's assertion rather than presentation. Its scenes are entirely composed of narrative prose, and Lewis makes liberal use of the block capitals that are typical of *Blast*'s manifestoes. The text is not divided into autonomous speaking parts. Passages of abstract description alternate with more conventional dialogue that is nonetheless presented novelistically, spoken passages placed between quotation marks rather than cued as speeches by particular actors. *Enemy of the Stars* is fully presented in readerly form, and is a play only insofar as Lewis declared it to be so.

Attention to *Enemy of the Stars* has tended to diminish the theoretical problems raised by this overt assumption of a form that it only problematically occupies. Critics who consider the play seriously tend to underemphasize the concerns of its narrative in favor of analyzing the audacity of its style.[24] Yet the relationship between its narrative and style illuminates with surprising intensity the paradigmatic paradoxes we have been tracing in Lewis's early work. The concerns of his nascent Vorticism are theoretically and practically incompatible with the chosen genre, particularly in its presentation of the individual artist as self-reliant creator of new forms. This mode is made clearer when the play is positioned first within Vorticist ideology and then, surprisingly, within the tradition of Romantic closet drama. We shall see that the form that *Enemy of the Stars* implicitly repudiates is also the form that it obliquely follows.

*Enemy of the Stars* at first glance replicates the polemic of the manifestoes. Arghol, the protagonist, is an intellectual who stands against the crowd, one who "has come to fight a ghost, Humanity" (*B*1, 61). He represents the possibility of personal independence, standing against nature even as he uses it for his obscure and metaphorical purposes. He is the "enemy of the stars" of the title, and stands alone as a "MAGNET OF SUBTLE, VAST, SELFISH THINGS" (*B*1, 61). He attempts to give some shape to the "archaic blank wilderness of the universe" (*B*1, 64), and Lewis stresses that Arghol is discontinuous with the world around him in the descriptions of the landscape: "The canal ran in one direction," Lewis writes, "his blood weakly, in the opposite."[25] Arghol rejects the world of desire to achieve a transcendent distance from the world. Like the Vorticist, he wants to leave "life" behind to enter the void that is the merging of paradoxical opposites, to "take header into the boiling starry cold" (*B*1, 67). He hopes to achieve this transcendence through solitude, with which, he explains to his disciple Hanp, he will "reach the stars" (*B*1, 67). On the other hand, Hanp epitomizes the "BLACK BOURGEOIS ASPIRATIONS" that threaten to undermine Arghol's "BLATANT VIRTUOSITY OF SELF" (*B*1, 59), an indistinct form who merges with all around him. Arghol castigates him in the same metaphoric terms with which Lewis dismisses the Romantic artist: "You cling to any object," he says, "dig your nails in earth, not to drop into it" (*B*1, 67). Arghol sees in Hanp only a general portrait of an anonymous and homogeneous mankind whom he must counteract with his theories of selfhood, asserting that selfhood represents the opposite of Hanp's mass mediocrity. "Between Personality and Mankind it is always a question of dog and cat," Arghol states, "they are diametrically opposed species" (*B*1, 66). He rejects all that is not the self as repulsive to individual purity, blaming the other for its gradual destruction: "The process and condition of life, without any exception, is a grotesque degradation, and 'soillure' of the original solitude of the soul. There is no help for it ... Anything but yourself is dirt. Anybody that is" (*B*1, 70).

In living out this startlingly egoistic and misanthropic philosophy, Arghol rejects all action, even self-protection. When Hanp suggests that he avenge himself against the uncle who regularly arrives to beat him, Arghol declines, for any contact with the other, however defensive, can only tarnish selfhood. Arghol considers himself to be a superior force, "too superb ever to lift a finger when harmed," he argues, and cannot lower himself by responding to the world (*B*1, 67). In rejecting the kinetic impulses of life he believes he can ultimately transcend mortality, trusting that the metaphysical weight of his adopted symbols can oppose his dissolution. His intellectual activities are a form of exercise to ward off destruction, the production of an art that can transcend time. "The stone of the stars will do for my seal and emblem," he says, "I practice with it, monotonous 'putting,' that I may hit Death when he comes" (*B*1, 70). Yet as the play progresses it becomes clear that Arghol, unlike the ideal artist of Lewis's manifestoes, cannot protect himself from the world through his trust in self and symbols. When Hanp attacks Arghol after Arghol contemptuously dismisses him as a parasite, Arghol has no choice but to fight back in Hanp's sphere of "life." Arghol becomes an extension of the world rather than its opposite, a "soft, blunt paw of Nature" (*B*1, 75) who loses his distinctiveness, falling into Hanp's condition of integration with the surrounding landscape. This grudging acceptance of nature seals Arghol's downfall. Infuriated by his inconsistency and in "sullen indignation at Arghol ACTING, he who had not the right to act" (B1, 80) Hanp turns against him a second time and murders him as he sleeps.

Arghol's defense against Hanp foreshadows his own destruction. Hanp cannot resolve the contradictions between Arghol's transcendent theories and worldly actions without obliterating their source. Arghol's death is Hanp's dramatic proof that despite his opposition to nature, Arghol is still "imprisoned in a messed socket of existence" (B1, 64). Yet although Hanp is the direct agent of his death, Arghol's downfall results logically from his programmatic rejection of otherness. This is implicit in the dream that Arghol has before his death. He remembers himself as a student in the city, furious with the confinement of his room, who rejects the book that lies "stalely open" before him, *Einege und Sein Eigenkeit* [sic] by the German philosopher Max Stirner (B1, 76).[26] Disgusted with the book as yet another of the tarnishing influences of the external world, Arghol flings it from his window, dismissing it because it is a drain on the authenticity of the self and because its otherness is a perverse call to external experience. A dream figure appears at the door to return the book. This figure appears first as a figure from town, changes into Hanp, and then transforms into Arghol's imagined image of Stirner. The figure ignores Arghol's repeated attempts to eject him, and, as Stirner, provokes Arghol into a repetition of his recent struggle with Hanp.

Although Arghol succeeds in banishing the dream figure from his room, his rejection of Stirner is puzzling. As Tom Kinnimont has noted, Stirner's ideas are substantially those of Arghol, and, insofar as Arghol is a figure of Lewis, of Lewis himself.[27] *Der Einzige und Sein Eigentum* asserts the truth of the self, and attempts to establish its independence from society's falsehoods and reality's limitations by declaring that the self is all-sufficient, its own master and owner. For Stirner, as for Arghol, the self is an ultimate good that can be achieved only by egoistically conserving one's power. "*My own* I am at all times and under all circumstances," he writes, "if I know how to have myself and do not throw myself away on others."[28] He emphasizes that man needs to cast off the bonds of externality, rejecting desire and the societal constructs that limit his autonomy. "I am my *own* only when I am master of myself," Stirner writes, "instead of being mastered either by sensuality or by anything else...what is of use to me...my selfishness pursues" (Stirner, 125). The similarity of Stirner's formulations to those of Arghol is striking. *Der Einzige* further provides the actions of *Enemy of the Stars* with their underlying metaphor. Stirner describes man as a slave who must endure the torments of a mastering reality in order to assert his natural power:

The fetters of reality cut the sharpest welts in my flesh every moment. But *my own* I remain. Given up as serf to a master, I think only of myself and my advantage; his blows strike me indeed, I am not *free* from them; but I endure them only for *my benefit*, perhaps in order to deceive him and make him secure by the semblance of patience, or, again, not to draw worse upon myself by insubordination. But, as I keep my eye on myself and my selfishness, I take by the forelock the first good opportunity to trample the slave holder into the dust. (Stirner, 112–13)

This response to the self's limitations is also shown in the play by Arghol's rejection of action and Hanp's revenge. Arghol refuses to fight against his uncle, his "master," for Stirner's reasons. He will not condescend to act because his uncle is of use to him, for he feeds him. Moreover, like Stirner's self, Arghol obscurely intends to use the energy of the attacks to his own ends, to liberate himself from mastery, "as prisoner his bowl or sheet for escape: not as means of idle humiliation" (*B*1, 68). Yet Arghol is also a master, to Hanp, and he abuses his disciple as severely as he is himself maltreated by his uncle. Hanp's revenge is therefore also a response to the play's avowal of the self's power. He endures Arghol's abuse, like Stirner's selfhood, for his own benefit, eagerly accepting it because it is the only way he can gain knowledge about the city, the desire for which has placed him in Arghol's control. Only when Arghol dismisses Hanp completely does Hanp take advantage of Arghol's sleep to "trample him into the dust." Both Arghol and Hanp enact Stirner's ideas of the self. Arghol explicitly presents the theoretical side of philosophical egoism, while Hanp embodies the destructive action that those ideas imply. "I secure my freedom with regard to the world in the degree that I make the world my own" (Stirner, 120), Stirner concludes; both Arghol, who dominates the stars, and Hanp, who murders his master, are versions of the ego that seeks its freedom through domination of its environment.

Arghol's rejection of Stirner exposes the limiting contradictions in his own thought. If Arghol rejects the other simply because it is not the self, then he blinds himself to the possibility that the object of his scorn, in this case Stirner, may be an equal who shares his ideas and therefore his power. When he rejects Stirner on the automatic grounds of his externality Arghol thus unwittingly rejects his own selfhood. The dream figure, who initially appears as "a young man he had known in the town, but now saw for the first time, seemingly" ($B1$, 77) can be interpreted as a figure of Arghol's internal inconsistency. As an aspect of the self he "had known in town" the figure offers him the literal opportunity to "see himself" for the first time. He gives Arghol the chance to reintegrate his personality by reaccepting the book that he has rejected, offering him the awareness that his self is also, in a sense, other. Their fight, however, demonstrates that Arghol refuses to recognize the contradictions implicit in the cult of selfhood. By throwing Stirner's book from the window he inescapably adheres to his philosophy of selfhood and also transgresses it. By refusing to reaccept it he completes his destruction. Arghol emerges from the fight with only a partial understanding of his endangered self. He tears up his books, and in a paradoxical effort to reclaim his identity he wanders through the streets of the city denying himself to those he meets – "I am not Arghol," he claims, "This man has been masquerading as me" ($B1$, 78). As Arghol believes he can control the logic of selfhood with his paradoxes, his avowals only underscore his actual loss of control. Lewis has described him earlier in the play as "a large open book, full of truth and insults" ($B1$, 71). When Arghol destroys all of his books the reader understands that he has metaphorically completed the eradication of the self that began with his rejection of Stirner. When Arghol returns from the city to the wheelwright's yard at the play's beginning he has already been defeated. In rejecting the other he has already rejected himself.[29]

*Enemy of the Stars* is therefore a narrative about failure. Arghol's theories foreshadow his destruction, for he can no more overcome the material world than he can be consistent with himself. Arghol's fall, as Lewis warns the reader in the play's first line, is part of an "IMMENSE COLLAPSE OF CHRONIC PHILOSOPHY," not simply an implosion of temporal philosophy but of continuous and excessive thought (*B*1, 59). For these reasons *Enemy of the Stars* occupies a problematic position within *Blast*. Where the manifestoes insist that the autonomous self is the basis of the artist's power, the play rejects the efficacy of that philosophy and exposes the Vorticist self as a divisive delusion. Arghol's theories serve only to divide him from himself, and he and Hanp are unified only in their mutual obliteration. The play's content is opposed to that of the manifestoes. In the play opposites are irreconcilable, for they result only in destruction; in the manifestoes the balance of oppositions leads to a higher creativity. *Enemy of the Stars* presents the reader of *Blast* with a fundamental paradox. If the manifestoes' version of opposition is authentic, then the play's apparent contradiction of that truth is not a real contradiction. It can be understood as one of the "opposite statements of a chosen world" (*B*1, 30) that the artist erects as part of his power, an extreme whose denial makes the self stronger. Yet the struggle between apparent opposites has quite different results within the play. The intellectual is unable to balance himself against his negation, and the powerlessness of his rhetoric leads to his destruction. *Enemy of the Stars* threatens to invalidate the very principles upon which the manifestoes are erected even while formally fulfilling them.

The paradox is underlined by Lewis's presentation of his failed hero as a quintessential practitioner of the manifestoes' doctrines. Like Lewis's ideal artist, Arghol tries to use a studied inactivity to escape from the action and reaction of common life. His approach to the world is familiarly figurative and double. According to Hanp, Arghol's logic is mysterious, his association of opposites inscrutable – like the Vorticist "He gave men one image with one hand, and at the same time a second, its antidote with the other" (*B*1, 80). Moreover, the play takes place in a wheelwright's yard, a setting for the creation of whirling objects, metaphorical versions of the Vortex. Like the Vorticist – or at least the Vorticist author of *Enemy of the Stars* – Arghol is a metaphorical playwright, creating from the materials of nature that he paradoxically attempts to rule while eluding their authentic and autonomous power. Lewis states "The stars are his cast" (*B*1, 61). Arghol's struggles are unequivocally Lewis's struggles, an identification made explicit directly before the play. In the "advertisement" Lewis writes that *Enemy of the Stars* is a version of the conflict between the artist and his audience. He informs the reader that the play is "VERY WELL ACTED BY YOU AND ME" (*B*1, 55). (One notes already the element of agon with an unsympathetic readership in *Blast* at large, where Lewis lambastes his own scoffing readers: "CURSE those who will hang over this Manifesto with SILLY CANINES exposed" [*B*1, 17]). Lewis thus appears to implicate himself in his own fictional designs. Just as Arghol falls prey to self-contradiction by dismissing the text of himself as his opposite, Lewis seems to negate himself by creating a text whose content suggests his own necessary failure.

The play's narrative of division and failure, however, can be read as a reflection of its problematic double position within Lewis's artistic canon and the larger generic tradition of "readerly" drama. Lewis wrote *Enemy of the Stars* with the goal of inventing a Vorticist prose, and it stands out strikingly from the other fictions in *Blast*, stylistically conservative efforts by Ford Madox Ford and Rebecca West. Lewis hoped to create a language analogous to his painterly abstractions, revivifying literature with non-representational techniques borrowed from other forms of modernism. "My literary contemporaries I looked upon as too bookish and not keeping pace with the visual revolution," he later explained, "A kind of play, 'The Enemy of the Stars'... was my attempt to show them the way."[30] The relative conservatism of the resulting abstraction of language is striking, however, next to the visual experimentation of the canvases that Lewis reproduced in *Blast* under the play's rubric.[31] Here, for instance, is an example of description from the middle of the play:

Throats iron eternities, drinking heavy radiance, limbs towers of blatant light, the stars poised, immensely distant, with their metal sides, pantheistic machines. (*B*1, 64)

In this passage Lewis distorts expected structure and connotation, much as he rejected expected shapes in his canvases. He places short phrases in apposition without consistent grammatical markers, juxtaposes nouns illogically, and uses verbs to shape disjunct fragments within the sentence rather than to relate them to one another. Yet the sentence's grammar can be easily normalized. If one places the word "are" between "Throats" and "iron," "limbs" and "towers," "stars" and "poised," the apparent idiosyncrasy of the sentence's structure is re-contained as "proper" English. Its effect depends upon the elision, rather than the subversion, of traditional perceptual markers, and its syntax can still be perceived through its apparent discontinuities. The abstraction of its content is similarly limited. A phrase such as "throats iron eternities" depends entirely upon juxtaposition for its abstract effect. The words invoke three distinct images, whose proximity create an aggregate non-representational image. Even if the phrase as a whole has no direct corollary in the world, however, its components remain indivisibly referential. The words "throat," "iron," and "eternities" always evoke real objects or concepts that are separate yet pragmatically connected to the words themselves, even when they are juxtaposed in otherwise extravagant contexts. Lewis himself condemned juxtaposition for artistic effect in his later criticisms of Surrealism. Its interest was psychological rather than pictorial, he wrote, for it arranged "the same old units of the same old stock-in-trade" in novel patterns but added nothing to the vocabulary of representation.[32] By Lewis's own stringent criteria, abstraction and language are intrinsically incompatible. Words, more than visual symbols, are inseparable from their logical systems and fixed referents. Sentences cannot be distorted radically without obliterating their structural sense, while words themselves can never be separated entirely from their signifieds.

Lewis later would admit the hopelessness of the experiment. The writing of *Tarr*, he explains in *Rude Assignment*, made him see "that words and syntax were not susceptible of transformation into abstract terms."[33] Later in *Men Without Art* he states the more general disbelief "that anything in the literary field can be done that will correspond with what has been called 'abstract design'" (*MWA*, 115). Yet the form as well as the content of *Enemy of the Stars* has already suggested its contradictions with his ideal art. By designating his prose experiment a "play" Lewis emphasized the work's visual origin. It is intended to be "seen" rather than read, "acted by you and me" rather than confined to the page. By presenting *Enemy of the Stars* as both drama and printed text Lewis draws particular attention to its features that coexist uneasily with Vorticist ideals. As prose narrative it necessarily unfolds over time; its linearity emphasizes and replicates the temporal nature of the signs with which it is constructed. As drama, moreover, it necessarily places action in its foreground. Its visual and narrative interest must be propelled by the same kinetic surrender to desire that the manifestoes associate with fragmentation. If Arghol is condemned by his ideas, then, he is also condemned by the logics of his fictive and dramatic form. He cannot avoid nature or mortality for the language in which he is described cannot transcend asynchrony or the necessary presentation of action. His failure of transcendence within the play mirrors Lewis's self-created failure of form. As author Lewis cannot escape the demands of the word and its related structures of syntax and narrative. His use of narrative language is a capitulation to the temporal desire and explicit representation that Vorticism elsewhere rejects. Like Arghol's unwilling acceptance of nature, Lewis's use of the signs of language intrinsically contradicts his claims to power.

This contradiction in Lewis's claims for the power of the self is, however, already implicit in the manifestoes' language. In the play Arghol lives according to a false idea of his ability to stand against the other, yet inevitably gives in to desire and destroys himself. The same conditions obtain in the manifestoes in analogous form. When Lewis advises the soldierly erection of dualities his diction consistently describes a system of desire and fragmentation:

3. We discharge ourselves on both sides.
4. We fight first on one side, then on the other, but always for the SAME cause, which is neither side or both sides and ours. (B1, 30)

The phrase "we discharge ourselves," as alluded to previously, invokes not only military force but secondary associations of male sexuality. The artist's creative force is both destructive, yet informed by an externalized and metaphorical desire. The language renders desire self-reflexive. The artist acts not only against the external but also against himself. As he "fights" on both sides, he is not only the creator of his interrelated violence and desire, but also its ultimate object; if he is a soldier then the rhetoric's language of doubleness locks him in mortal combat with himself, as a version of his own despised Narcissus.[34] Lewis's use of figuration implies what the narrative of *Enemy of the Stars* makes explicit. The artist is divided against himself not because he chooses a programmatic doubleness, but because he cannot transcend the self's warring impulses. The structures of nature or "life" even creep into the language of his power. Despite Lewis's dismissal of psychoanalysis, the Vorticist does not elude the rules of the psyche. He emerges rather as an archetypal selfhood who corresponds exactly to Freud's late, and roughly contemporaneous, formulation of the dual drives. Both sexual and outwardly directed, his actions are figurations of a violence that is both externalized and self-reflexive. Like the model of selfhood that Freud describes in *Civilization and its Discontents*, the Vorticist's drive towards creativity, described here in implicitly erotic terms of "discharge," coexists with an aggressiveness that he directs both outward against the external, and inward towards his own dissolution. Lewis's artist, who relies upon the validation and actions of the self, shares the structures of the self's defensiveness. His insistence upon his unity and his ability to contain contradiction compensates for the self's insecurity in the face of the real with a language whose discourse nonetheless subverts its content. Lewis proclaims his power as his rhetoric and narrative imply his weakness. They implicate the artist in the world of the other that he tries to oppose.

This falling into the conditions of Romance at the level of individual psychology meets its generic analogy in the form of *Enemy of the Stars*. In his study of English poetic drama from Wordsworth to Beddoes, Alan Richardson abstracts the narrative features that bind together prominent representatives of the genre. Such plays deal with the history of an individual protagonist's consciousness. They hinge upon highly rhetorical confrontations between the protagonist and his opposite, who represents an aspect of the hero's divided consciousness. The hero is seduced into transgression by his daimon and lapses into a repetition of that transgression, having become dependent upon his other, as Hegel's master and slave come to depend dialectically upon one another. Finally, the divisions within the protagonist revealed, he becomes destructive, either towards others (cynically replaying his own seduction into transgression with another) or towards himself.[35]

The very unperformability of *Enemy of the Stars* serves to underline its thematic and generic affiliations with Romantic genre. As a programmatically unperformable "play," it is surprisingly closer in intent to the verse drama of the English Romantics – in which an essentially non-narrative form is pressed into narrative service – than to the theatrical experiments of contemporaneous European avant-gardists. Like the Romantics, Lewis was attempting to forge a style that was by definition private, to construct a personal language. Yet this essentially lyric impulse is in conflict with the dramatic necessity of the artist's public pronouncement of that style. The verse or readerly drama is caught between the private realm of abstract contemplation and the public realm of narrative, and is the problematic product of that dialectic. The divisions between ideal and actual, private and public, are enacted in Lewis and in the Romantic plays that share his representational concerns by the work's characters, who are themselves rent by self-destructive yet potentially transcendental division. This in turn may be seen as part of the legacy of the English theater, which traces its heritage not from the interplay of individuality and society that is implicit in the Greek tension between chorus and individual performer, but from Senecan dialogic drama. Unlike Aeschylus and Sophocles, Seneca divides issues of philosophy into characters that reify, through the logic of dramatic form, the spectacle of mutilation rather than cultural affirmation. When Arghol and Hanp wear masks "OF ANTIQUE THEATRE" (*B*1, 60) they recapitulate eternal struggles in the dramatic garb of Greek tragedy and its later Roman resolution into internalized philosophic struggle.[36]

We may see in the patterns of *Enemy of the Stars* the mechanisms that obtain in *Manfred* and plays like it. Arghol is seduced into action by Hanp in an atmosphere of intense rhetorical opposition, including the stylistic opposition of nonnarrative Vorticist prose against the demands of action, which betrays Arghol into his own repetitions. The dream of struggle repeats Hanp's attack, as Hanp's attack in turn repeats that of Arghol's uncle. Arghol's dependence on his uncle – "he loads my plate" – is a Hegelian reduplication of Hanp's dependence upon Arghol, as the importance of Stirner's work, formatively influenced by Hegel, grudgingly suggests. And Arghol recognizes overtly that Hanp is a part of himself. The narrative of Hanp's murder of Arghol is, as Richardson notes of *Manfred*, "less a celebration of isolated subjectivity than a critique of the false assumptions behind psychic autonomy."[37] The unitary protagonist is revealed to be divided, and his transgressions against the self destroy him.

Hanp's vengeance upon Arghol thus can be understood as a generic figuration that follows from Lewis's stance of opposition. The figure in Arghol's dream appears as Hanp before it turns into Stirner. Arghol must by implication accept that his disciple, whom he has rejected, is bound to himself. Lewis emphasizes throughout *Enemy of the Stars* that Arghol and Hanp, as he added in the 1932 revision, are "improperly separate."[38] "You are an unclean little beast, crept gloomily out of my ego," Arghol tells Hanp, and he questions explicitly whether his tirades are directed at Hanp or at himself – "'Why do I speak to you?' It's not to you but myself" (*B*1, 73). Arghol recognizes too late that the self he believed he left behind in the city has been replicated in his disciple. Immediately before he dies he recognizes that the other is merely a version of himself – "suddenly he had discovered Arghol who had followed him, in Hanp" (*B*1, 80). Hanp has a similar difficulty in differentiating himself from his master. When he decides to kill Arghol he cannot distinguish between murder and suicide. Lewis writes that Hanp "could hardly help plunging [the knife] in himself, the nearest flesh to him" (*B*1, 34). Hanp is drawn to act as though he is an inextricable and rejected aspect of his master. For this reason Arghol's death implies Hanp's necessary dissolution as well. When Hanp throws himself from a bridge at the play's end, Arghol's cycle of self-destruction is complete. His murderer's suicide is the final silencing of Arghol's demanding self.

Hanp acts as Arghol's destroying double, a Gothic version of the self that Arghol has projected into the world to act out the destruction of his own contradictions. Arghol denies nature, but since he cannot see his own connections to the world he does not recognize that in condemning the external he also condemns himself. He intentionally and wrongly assumes an alienation from the world, and is doomed to failure because his disassociation must necessarily be incomplete. By associating the artist with Arghol, Lewis falls into the same conditions. In his study of the motif of the double in Romantic fiction, Otto Rank summarizes the attributes of the psyche that projects its own dangerous similitude into the world:

[His disposition] is conditioned to a large degree by the splitting of the personality ... to which corresponds an abnormally strong interest in one's own person, his psychic states, and his destinies. This point of view leads to the characteristic relationship ... to the world, to life, and particularly to the love-object, to which no harmonious relationship is found.[39]

Rank seems here to paraphrase Lewis's description of the Vorticist. According to Lewis he is both explicitly and implicitly split – both a "duet in everything" and a fighter against himself

– while his power is erected upon the conditions of the abnormally isolated self. He rejects externality, and denies the world, life, and any desire that leads to harmony with any external object. If Lewis rejects the Romantic as the literary other, therefore, he does not escape its generic mechanisms. When Arghol is killed by Hanp, who is identified with both Stirner's book and Arghol's divided self, Arghol falls prey to the forms and philosophic concerns of his author's rejected Romanticism. When Lewis exposes his own weakness with *Enemy of the Stars* he destroys his model of the artist with a text that is both other and yet an inescapable aspect of a self that, like its signs, is powerless to enact an ideal transcendence. Lewis's narrative negates the self that produced it as its own vengeful double. It proclaims the self's division and collapse as a consequence, rather than an aspect, of its assumed power.[40]

As we close the book upon Lewis's mental drama we may return to Poe. "The Tell-Tale Heart" bears closer ties to *Blast* than the manifestoes immediately suggest. Like Poe's narrator Lewis declares his independence from otherness and the world of common action and reaction, yet despite his proclamations to the contrary he is not exempt from his metaphysical limitations. Nor do his protestations of wholeness and power hide his capitulation to the fragmentation he denies. He is subject to the vengeance exacted by his inevitable division. The language of *Blast* suggests that the Vorticist, like Poe's narrator, is defined not only through his opposition but also through his similarity to that which he presents as his opposite. If he rejects the determination of the self by psychoanalysis, the genres of Romance, or the external world, his opposition nonetheless contains the fulfillment of the laws he rejects. Lewis's early references to Poe mark the textual tension that is built into Vorticist ideology and its narratives from their inception. The Vorticist's reaction against the external is an aspect of his identity with the other, which Lewis overtly denies yet cannot efface – or perhaps more interestingly, chooses not to efface – from the language of his exposition.

Lewis's question in "Some Innkeepers and Bestre," about whether Bestre has discovered "the only type of action compatible with artistic creation" (*WB*, 231) remains without an answer because its solution is as ambiguous as Vorticism's double presentation of itself. Judged by the explicit standards of the manifestoes the answer must be "yes," for Bestre stands against externality with a visual power that triumphs over others through the sheer force of will. Yet Vorticism's subtext, reinforced by the story itself, suggests that Bestre's confrontations are actually failures. Although he admires Bestre's actions, the unnamed narrator of the earlier version notes that the innkeeper deludes himself:

[He] has the common impulse of avenging the self that was starved and humiliated by the reality, in glorifying and satiating the self that exists by his imagination. (*WB*, 232)

Bestre's offenses are finally revealed as defenses. His triumphs are the functions of a desire for "satiation" that is real only to himself, for the self he constructs through his opposition is an illusion that compensates for an actual inability to control what he perceives. As Ker-Orr concedes, Bestre's vision has little to do with actuality. Bestre looks at life with the eye of a "professional liar" (*WB*, 87). Yet if Bestre fails to vanquish his imagined enemies, his transformation of his own failure is itself a form of heroism:

the more cramped and meagre his action has been, the more exuberant his account of the affair afterwards. The more restrictions reality has put on him, the more unbridled is his gusto as historian of his deeds, immediately afterwards. (*WB*, 87)

If Bestre provides the pattern for art it can only be for an art of compensation that erects imaginative figurations as a substitute for reality. His tales are misrepresentations of the self, "disfigurations" of the ego that occlude a reality of dependence with fictions of power. Lewis's early narrator leaves undecided whether this art is sufficient to disguise that failure. The elimination of the question in the final version of "Bestre," written after *Enemy of the Stars* and the period of Lewis's most abstract painting, seems to provide its own tacit denial. In his heightened awareness that the artist's programmatic opposition of the other is ultimately contradictory, Lewis concedes by default that narrative, and the rhetorical assertion of the power of selfhood, cannot evade successfully the fragmentation of Bergsonian or Romantic reality. For Lewis, as for Bestre, the Eye that is art's ultimate justification is inseparable from the "I" that tells its tale. Its figurations, and disfigurations, are the artist's only flawed defense against an other whose opposition is inextricable from one's own identity.

CHAPTER 2

# *The mirror and the razor*

> By what reflections did he, a conscious reactor against the void of incertitude, justify to himself his sentiments?
>
> ... [T]he presupposed intangibility of the thing in itself: ... the apathy of the stars.
>
> James Joyce, *Ulysses*, 17.2210–26
>
> "[I]t is impossible not to commit 'adultery.'"
>
> James Joyce, *Stephen Hero*, 191

Joyce tells the reader of *Ulysses* three times that Leopold Bloom had once planned, among his many other lapsed schemes in the realm of phenomena, to answer a newspaper's challenge to "square the circle" (*U*, 15.2401, 17.1072, 17.1696). Bloom is of course preoccupied with financial gain, and the prize, according to a document in his desk, would have been a million pounds. Yet unlike the more mundane puzzles with which Bloom amuses himself on June 16, 1904 – how to cross Dublin without passing a pub, for instance – the challenge of squaring the circle suggests a deep connection with the workings of *Ulysses* itself. The problem first enters the text in "Circe" when Virag, the apparition of Bloom's grandfather, claims that Bloom had once "intended to devote an entire year to the study of the religious problem and the summer months of 1886 to square the circle and win that million" (*U*, 15.2399–401). The specific nature of that "religious problem" remains only implicit in *Ulysses*, but Virag's rhetorical association of the ancient problem of quadrature with theology is reiterated by the symbolic context of its later appearances in "Ithaca." When Stephen leaves Eccles Street chanting "*In exitu Israel de Egypto*" and confronts with

65

Bloom the spectacle of "The heaventree of stars hung with humid nightblue fruit" (*U*, 17.1039) both Stephen and Joyce draw upon Dante, sardonically but also seriously. "*In exitu*" is the psalm sung by Dante's souls as they enter purgatory and the verse Dante uses as the model for his theory of allegory in the famous letter to Can Grande. The "heaventree of stars" suggests that Stephen and Bloom, among their other symbolic and parodic analogues, emerge from their day's Inferno as a Dante and Virgil who, like their originals, "*riveder le stelle.*"[1]

In this Dantean context the quadrature of the circle raises issues that are simultaneously theological and linguistic. When Dante gazes into the heart of the Eternal Light in the final canto of the *Commedia* he mourns that his language pales before his conception of the divine presence ("*O quanto è corto il dire e come fioco / al mio concetto!*" [*Paradiso*, XXXIII, lines 121–22]), and he describes the impossible task that faces him with the simile of the geometer:

> *Qual è 'l geomètra che tutto s'affige*
> *per misurar lo cerchio, e non ritrova,*
> *pensando, quel principio ond' elli indige,*
> *tal era io a quella vista nova...*

(Like the geometer who sets all his mind to the squaring of the circle and for all his thinking does not discover the principle he needs, such was I at that strange sight)[2]

Dante likens his inability to represent the substance of revelation – if not without a certain rhetorical disingenuousness – to the geometer's inability to transform one fixed shape into another using only the limited tools of straight edge and compass. The simile presents language, which although written is presented as spoken ("*O quanto è corto **il dire**,*" my emphasis), as a tool of representation that is separate and estranged from its referent. Although a potential tool of mediation between man and reality, here language is unable to register ultimate meaning, which for Dante is the teleologic struggle of the poet and pilgrim towards apprehension of the order of God. Dante fulfills his quest in the *Commedia*, to "see how the image was fitted to the circle and how it had its place there" ("*veder volea come si convenne/ l'imago al cherchio e come vi s'indova*" [*Paradiso*, XXXIII, lines 137–39]) only with the help of a divine knowledge that exceeds "*fantasia*," man's ability to represent.³ At the heart of the Rose the distance between language and the thing-in-itself is dissolved, as the movement of the spheres incorporates the poet's desire and will ("*disio e velle*").

In borrowing the figure of the circle's quadrature Joyce implicates his own characters in the Dantean struggle to gain sense of place in a transcendent order. This longing has been manifested previously in *A Portrait of the Artist as a Young Man*, where the young Stephen creates a naive taxonomy that embeds his schoolboy identity within the hierarchy of his perceived universe. He writes on the flyleaf of his geography book:

> *Clongowes Wood College*
> *Stephen Dedalus*
> *Class of Elements*
> *Clongowes Wood College*
> *Sallins*
> *County Kildare*
> *Ireland*
> *Europe*
> *The World*
> *The Universe* (P, 15–16)

Although Stephen positions himself within the coordinates suggested by the subject of the geography book – town to county, to country to continent, to world – the implications of the list go beyond the world, implying selectivity of self-definition within a yearning for overarching order. The second entry particularly invites symbolic interpretation. To be a member of the "Class of Elements" is literally to be a member of a group defined pedagogically within Clongowes, but also to be positioned emblematically within the most inclusive of categories. Like the chemical elements, from which the largest structures of the world are created, the young Stephen is positioned within both microcosm and macrocosm. Not merely a member of Conglowes, he is also a vital part of the largest order he can contemplate. It is symbolically fitting that Stephen, raised in part by a woman named Dante, defines himself in terms of ascending concentric categories. Given Stephen's future struggles with Catholic doctrine, it is significant that Joyce stops the list one sphere short of the Dantean nine. Even a childish vision of the universe permits Stephen no divine Mover to encompass and give meaning to the rest.

Where the child Stephen is a kind of naive spiritual taxonomist, in *Ulysses* both Stephen and Bloom are fully mature pilgrims, even if unknowing ones. They travel through the day of June 16, 1904 seeking answers, and are used by Joyce as elements of symbolic solutions, to puzzles of identity and language that are manifested, as in Dante, by those structures of culture and signification from which they feel most alienated: theology, politics, and family. Joyce presents Stephen and Bloom as exiles who are excluded, or exclude themselves, from their literal homes as well as from the various forms of metaphysical unity those homes represent. Stephen abandons the key of the Martello tower to Buck Mulligan, and Bloom inadvertently leaves his housekey in a pair of trousers he has left behind. The narrative registers the loss of their "keys" as a symbol of their larger exclusion from the validating orders of their cultures, a sign that they lack the tools to regain a lost center from which they could recognize "how the image" – which is the image of man – has its place in the orders that exceed individual identity.

As in Dante, moreover, the author's ideals of figuration are inseparable from the characters' awareness of the powers of language. Through the narrative concerns of his characters, as well as his own manipulations of style, Joyce explores in *Ulysses* the natures of unity and artistic voice in terms of the limitations and doubleness that are implicit in Dante's symbol of representation. Joyce consistently figures the validity of art and self within *Ulysses* in terms of doubleness and the desire for synthesis, which is also the attempt of the ego to mediate the forms of experience which, like the square and circle, stand estranged on either side of language's division. Through Stephen's and Bloom's meditations on the nature of language – and especially in Stephen's lecture on Shakespeare – he creates a model of literary language that explores the role played by dialectic in the search for coherence between word and world: an exploration of doubleness that both motivates and results from *Ulysses*' most important themes and techniques.

While Joyce articulates the problematic relationship between language and selfhood most directly in "Scylla and Charybdis," he establishes the theoretical and symbolic terms for that exploration in the book's opening. During the morning Stephen is frequently confronted by the ambiguous split manifested within language by its dual status as speech and writing. This distinction is implicit in the traditions of biblical and philosophical exegesis inherited by both Dante and Joyce. William T. Noon, for instance, noted in the 1950s that the sign's arbitrary relationship to the signified, and the allegorical doubleness of poetic language are implicit in Joyce's Thomistic inheritance. In the *Summa Theologiae* Aquinas remarks that the "'referential meaning' of a word is not an inevitable meaning," and that the "boldly bifurcated language that poets use" leads to an "opaqueness for the intellect" that frustrates the mind's quest for unity.[4] These dichotomies also have held much interest for post-Saussurian theories of language and sign-making systems. Most notably, Jacques Derrida has claimed, building on a distrust of the absolute that can be traced back to Aristotle's revisions of Plato, that the metaphysical tradition of western culture consistently has viewed speech as ontologically distinct from, and superior to script. Speech has been considered as interior, natural, and unmediated, "present" to the self, whereas writing is exterior and intermediary, deferring and betraying "natural" meaning. Derrida's work strongly implies that the cultural mythology that privileges speech over script is inseparable from the problematic oppositions that undergird the hierarchies of the human sciences, which include philosophy and, implicitly, politics.[5]

These categories of value and hierarchical power are useful for the consideration of *Ulysses*. The very beginning – Buck Mulligan's parody of the Catholic Mass – suggests the categories' importance to Stephen's sense of his lack of power. Mulligan, the "Usurper" (*U*, 1.744), demonstrates his own preeminently verbal power by usurping the written ritual of the

Church and turning it into his own mode of ironic speech. His manipulation of the mass establishes his insouciant character in stark contrast to Stephen's Jesuitical sobriety, but it does more than that. It is a sign of Mulligan's enactment of power and centrality through voice. His appropriation of ritual into ironic speech is another manifestation of the egoism that leads him to declare that the Martello tower on a provincial coast is the "*omphalos*" of a new society. Mulligan constantly displaces the center onto himself, claiming that he is both a sufficient source of value and his own self-enclosed order, both "*Fertiliser and Incubator,*" as he has printed on his calling cards in "Oxen of the Sun" (*U*, 14.660). Intoning the Mass, Mulligan demonstrates not only the power speech plays in the orders from which he gladly excludes himself, but flaunts his ability to elude those powers by using them for his own ends. The words of the Church maintain a secondary and reflected power with their content inverted, for Mulligan uses the words of ritual to reflect only the power of the self who expropriates them for his own ironic purposes.

For Stephen, who also wishes to distance himself from the Church, Mulligan's independent and usurping speech carries both religious and social weight. His speech is inseparable from the privilege and cultural power that Stephen both wishes for and resents. Like that of the youths whom Stephen pictures at the Oxford ragging of Clive Kempthorpe (*U*, 1.165–71), Mulligan's ability to master and even torment is associated with his ability to live within and manipulate the rituals of class. On the other hand, Stephen is inconsistently concerned with the trappings of bourgeois respectability. When he learns that Haines wishes to make a collection of his sayings he muses merely about its potential profitability, and although Mulligan taunts him, Stephen insists upon wearing black for the full year after his mother's death. Yet he is unable to adapt language to social expediency, as Mulligan suggests, to "play them as I do" (*U*, 1.506). For Stephen the words of the Church are so charged with power that he refuses to step within their bounds by praying at his mother's deathbed. For him language is an agent of its culture rather than a servant of the self that temporarily inhabits it. Language delineates a region of inhibition and threat. Stephen's faith in its intrinsic power thus bars him from Mulligan's realm of play. Stephen cannot accept that language's value is relative and that the shifting of signification can be innocuous.

In *A Portrait of the Artist as a Young Man*, Stephen has already viewed speech as culturally divisive. While speaking with the dean in chapter 5 he thinks of the political and ontological differences created by the distinction between the words "funnel" and "tundish," because of the priority of English and its inevitable difference from an Irish tongue:

The language in which we are speaking is his before it is mine. How different are the words *home*, *Christ*, *ale*, *master*, on his lips and on mine! I cannot speak or write these words without unrest of spirit. His language, so familiar and so foreign, will always be for me an acquired speech. I have not made or accepted its words. My voice holds them at bay. My soul frets in the shadow of his language. (P, 189)[6]

To Stephen the dean's English carries a pressure of cultural authenticity. Although he resents the dean's implicit cultural paternalism just as he resists Mulligan's blasphemies, he cannot consider his own speech to be other than inferior and secondary, exceeded by a language that overshadows the aspect of the self – "the soul" – that is most inextricably his. Yet it is significantly speech itself rather than the more general condition of language to which Stephen responds so strongly. Although he also thinks that he cannot "write these words without unrest of spirit," the specifically verbal difference of "acquired speech" marks Stephen's sense of division. He recognizes that he inhabits the "language in which we are speaking" without controlling it, as he will later inhabit Buck's Martello tower without controlling its key. He notes particularly that spoken English differs "on his lips and mine," for speech is inevitably branded by a national accent that lays bare the status of political origins and marks off native from pretender: the subject whose subjugation is marked by the loss of his original language. Aware that speech brands his distance from its origin, Stephen is also aware that he cannot escape its impositions. He cannot divorce himself from his language – and this marital metaphor, as we shall see, has general ramifications for *Ulysses* – for it is the only one he has. It is not simply foreign but also "familiar," with that word's etymological suggestion of intrinsic bond.

Stephen figures his position towards the cultural conditions of language doubly. He is interior and exterior to language, contained within it yet also standing outside of it in grudging defense. He "holds words at bay." His voice is a warrior who faces an invading army, able to fend it off but unable to negate its threat to the self through whom it speaks. If Stephen recognizes that he exists inevitably within the English language, he simultaneously exists at an ontological distance from speech rather than as speech's powerful inhabitant. Language is less his "home" than his "master," even if it partakes of both. As Jules David Law has suggested, Stephen is trapped uncomfortably by metaphors both of belonging and of exile.[7] Stephen is unwilling to "accept" a discourse that his tongue tells him is alien, and lacking Mulligan's faith in ironic expropriation, he is unable to extricate himself from language or feel unthreatened by the otherness that his voice cannot defeat.

Stephen's defensive positions have manifested themselves earlier in metaphors of armament and retreats to figurative language. In the last chapter of *A Portrait of the Artist as a Young Man*, Stephen refuses McCann's attempt to coerce him into signing the Czar's petition for universal peace, rejecting McCann's attempt to label him "reactionary" as a "wooden sword" (*P*, 197). This association of the speech of the powerful other with figurations of attack appears with renewed vigor in *Ulysses*. Both Mulligan's and Deasy's speech take on the literal attributes of arms to be "held at bay." As is suitable for companions who begin their day in the unlikely setting of a fortified tower, Mulligan's speech leaves "gaping wounds" in Stephen's heart against which he must "shield" himself (*U*, 1.216–17), as though Mulligan's words were penetrating weapons against which Stephen can launch only a belated defense. Deasy, who heads the school in which Stephen works and who speaks with the voice of received political wisdom, similarly presents his speech as an instrument of war and penetration. After his one-sided and prescriptive conversation with Stephen he says "I like to break a lance with you" (*U*, 2.424–25), suggesting (as does Mulligan) that political opposition and speech are closely related, a battle analogous to the "joust" being played outside the window by the boys at hockey. Deasy's use of "breaking a lance" suggests a habitual condition. Although as Stephen's employer he exerts undeniable power (Deasy convinces Stephen to deliver a letter on foot and mouth disease to his literary friends) his use of a cliché suggests that he refers not solely to the matter at hand but to all of his discourse. His sense of the potency of his speech, like the dean's, is so inbred as to be frozen into unthinking figuration. Mulligan similarly observes that the act of speech itself, rather than specific content, wounds Stephen. "[Y]ou sulk with me because I don't whinge like some hired mute from Lalouette's," he says (*U*, 1.213–14), attributing Stephen's dismay not to his words but to the fact that he speaks at all. Mulligan significantly associates restraint of speech here with subservience. One "whinges" if one is a servant or under hire by a temporary master, and Mulligan's speaking against the conventions of mourning, as permanent a part of culture as the Mass, is as much a gesture of control and opposition as his earlier appropriation. Stephen finds himself trapped in a double bind, in which his metaphorical opposition to speech has become literalized in his day-to-day discourse with his nominally powerful companions. He thinks that when meeting Haines he must come up with "talk, to pierce the polished mail of his mind" (*U*, 2.43). If he can neither master the speech of his culture nor meet others' speech with his own historically powerful thrusts, he will be condemned to his own kind of silence: a cultural exclusion that is both personal and political.

This relationship between language, politics, and personal attack becomes climactically literal later in "Circe" when Stephen is knocked unconscious by British soldiers who speak their own brutal and obscene version of the "King's English" (*U*, 15.4746). Stephen's position in the classroom of "Nestor" dramatizes his powerlessness with proleptic acuteness emphasizing, in a chapter rife with history and images of battle, his inability to speak powerfully for himself.[8] As a teacher he finds himself in a position of nominal hierarchical power, one of Deasy's unwilling allies. Yet he is an ineffectual leader. He thinks of Pyrrhus at Asculum in terms of his own rhetorical position, his ashplant become armament: "a general speaking to his officers, leaned upon his spear... They lend ear" (*U*, 2.16–17). However, he is unable to control his students, to play general to the small officers whose economic and social privilege he envies. Stephen's voice is unheeded. For example, Armstrong confuses his request for historical information with a lesson in Latin. Even when Stephen makes a self-referential jest about the difficulty of making connections, describing a pier as a "disappointed bridge," the class misses the joke as though there were "No-one here to hear" (*U*, 2.42). They show interest in his voice only when they request a story. But they do not grant Stephen an opening to demonstrate creativity, since they are presumably ignorant of his literary aspirations. They wish to listen rather to a narrative that pre-exists Stephen, for which he would merely act as interpreter. The only voice able to muster the children into engagement and action is the anonymous voice that announces "Hockey!" from the corridor. Stephen crumples readily before the voice from the hall – an exterior voice – that announces ritual and gamesmanship, speech that combines a call to pseudo-military battle with Mulligan's valorization of privileged play.

As in *A Portrait of the Artist as a Young Man* Stephen's awareness of the ambiguous relationship between culture and language is inseparable from his sense that he is secondary, and disenfranchised both by the anonymous voice of history and by the usurping language that lends it speech. Yet while in *A Portrait of the Artist as a Young Man* the practical politics of linguistic division overshadow its associated metaphysics – the imposition of an alien language upon the Irish voice rather than the fragmenting power of speech itself – in *Ulysses*, as the voice in the corridor suggests, Stephen's sense of exclusion is an effect of the ontological properties of voice itself. An incident in the first chapter marks an instructive parallel to Stephen's musings in *A Portrait of the Artist as a Young Man*. When the milkwoman appears at breakfast, the Englishman Haines enacts a more severe form of the dean's cultural imperialism. Like Mulligan expropriating the language of the Mass for his own ends, Haines takes over the milkwoman's native language itself. He speaks Gaelic to a woman who not only believes it is French – confusing that which should be "familiar" with that which is "foreign" – but cannot even understand the patronizing gesture. Rather than resenting the political conditions that allow a foreign country to colonize a native culture for its own picturesque purposes, Stephen's consciousness surprisingly attends to the properties of voice itself:

> Stephen listened in scornful silence. She bows her old head to a voice that speaks to her loudly, her bonesetter, her medicineman: me she slights. To the voice that will shrive and oil for the grave all there is of her but her woman's unclean loins, of man's flesh made not in God's likeness, the serpent's prey. And to the loud voice that now bids her be silent with wondering unsteady eyes. (*U*, 1.418–23)

In Stephen's imagination Haines's and Mulligan's voices have become instruments of pure power. Mulligan's position as medical student has granted him the ability to provide a kind of secular absolution. Ironically, given his cavalier expropriation of the Church's rhetoric, his ability to "shrive and oil for the grave" places Mulligan in a position of priest-like authority, from which he can demand an implicit obeisance. Yet Stephen associates this power not with Mulligan himself, but with the absolute condition of voice. The milkwoman bows her head, as though a "voice," not Mulligan, were the bonesetter and medicine man. The voice itself usurps the priest's prerogative, shriving and granting benediction. It seems to float free from its speaker, embodied by "wondering and unsteady eyes" that are neither clearly Mulligan's nor Haines's. Stephen imagines voice in this passage as though it were not only contingent upon historical and cultural order but as though it were actually separate from its speaker, not only exceeding those through whom it speaks but pre-empting them as well. If Haines proves that the milkwoman has become radically separated from a language that should be authentically hers, the rhetoric of the passage suggests a surprising similarity between nominal ruler and nominally ruled. Those who speak with the powerful voice of culture are themselves usurped, occluded as individuals by the very voice that grants them their power.

This separation of self from voice is not merely an artifact of Stephen's self-involvement. Throughout the opening chapters Joyce's rhetoric emphasizes the degree to which voice usurps the individuals who attempt to use it as an agent of power. Through his transcription of Stephen's consciousness and in omniscient narrative Joyce transforms those who speak most powerfully into objects replaced by, or separated from their voices. Haines appears in the text first as "A voice within the tower" (*U*, 1.227). Joyce attributes his first reported words, a question of priority and control, to voice itself – "Have you the key? a voice asked" (*U*, 1.322). Like his Oxford classmates, reduced to "moneyed voices" in Stephen's imagination (*U*, 1.165), Haines becomes a function of speech, defined and replaced by voice. When he proclaims his political identity, it is his voice, not himself, that announces who he is – "Of course I'm a Britisher, Haines's voice said, and I feel as one" (*U*, 1.666). Mr Deasy is similarly abstracted when he broaches issues of power and identity. He restores order among the bickering hockey players with his "old man's voice" (*U*, 2.193), while his "thoughtful voice," rather than he himself, explains his conservative views (*U*, 2.268). More than any other character, however, Mulligan is defined and occluded by voice. By the second page Joyce objectifies Mulligan's banter – "Buck Mulligan's gay voice went on" (*U*, 1.40) – and grants it an existence that supersedes his physical presence. Mulligan stands beside Stephen as a "wellfed voice" (*U*, 1.107), and when he vanishes down the staircase the "drone of his descending voice" (*U*, 1.237) remains to boom out a poem by Yeats, to "[sing] from within the tower" and to climb up again as though independent from Buck himself – "It came nearer up the staircase, calling again" (*U*, 1.281–82). By the end of the chapter Mulligan disappears completely as a character on the page. As he swims he is simply "A voice, sweettoned and sustained" who calls from the sea, deprived of gender and identity – "It called again" (*U*, 1.741–42).

These consistent figurations suggest that independence of

voice disunifies the individual. When Haines claims to "feel as one," for instance, the ascription makes it clear that "one" is precisely what he cannot be. The rhetorical separation of voice suggests that Haines's speech emanates from a place other than himself. Not only does Haines submerge his individuality in a stereotypical adherence to national identity, but his usurpation implies that his political voice lives at a remove from the self within the narrative, operating, like a metaphorical Mr Duffy from "A Painful Case," at a "little distance from his body."[9] Mulligan's "own" voice, so often abstracted from his narrative identity, similarly becomes an external subject that takes Mulligan himself as its grammatical object rather than its source. "He had spoken himself into boldness" (*U*, 1.216), we are told in "Telemachus," while Mulligan's laughter, another expression of voice, acts upon him entirely from without, reducing him to both grammatical and literal object – "Laughter seized all his strong wellknit trunk" (*U*, 1.132–33). When Stephen finds himself "depressed by his own voice" (*U*, 1.188) his feeling that he is an object to his speech reinforces his sense of existing both within and outside of his language. Joyce's rhetorical treatment of Haines, Deasy, and Mulligan suggests that Stephen suffers more from self-awareness than from radical difference. His consciousness of linguistic disenfranchisement is only a more urgent version of the metaphysical disunification that is implicit even in the others' use of "powerful" speech.

Voice and speech are no longer unproblematic vessels of "presence" in these chapters, neither naturally accessible to the self nor unequivocal in their ability to express truth. Although Mulligan, Haines, and Deasy treat voice as though it were revelatory, Stephen and the narrative of *Ulysses* know it to be disunifying, and dangerous. When Stephen counters Mr Deasy's teleological view of history with a God that is "A shout in the street" (*U*, 2.386), the "one great goal" of history reduced to the goals in a game of hockey, he not only revises Deasy's theology and mistaken historical sense but also the schoolmaster's faith in the intrinsic valorization of signs. By replacing the headmaster's immanence with a divinity both random and external, Stephen associates the Word – replaced by boys' shouts – with the opposition and violence of radical disunity. This conception of false unity within the Word has already appeared in Stephen's attitude towards the voice of the Church, whose power he cannot bring himself to deny. While walking with Haines on the beach Stephen constructs a musical vision of its "potent titles" and "brazen bells" (*U*, 1.650–51). They are "Symbol of the apostles in the mass for pope Marcellus, the voices blended, singing alone loud in affirmation: and behind their chant the vigilant angel of the church militant disarmed and menaced her heresiarchs" (*U*, 1.653–56). The reference to Palestrina, whose *Missa Papae Marcelli* supposedly proved to the Council of Trent that polyphony in the Church's music was not inimical to the understanding of its spiritual messages, becomes in Stephen's reconstruction an emblem of the Church's resistance to those who challenge its arbitrary center. By insisting upon the monody of Gregorian chant and outlawing polyphony in its music – literally, the existence of many voices – the Church grafts artificial singularity upon that which is naturally multiple. It uses an artificial blending of voices – polyphony become plainchant – as a smokescreen behind which it can "disarm its hieresiarchs." Palestrina's modified polyphony is co-opted by the Church as a kind of pretense to innovation that accomplishes a thorough oppression of difference and multiplicity in the face of aesthetic and historical challenge.[10]

The Church's immanence is thus as inauthentic as Mulligan's, and for the same reasons. Although Mulligan calls Stephen a "mummer" (*U*, 1.98), accusing him of taking on masks and costumes to occlude his authentic self, the narrative makes it clear that it is Stephen's opponents, Mulligan himself and the Church, who are created in a succession of speech, their identity subsumed by a multiplicity of voices, none of which are authentically theirs.[11] Like the Jewish merchants at the Paris stock exchange of whom Stephen thinks "Not theirs: these clothes, this speech, these gestures" (*U*, 2.367), voice emerges in the syntax and figuration of these chapters as an instrument of division and inauthenticity that clothes itself in the garments of origin. When Blake's "*The harlot's cry from street to street/ Shall* weave old England's windingsheet" (*U*, 2.355–56) passes through Stephen's mind in "Nestor," Joyce merely reaffirms through quotation what his rhetoric has already made clear – voice partakes of death as well as life, cover as well as revelation.

In these early chapters speech is not exempt from the metaphysical associations of fragmentation and externality that post-structuralism has associated with writing. Yet the chapters' figurations do not grant writing metaphysical priority over voice in a simple undoing and reversal of hierarchies. Instead Joyce bounds writing – which appears in the narrative both as the literary tradition and as the physical manipulation of signs – with similarly indeterminate and opposed figurations. Particularly in the early chapters writing maintains powerful associations of fragmentation, belatedness, and suppression of origin. Those most fragmented by voice are those who most fragment texts. Mulligan and Deasy misuse theological and literary quotations in their speech, inverting their context, as when the schoolmaster quotes Iago's "*Put but money in thy purse*" to Stephen as positive advice (*U*, 2.239). Writing appears in their discourses as disassociated fragments, reduced either to the objects of Mulligan's play or decayed into unthinking maxims. Haines's proposed book of Irish quotations and folklore is similarly reductive. Haines plans to contain and preserve speech within his own script, yet his book embodies writing as doubly alien. In recasting speech into the foreignness of another language as well as into the distancing medium of print Haines will kill what he tries to preserve under its own academic weight, as Mulligan notes, burying "Five lines of text" under "ten pages of notes about the folk and the fishgods of Dundrum" (*U*, 1.365–66).

These characters' writing is implicitly subservient even when it is nominally original rather than quotation. Mr Deasy fills his letter to the press, for instance, with a nostalgia for the presence of voice that exceeds the mechanism of his own typewriting. He commands his typewriter as though it were an extension of speech, ordering as is his wont in the classroom – "Full stop, Mr Deasy bade his keys" (*U*, 2.305). Deasy asks his projected reader to heed "*the dictates of common sense*" (*U*, 2. 294–95), implicitly opposing what is "dictated" – both a secretarial and a political term – against the letter of the law as a carrier of natural ethics. Deasy even calls himself a "Cassandra" (*U*, 2.329) associating his writings not with script but with prophetic voice – a voice, ironically, like Deasy's "actual" voice, that fails to communicate.

Nor is Stephen freed from the distortions of writing, which in his classroom is battered and alien. His history book is "gorescarred" (*U*, 2.12) and serves him only as a crutch for information that, as a teacher, he should already know. He is unable to tell a student where to begin to read, and Milton's "Lycidas," with its elegiac intimations of resurrection, is reduced to "jerks of verse" (*U*, 2.62) by the student's mechanical and faulty reading. Even the children's request for a story associates writing with posthumousness. They want a "ghoststory" (*U*, 2.55), a narrative of mystery and veiling, while Stephen responds with a riddle that not only takes death and cover as its answer – "The fox burying his grandmother under a hollybush" (*U*, 2.115) – but which itself enacts repression, promising solution but offering only a further enigma.

When Stephen helps Cyril Sargent with his algebra homework, script further excludes and makes strange. The student's name is ironically emblematic. His surname echoes Stephen's status as a powerless officer, for he is a "sergeant" who cannot marshal signs any more than his teacher can marshal students. Although he shares the name of Cyril, inventor of an alphabet, the machinations of signs lie beyond Sargent's comprehension. Even his signature, the text that should be most intimately connected to the self, is only "crooked ... with blind loops and a blot" (*U*, 2.129–30). The algebraic signs that he copies mechanically are crippled, "unsteady symbols" whose signification depends not upon his comprehension, but, like Deasy's script, upon validation by speech – they stand, as does Sargent, "Waiting always for a word of help" (*U*, 2.163–64).

These disjunctions established by the figurations of the classroom also haunt Stephen outside of it. In "Proteus" he expresses his fears of alienation from writing in the same symbolic terms that prevail in the schoolroom:

Books you were going to write with letters for titles. Have you read his F? O yes, but I prefer Q. Yes, but W is wonderful. O yes, W. Remember your epiphanies written on green oval leaves, deeply deep, copies to be sent if you died to all the great libraries of the world, including Alexandria? (*U*, 3.139–43)

Like Deasy, Stephen alludes to writing as prophecy. Yet where Deasy naively considers his script to be the servant of an authentic immanence, Stephen's "green oval leaves" are rather the leaves of Virgil's Sybil, which scatter if read, turned into the "blind loops" of Sargent's script. Written language decomposes even in his ironic titles. Their single letters juxtapose a literal fragmentation of the alphabet with a metaphorical rejection of writing as revelation, dismissing his epiphanies, like the fox's grandmother, as "deeply deep," buried rather than profound. Writing, for Stephen, has become its own "ghoststory." It can only offer a posthumous and implicitly futile revelation, relegated from an absent self to the equally absent repository of a library long destroyed. When Mulligan early in the morning laughs that Haines's book will be printed by "the weird sisters" (*U*, 1.367) he jokingly declares script unnatural and strange. Stephen's musings similarly associate writing with the deathly absence of the self, the anti-revelatory, the excluded.

This distrust of writing allows us to make a preliminary leap from the themes within the narrative of *Ulysses* to its own status as writing, as a book whose narrative movements, to which we shall return, reflect its distrust in the truth-value of any singular written style.[12] Indeed, Joyce particularly associates the physical reproduction of signs – both printing and iconic representation – with decay and exclusion throughout *Ulysses*. Linguistic decay particularly clusters around Bloom. The legend on the "sweated band" of his hat has turned "hat" into "ha" (*U*, 4.69–70), while a sign in a urinal is disfigured from "POST NO BILLS" to "POST 110 PILLS" (*U*, 8.101); later in the day his name is misspelled in a newspaper that also contains a passage of botched type (*U*, 16.1260). The newspaper, presumably an organ of cultural inter-communication, becomes instead a focus of alienation. Neither Bloom nor Stephen finds a place among the newspapermen, Bloom feeling particularly excluded by the typesetter Nanetti, who can say "we" in a sense that Bloom cannot (*U*, 7.35). This exclusion extends to other forms of political and social disenfranchisement. Kevin Egan, the exiled Irish nationalist, rolls cigarettes "through fingers smeared with printer's ink" (*U*, 3.216–17). Gerty MacDowell, an outsider because of her handicap, carries "cork lino letters" past a printinghouse for her father, who is himself excluded, "laid up" (*U*, 10.1207). Even Milly Bloom, whose apprenticeship in the photo business is an extended lesson in a different kind of reproductive printing, is excluded from *Ulysses* by her absence from Dublin and her absence from the foreground of the narrative. Finally, the gramophone and pianola – both mechanical reproducers, like printing, in the absence of originating consciousness – claim their associations with death. The gramophone, like the ghost of Hamlet's father, brings back the voice of the dead (*U*, 6.964–67) while the "*coffin of the pianola*" in "Circe" (*U*, 15.3667) plays the dead march from *Saul* (*U*, 15.3500) and the "Dance of death" itself (*U*, 15.4139).

While these images associate the reproduction of signs with exclusion and deathly disjuncture, moments in the text nonetheless suggest that this very weakened and imperfect script is also the key to issues of community and cultural transmission that are elsewhere claimed – although ambiguously enacted – by speech. When Stephen helps Sargent with his algebra in "Nestor" the symbols on the page, despite their opacity for the student, surprisingly maintain the power to cohere and represent origin that Stephen elsewhere rejects:

Across the page the symbols moved in grave morrice, in the mummery of their letters, wearing quaint caps of squares and cubes. Give hands, traverse, bow to partner: so: imps of fancy of the Moors. Gone too from the world, Averroes and Moses Maimonides, dark men in mien and movement, flashing in their mocking mirrors the obscure soul of the world, a darkness shining in brightness which brightness could not comprehend. (*U*, 2.155–60)

These signs cause Sargent's incomprehension and exclude him from the community of his fellows, but in Stephen's imaginative recreation they also give allusive life. Although they form the subject of the enigma they also allow Stephen to "[solve] out the problem" (*U*, 2.151). When the symbols dance "in grave morrice" the adjective echoes the metaphors that relate writing to burial, but also transforms them into an image of productive seriousness, the vitality of movement and art. The characters "give hands," and "bow to partner," creating a metaphorical community within themselves, while their dance establishes its own community between past and present, transmitting the culture of its creators.

That this continuity is of historical and even nationalist significance is implied by the nature of the dance. The "grave morrice" is not merely Moorish, as the immediate context suggests, but the "mummery" of the Morris-dance, a ritual performed in villages in the English Midlands, whose name is thought to derive from Moorish models. A particularly communal activity and spectacle, the Morris-dance originated in fertility rituals and the continuity of the harvest. In the 1904 of *Ulysses* it was part of a tradition that had largely lapsed, falling into disuse in the mid-nineteenth century and only becoming at the turn of the twentieth century the subject of a nationalist revival. As an emblem of fertility, the Morris-dance of the algebraic symbols suggests not only the viability of signs, but the potential re-establishment of a form of nationalist art. It implies the possibility of cultural rebirth – here ironically under a British imprimatur – with origins in a surprisingly alien culture, the Moorish becoming domesticated, the alien made familiar.[13]

Stephen's fantasy of script's transmission of history therefore differs from voice's temporal power. Where Joyce earlier establishes voice as mediating between the powerful and the subservient in a dialectic of command, Stephen envisions script here as a provisional bridge, a dance of partners that traverses times and cultures as it traverses the page. Its system is independent and external from conventional western history, associated with Moorish and Jewish thought rather than the Roman and Christian paradigms of voice, but is capable of restoring lapsed cultural value within western modernity. Although Stephen figures its power as exterior play rather than interior command, this externality is positive rather than diminishing. It reverses the ontology of inauthenticity that

Joyce and Stephen have hitherto associated with the play of Mulligan's voice. Averroes and Maimonides, called up through association with their symbols, live on through the "flashing [of] mocking mirrors," much as Mulligan "flash[es] the tidings abroad in sunlight" in his own mirror after shaving (*U*, 1.130–31). Where Mulligan's verbal mockery threatens to turn in upon itself and invalidate both subject and self, Stephen here grants script's similar attributes the paradoxical ability to preserve. The ambiguous genitive in the phrase "their mocking mirrors" suggest that the symbols of Averroes and Maimonides have the power to reflect not only the world but also their creators. It implies that writing is the exterior image of the self, which acts as the potential key to a reality possessed of its own core of irreducible meaning, an "obscure soul." The symbolic logic of the passage, therefore, suggests that exclusion – externality rather than internality – is the key to the illumination, however obscure, of the "darkness shining in brightness" that ever exceeds unriddling or representation. If script in this passage is external and belated its disjunction from self and referent becomes its strength. It stores and reconstructs value in a ritual of serious play whose ability to mirror the self and the real depends upon the "mockery," the imitation, of its distance from both.

Disunifying and alien, then, writing is also implicit in *Ulysses* as provisionally strengthening and politically healing. Usurped and excluded by a voice whose autonomy and internality are themselves in question, script in Joyce's figurations is estranged from origin, yet is provisionally able to reflect and penetrate, to establish symbolic continuity within the structures of self and history from which it is excluded. The silence, cunning, and exile that Stephen claimed for the creative artist are recapitulated by the symbolic paradoxes of textuality, which though divorced from selfhood are able to reconstitute its source, much as the artist in literal exile claims the ability to represent his homeland more tellingly from without.

This is the metaphysical substratum of *Ulysses* as a whole. However, in Stephen's case writing remains ironically unsuccessful. Although he finds solace in Yeats's "Who Goes with

Fergus?," whose call for a retreat from solipsism echoes the figurations of dance and fruitful penetration that elsewhere adhere to script,[14] his attempts to comfort and reflect through his own writing remain strangely disjunct. The poem he writes on the beach, his sole act of inscription in the early narrative, figures writing not as healing but as parasitism, depletion rather than reconstitution. Its figure of the "*pale vampire, / Mouth to my mouth*" (*U*, 7.524–25) posits creation as an unnatural penetration, a sucking out or mutilation of the self. Authorship is a leeching upon an authentic and preverbal inspiration, a "breath, unspeeched" (*U*, 3.402–03), that betrays the author even as it creates a bridge between self and other. Moreover, as the poem reveals anxieties of writing as vampirism, a leeching upon "blood not mine" (*U*, 3.394), it enacts a deeper inauthenticity of form. Aside from the introduction of the vampire, Stephen's lyric is almost identical to "My Grief on the Sea," a Celtic poem translated by Douglas Hyde in his book *Love Songs of Connacht*, which was published in Dublin in 1904 and appears within the narrative of *Ulysses* as the book that leads Haines, who is involved in a similar project of collection, away from Stephen's lecture on Shakespeare.[15] The lyric performs through plagiarism the very betrayal of the artistic self that it portrays. As an adaptation of a translation it steals inspiration both from a mediating author and an original model, obscuring through its transformations the authentic connection between writing and subject. The figure of the vampire acts as a poetic correlative for the inauthenticity of the language in which it is described. It is not only extrinsic to the Celtic of the original but is doubly extrinsic to Stephen, for he is not only excluded by the English language, but he creates a poem that exists aesthetically at two removes from its source. Like the telegram that Mulligan recognizes Stephen has plagiarized from Meredith, Stephen's writing in these early chapters does not reflect authentically either himself or the "signatures of all things" that he so wishes to interpret. Presented as mediation and healing – the lyric's composition allows Stephen to feel that "Pain is far" (*U*, 3.444) – his writing implicitly claims an undeserved originality. Produced by a compatriot of Hyde but also of Bram Stoker and Sheridan Le Fanu, Stephen's vampire reflects within itself only the order of the previously written.

In "Scylla and Charybdis," however, Joyce provides a model for the reconciliation of the dualities of self and sign that are implicit in the earlier chapters' treatment of the disjunctions of voice and script. This chapter's placement within *Ulysses*, and the schema that Joyce sent to Stuart Gilbert, suggest that Joyce viewed this ninth of eighteen chapters as a structural and symbolic culmination of what had come before. Joyce wrote in his manuscript that it was the "End of first part of *Ulysses*."[16] In the schema he lists this chapter's respective "technique" and "art" as "dialectic" and "literature," suggesting not only that the chapter's central concern is mediation and synthesis (as its Homeric title already implies) but also that such an inquiry is associated with linguistic representation, which has already been framed by the preceding narrative in terms of metaphysical oppositions. This link between dialectic and language is stronger than the mere juxtaposition of terms. Although they are only implicitly connected in the schemata, the symbols that Joyce elucidates for Gilbert imply a deeper structural connection between their oppositions and the explicitly linguistic oppositions of the earlier chapters. "Plato, mysticism, and London" are the chapter's analogues for Homer's "Whirlpool," Joyce explained to Gilbert, while "Aristotle, dogma, and Stratford" act within the chapter as "The Rock."[17] Significantly, these symbols array themselves into the same dialectical pairings that are active in the preceding chapters, which suggests that the early oppositions of voice and script are now at the symbolic center of the narrative. Joyce's terms fall into similar patterns: of powerful and usurped, inside and outside, central and emarginated, original and belated. He opposes "Plato," the original teacher of the interiority of form, against "Aristotle," who as "Plato's schoolboy," as Stephen calls him (*U*, 9.57), is both a "belated" philosopher and the standard bearer for the exteriority of particulars. Similarly "mysticism," which posits a central and indwelling faith, stands opposed to "dogma," faith's external impositions in the form of written law. "London," finally, the political seat of Britain and locus of English's most "central" accent, is juxtaposed against the provincial, and therefore marginal, Stratford.

Moreover, these "secondary" symbols of the "Rock" with which Stephen identifies himself share script's symbolic potential to reconstitute itself, to establish a new origin out of seclusion. Each of the symbols creates its own tradition or centrality, usurping or reversing from without the ontological status of its "primary" opposing symbol. Aristotle, who is jokingly validated within the chapter by the script of the "diploma" received from his master Plato ($U$, 9.59), is followed by a line of "revisionist" philosophers who stand equally with, if they do not replace, the Platonists. The Catholic Church's dogma, however much Stephen distrusts it, has replaced mysticism as the source and center of modern Catholicism. Stratford's new centrality is the most explicitly linguistic of these symbolic reconstitutions. It literally gives birth to an "external" script that establishes itself as a new center. It gives the world Shakespeare, whose distance from London, according to Stephen's lecture, is inextricable from his place as the new "center" of his national literature.

As Joyce identifies Stephen with these "secondary" but potentially triumphant symbols, he similarly arrays the opposing "primary" and powerful symbols in directly linguistic contexts around the poets and other literati who come to hear him lecture. Like the powerful members of the community elsewhere in the narrative from whom Stephen feels excluded, these writers associate themselves through these symbols with a theological access to origin, which they find in the natural immanence of voice. To Russell, the strongest opposing voice in the library, Stephen's inquiries into Shakespeare's life are like "Clergymen's discussions of the historicity of Jesus" ($U$, 9.48). Imaginative biography is for Russell a perverse attempt to create a pragmatic context for an artistic language that must, if it is to be worth anything, reveal "formless spiritual essences," validated by the secular divinity of its creator. As theosophists, Russell and the others are dedicated to "Father, Word and Holy Breath... the Logos who suffers in us at every moment"

(*U*, 9.61–63), Stephen thinks. Language itself is for them a mystically trinitarian product of inspiration, self, and source linking utterance to origin, which is both God and the self in which it dwells. As the word is naturally present, informed by the Platonic ideal rather than the Aristotelian accident, Russell also conceives of art as the product of a society whose artistic and political voice has become perverted by the cultural appurtenances of writing. The powerful movements that "work revolutions in the world," come not from the "rarefied air of the academy," he warns, but from the natural art of the love songs produced spontaneously "out of the dreams and visions in a peasant's heart on the hillside." The "sixshilling novel, the musichall song," in contradistinction, are artifices imposed upon a natural society, and implicitly a natural language, by the intelligentsia (*U*, 9.108). Russell compares the "desirable life," which is revealed only to "the poor of heart, the life of Homer's Phaeacians" (a curious description of Odysseus' abundantly gifted and wealthy listeners) to the culture of symbolism that produced Mallarmé (*U*, 9.109) and finds the French poet corrupt. Yet his comparison again sets the idea of a natural voice against the specter of an unnatural script. He implicitly condemns Mallarmé's poetry of artifice, which in poems such as "*Un coup de dés*" is also experimentation with print itself, while lauding the paradigmatic oral culture of western literature – those who listen to Odysseus' words – as the natural recipients of Platonic revelation.

The writers object to Stephen's theory not only because it deals with the particular and the biographical, but because its excessive ingenuity imposes falsehood upon the presence of the artistic self in a natural language. Earlier in the morning Mulligan jokingly described Stephen's lecture as "algebra," a paradoxical attempt to establish correspondence and identity through signs (*U*, 1.555). Stephen's audience similarly accuse him of manipulating symbols in bad faith in order to provide a pragmatic basis for art. Russell declares that Stephen's ideas are of interest only to the "parish clerk" (*U*, 9.184), relegating him to the level of the mechanical scriptors of conventional history, while Eglinton accuses Stephen of leaning "towards the bypaths of apocrypha" (*U*, 9.407), trusting in and re-creating an inauthentic writing. If Stephen attempts to speak with originality or authority in his lecture, Eglinton implies at its opening, it can only be with an artificial and grotesque power that he models after the previously written. "Like the fat boy in Pickwick," Eglinton says of Stephen's "ghoststory," "he wants to make our flesh creep" (*U*, 9.142–43).

Yet Stephen's relationship to writing and speech in the library is more complex than these writers credit. Certainly in his unfamiliar roles as lecturer and teacher Stephen has to mediate between the pressure of the "writing" he is accused of championing and the newly varied implications of his voice. He is not only attempting to create, he is also trying to enter a group that excludes him, as well as to oppose them. As Eglinton intuits, he wants to "make their flesh creep." When beginning to lecture he feels the same uncertainty and distrust of voice that he felt in the classroom. As a silent revenge against Eglinton's witticism he thinks of the passage from Canto XXI of Dante's *Inferno* in which the leader of the devils "*avea del cul fatto trombetta*," musters a scripted quotation to invert the poet's Platonic equation of power and voice into a farcical perversion of speech's role in hierarchy and control. Although he continues to think of himself as disjunct from voice and artistic power, a "mute orderly, following battles from afar" (*U*, 9.136), as his lecture continues he begins to recognize that he too can use voice as a provisional instrument. He becomes aware that his voice is not only a mark of inauthenticity but also an ambiguous vehicle of power. He thinks of his voice as a weapon that unsheathes "dagger definitions" (*U*, 9.84), an instrument of revenge that can use words as a kind of poison. "And in the porches of their ears I pour" (*U*, 9.465) Stephen thinks as he speaks, refiguring his voice in terms of the murder in *Hamlet*, a mechanism that he can turn against those who, like the king in the play, are most powerful. Stephen's relationship to his voice in the library is therefore newly double. He continues to feel that he speaks with a usurped or stolen voice, "the voice of Esau" (*U*, 9.981), but he also recognizes that in that theft his subject charges him with an authentic and vivifying power. He recognizes the deathliness inherent in the writing of the library. The books around him are "coffined," embalmed in the "spice of words." Yet Stephen nonetheless experiences them as a powerfully speaking presence. Like the ghost in *Hamlet* they "tell me in my ear a maudlin tale, urge me to wreak their will" (*U*, 9.357–58). In his figurations his lecture becomes a vocalizing and reinvigorating of the writing around him, a conversion of the dead letters of the past into the living and authentic speech for which Stephen, like the theosophists to whom he speaks, acts as mediator. If the previously written threatens originality, as Eglinton has hinted, Stephen also registers the written as the only metaphoric "voice" within whose history he can posit himself: the only tradition that can teach him a powerful and oppositional language of his own.

Stephen's lecture presents its own Scylla and Charybdis of opposed critical interpretations. Many critics have seen in it the successful avoidance of the extremes that are promised by the content of Stephen's commentary and by the symbolic and thematic parallel that surround Stephen's experience. Stuart Gilbert, who began the tradition of emphasizing the "paternity theme" in the chapter, and William T. Noon, who brilliantly explains its trinitarian dimensions, read Stephen's disquisition against the theological figures that obtrude into his religious and familial life, and find in art's correlative the symbolic solutions that elude Stephen in life.[18] The equation of art and life surfaces more explicitly in later criticism, inevitably harmonious with the critic's sense of the nature of *Ulysses* as a whole. For S. L. Goldberg, whose *The Classical Temper* treats *Ulysses* with Leavisian fervor as a piece of naturalism gone stylistically wrong, the Shakespeare lecture reveals that "self-knowledge, self-realization, detachment, human completeness, balance, are Joyce's key-concepts" before the deterioration of the latter part of the book into stylistic mannerism. The lecture restores meaningfulness and truth to art by restoring art to its context in experience, a restoration that emphasizes reconciliation.[19] Richard Ellmann presses a pattern of recontainment and metabiography yet more forcefully. In *Ulysses on the Liffey* he interprets the whole of *Ulysses* as a pattern of successful syntheses, and in his introduction to the 1986 Random House edition of the novel he borrows a phrase from Stephen's discourse as a generic description for the work as a whole: "Like other comedies, *Ulysses* ends in a vision of reconciliation rather than of sundering."[20]

More recently Robert Kellogg concurs that "by the end of the argument the opponents have reconciled the extremes," and John Paul Riquelme, usually scrupulously suspicious of singular perspectives, declares that "the episode's numerous dichotomies... combine into an all-inclusive whole."[21] Taken in the aggregate, these interpretations suggest that Stephen's tale and mental commentary upon it provide a successful model of the artistic self. Even if estranged from script and equivocally fragmented by voice, the artist nonetheless squares the circle by force of will, inserting himself into language's joint traditions. By accepting his own narrating self as an Aristotelian "form of forms" whose continuity is guaranteed by memory and self's fundamental identity with the materials of its perceptions, Stephen grants his imagination the power to evade the fragmentations that are thrust upon it. The ideal artist (that is, the ideal self) proves his coherence by mediating and rejoining oppositions through his mastery of language.

For these critics Stephen's Shakespeare is a mirror of Stephen's own self-image as artist: as synthesizer of opposites and discoverer of the symbolic middle ground between the oppositions of philosophy and life. Yet as Stephen explicitly states in his lecture, life is the product of both sundering and reconciliation, and to ignore the former in favor of the latter in interpreting his lecture is to privilege the symbolic potential of Stephen's lecture over performative evidence, intention over achievement. The opposite tendency – to emphasize failed performance over narrative intent – turns the lecture into evidence for an ironic vision of its generating text. To Hugh Kenner, for instance, Stephen's lecture "parodies classical dialectics," and the emergence of dichotomous oppositions in the chapter "brings the general dialectical impasse of the book to focus." David Hayman notes that Stephen is "rent and submerged" by his attempts to avoid the twin traps of Plato and

Aristotle, a performative failure that precludes analysis of the lecture's content.[22]

One is hard pressed to elude this critical dilemma. Readers who consider the figure of Shakespeare to be a successful emblem of the artist must ignore Stephen's inaccuracies or retractions, distortions of fact, and failed performance. Those who find him unsuccessful in his dramatic situation, however, tend not to read the content of his lecture with the same care as those who make it central to the meaning of the book. They tacitly accept the other camp's positive description of the Shakespeare of the lecture but deny its plausibility as narrative. William Schutte, the first detailed exegete of this chapter, reports this tension without attempting to discharge its paradoxical import. Although he presents Stephen's theory as proof of the "artist as a god of creation," he declares it a "defeat," noting the virtuosity of Stephen's lecture as well as its logical and historical deficiencies.[23] Hovering behind all else is Stephen's retraction, which must be ignored or argued away by those who support the content of the lecture, nowhere with more engaging, if perhaps disengenuous, elegance than by Richard Ellmann, who claims that "[Stephen] can disavow belief so easily because what he is offering here is not, as it seems, a biography of Shakespeare at all; it is rather a parable of art."[24]

There is much to be said for treating Stephen's performance as a parable of art, and as a reconciliatory parable at that. Shakespeare certainly represents a successful mediation of the linguistic problems with which Stephen has been grappling. As the central figure of English drama, Shakespeare provides the ideal model for a literature in which script and speech are simultaneously present as a unity. Shakespeare is for Stephen, in this respect, the model of an ideal linguistic practice. As both creator and actor he vocalizes a script for which he is himself the ultimate referent, invigorating his own signs without falling prey to the alienation of voice from self. Unlike Mulligan's plundering and parodic appropriations, Shakespeare's language is rooted in its originating consciousness and is formally whole in and of itself. This condition Stephen re-enacts by speaking his own "algebraic," or previously written, lecture. Moreover, Stephen's emphasis on reconstructing Shakespeare's biography through his language, suggests to many critics Joyce's faith not only in language's historical strength but also its power to bridge the gap between originating self and represented world. As Stephen suggests in his summation, Shakespeare "found in the world without as actual what was in his world within as possible" (*U*, 9.1041–42), and words were the means of connecting one to the other. The historical personage becomes the model Aristotelian whose ability to join together the disparate element of experience is part and parcel of his status as "lord of language" (*U*, 9.454).

One remembers, however, Stephen's tendency to fall into situations where the Gordian knot cannot be cut, from the moment on the schoolyard in *A Portrait of the Artist as a Young Man* when he is unable to provide the answer required by the boys who ask if he kisses his mother, and who tease him regardless of his reply (*P*, 14). Similarly, as Stephen appears to grant Shakespeare synthetic power in his summation, he shortly thereafter refuses to endorse his own theory. The reasons for this refusal are complex. The lecture tells a more ambiguous tale than Stephen seems to intend. In his introduction Stephen places Shakespeare firmly within the symbolic matrices of theology. He is the ghost of Hamlet's father speaking to his son, the paternal spirit giving voice to the redeemer who remains on earth. Yet Shakespeare's relationship to Hamlet as actor, and to *Hamlet* as playwright, render problematic the associated theological relationship of essence to letter. Stephen describes Shakespeare in the guise of Hamlet's father as a speaking presence, bound intrinsically to his creation. He is a "wellset man with a bass voice," speaking to "the son of his soul" (*U*, 9.165, 171). In a later passage Shakespeare as father becomes a natural voice that gives presence to the son, the spirit that motivates matter. He is the "sea's voice, a voice heard only in the heart of him who is the substance of his shadow" (*U*, 9.479–80). Correspondingly, Joyce associates the son Hamlet with matter and textuality. Before Stephen begins his lecture Best presents his own interpretation of *Hamlet*:

– Mallarmé, don't you know, he said, has written those wonderful prose poems Stephen MacKenna used to read to me in Paris. The one about *Hamlet*. He says: *il se promène, lisant au livre de lui-même*, don't you know, *reading the book of himself*. He describes *Hamlet* given in a French town, don't you know, a provincial town. They advertised it.
   His free hand graciously wrote tiny signs in air.

>                Hamlet
>                  *ou*
>              Le Distrait
>         Pièce de Shakespeare                (*U*, 9.112–21)

In this "French point of view" (*U*, 9.123–24), ironically tendered by one of Stephen's Phaeacian opponents, both Hamlet and *Hamlet* have become resolutely textualized, subjects for interpretation and further sign-making. The prince has become a metaphorical book, not only open to interpretation and "reading" but also the pretext for another set of interpretative signs, Mallarmé's "prose poem." *Hamlet*, meanwhile, obviously already a text, is further textualized as the subject of an "advertisement," a literal sign that Best in turn reproduces with his own "tiny signs" left hanging in the air. Both Hamlet and *Hamlet* share in the stigma of script. The self-interpreting prince is "*distrait*," absent-minded, or vacant, while the play, advertised with subtitle as though unknown, has become "provincial." If Shakespeare and father are speaking subjects, prince and play are both son and text, product and margin whose value (or, in the play, motivation) depends upon the presence of the originating voice of Shakespeare and the ghost.

   Yet Stephen's Shakespeare is anything but the pure authorizing presence of theology. As a character in Stephen's lecture, of course, Shakespeare exists only as the retrospective summation of his own creative signs, an extrapolated biography and psychology bound together by fiction. If Hamlet's father is for Stephen an intrinsic emblem for his creator so are, in other parts of his argument Shylock, Falstaff, John O'Gaunt, and Prospero. The historical Shakespeare, according to this line of inquiry, is the sum of his observable fragments. Yet by marshaling textual evidence to point towards a unifying Shakespearian truth

Stephen threatens to undermine his own implicit contention, for he emphasizes surface fragmentation rather than the underlying unity of the author. His postulated originating self threatens to disappear under the welter of character analogs and literary allusions that are all that can stand in his place.

This shadowy presence in the narrative, of course, is part of the point. If one cannot know the facts of the author's life but assumes that the self lies bound to its signs, then one can presume to reconstruct that self through its traces, examining not only *Hamlet* and the other plays, but Shakespeare's will, his epitaph, all one can know of historical origin. As such, Stephen's inquiry is fully recuperable within his stated aesthetic of *A Portrait of the Artist as a Young Man*, in which the artist withdraws behind his creation, and within the theological traditions by which God can be known only through his sacred signs. Yet Stephen's emphasis on Shakespeare's problematic coherence goes beyond the stylistic imperatives of his literary-historical dilemma. Surprisingly, given his announced intentions, Stephen emphasizes at every turn Shakespeare's distance from his signs, in denial of the very presence-in-absence that he seeks. Stephen stresses Shakespeare's absence not only from literary history but from his own life. As a speaking spirit he is a specter rather than a presence, taking on the garb of "a ghost by death" (*U*, 9.175) when he plays Hamlet's father, a "ghost by absence" (*U*, 9.174) in his life. Stephen emphasizes his "life of absence" (*U*, 9.1031) twice, pointing to the stage as the realm of facade, in which Shakespeare buried his identity in the borrowed selves of roles, wearing the "vesture of buried Denmark" (*U*, 9.175) without wearing an authentic vesture – the clothes, like Stephen's own clothes, are actually the "castoff mail of a court buck" (*U*, 9.165). If his language belongs to him in creation it does not belong to him in speaking. His writing makes him "a king and no king" (*U*, 9.166). Moreover, in Stephen's descriptions this language emerges as itself borrowed, part of a mechanism of covering and self-occlusion. Shakespeare's female characters have their "life, thought, speech...lent them by males" (*U*, 9.255), while the speech of Hamlet's father is the same "lean, unlovely English" (*U*, 9.471–72) that Douglas Hyde, appearing again in Stephen's consciousness during the chapter, contemns as the necessary corollary of translations and writing (*U*, 9.99). Finally and most importantly, Stephen describes Shakespeare's writing as a barrier to knowledge, a "creation he has piled up to hide him from himself" (*U*, 9.475). If the artist succeeds in installing part of his self into his signs – as is suggested by the ironic second meaning of *Hamlet* as a "*pièce de Shakespeare*" – then the reverse is not necessarily true. If meaning can be transmitted from father to son – speaker to listener or interpreter, self to sign – it may still be barred from its originating self. Stephen's Shakespeare remains "untaught by the wisdom he has written or by the laws he has revealed" (*U*, 9.477–78).

Shakespeare lies behind his own writings yet is displaced from them. This presents Stephen with an interpretative bind. While claiming to reconstruct an absent cause, he constructs instead a defense of absence. Shakespeare not only withdraws behind his creation but becomes disjunct from his writing's revelation. He does not disappear but is displaced and hidden by his signs, much as the ghost is a father displaced by his royal son, followed and threatened by what he has produced. As Stephen states, adumbrating Freud's *Totem and Taboo*, the artist/father fears his replacement by the image of himself that he has himself created – "He is the new male: his growth is his father's decline, his youth his father's envy, his friend his father's enemy" (*U*, 9.855–57). Shakespeare, in other words, loses through creation the very Aristotelian ability to mediate between self and world that Stephen has earlier claimed for the artist, explicitly as early as *Stephen Hero* and implicitly in the early sections of the lecture, and to which he harks in his conclusion.[25] Shakespeare emerges rather as a paradoxical figure, both powerful as source or "father" yet powerless as selfhood, a distinction Stephen registers in his own play with words. Shakespeare is both "*William the conqueror*" (*U*, 9.637) and "William the conquered" (*U*, 9.987).

While he gestures towards "the intense instant of imagination" (*U*, 9.381) and paternity's "legal fiction" (*U*, 9.844) as mechanisms that join father to son and speaker to sign, Stephen's faith in these totalizing constructs coexists only uneasily with his narrative's vision of Shakespeare as paradoxical source of both authentication and absence, both lord of language and language's victim. If there is an achieved dialectic in the chapter, therefore, one must seek it elsewhere. Yet even this inquiry is double, for it is dependent on the two distinct meanings of "dialectic." Stephen's immediate understanding of the term can be extrapolated from "Circe." When Stephen ineffectually confronts the enraged Private Carr at the climax of that chapter, Lynch says that he "likes dialectic, the universal language" (*U*, 15.4726). Dialectic here, Lynch implies, is argumentation used as weaponry. Stephen attempts to replace his stick with "pure reason" (*U*, 15.4735). Yet this martial and oppositional dialectic is not only separate but opposed to the project of synthesis. Earlier in "Circe" Stephen associates mediation not with his own project but with those of his enemies, the "priest and king" whom he must kill in himself: "Struggle for life is the law of existence but human philirenists, notably the tsar and the king of England, have invented arbitration" (*U*, 15.4434–36). Although there is bitter irony in nominating the tsar and the king as "philirenists" – "lovers of peace" – Stephen's understanding of dialectic is unambiguous. It is the active tool of the Socratic philosopher who uses language to turn one's opponents' arguments against themselves. The other dialectic – the search for synthesis or arbitration – is the post-Hegelian project of the powerful, those with a political interest in containing the violence of opposition with an artificial peace.

This is the distinction between Stephen's conception of his narrative and the conception of those who listen to him. Until his conclusion his miscomprehending listeners seek to recuperate his argument within a conciliatory framework. Lyster, who as librarian is unofficial moderator and as quaker is a programmatic "philirenist," consistently tries to "comfort" the listeners and gloss over the friction implicit both in Stephen's relationship to his audience and in his theory of Shakespeare (*U*, 9.1). For Lyster all interpretations are valid, containable within a framework that can include even Buck Mulligan's parodic interpretations – "He smiled on all sides equally" (*U*, 9.506).

For Best, Shakespeare is contained through allusion to Coleridge. He is "myriadminded," and therefore not subject to further scrutiny (*U*, 9.768–69). John Eglinton sounds the final and clearest note of Hegelian misinterpretation. After hearing Stephen's paradoxical exposition of the creative self he concludes "The truth is midway ... He is the ghost and the prince. He is all in all" (*U*, 9.1018–19), a naivety reaffirmed in "Circe," where Eglinton appears with a searchlight, seeking for "facts," and declaring "*with carping accent* ... 'I am out for truth. Plain truth for a plain man'" (*U*, 15.2257–59).

Stephen agrees with Eglinton that Shakespeare is "all in all" – indeed he quotes the phrase in his next paragraph – but he importantly does not respond to Eglinton's assertion that Shakespeare's truth lies in synthesis, "midway." Instead Stephen's response is troubling. He lists Shakespeare's attributes as a catalog of division, of arrayed opposites. Shakespeare is both "bawd and cuckold," he "acts and is acted on," he is "lover of an ideal or a perversion," never, in Stephen's exposition, the exemplar of a complete truth that lies midway between, or effectively joins, the oppositions he embodies. If Stephen's Shakespeare is a transcendent figure and not the product of a "delusion," the term with which Eglinton dismisses Stephen (*U*, 9.1064), then Stephen's catalogue suggests a curiously displaced transcendence, based upon the containment of the irreconcilable within a sundered self, not upon the unities in the Christian and mystical neo-Platonisms of his listeners. Shakespeare includes the unmediated Scylla and Charybdis within himself, rather than charting a safe course between the two.

To what degree can it be said that a dialectic is successfully achieved in the chapter? Stephen's attempt at an oppositional Socratic dialectic must be accounted for as a failure, for he neither carries his point nor overturns his listeners' narrative and historical presuppositions from within. When he laughs at the end of his lecture "to free his mind from his mind's bondage" (*U*, 9.1016) he confirms his failure to communicate, for he has laughed identically twice earlier in the day, both times after failing to engage other audiences with similarly gnomic narratives, the riddle of the fox and the "Parable of the Plums" (*U*, 2.116, 7.1028). Instead of forcing his ideas to their conclusion he concedes to the misinterpretations that attempt to recontain the subversive elements of his narrative within a vision of philosophic reconciliation. He gives in to an audience, including some critics of *Ulysses*, who ironically perceives in Stephen's narrative simply another straightforward "Platonic dialogu[e]" (*U*, 9.1069) filtered through a modern sensibility.[26] Whether this surrender is a calculated act of literary politics, a sign of Stephen's resignation to the deficiencies of his own exposition, or a surreptitious attempt to include opposed views within his own as an analogy to Shakespeare's doubleness, scarcely affects the question of dialectic in the chapter. For neither Stephen nor his listeners construct a vision of the artist that is dialectical in a Hegelian sense, capable of synthesizing the opposed elements out of which he is created rather than simply suspending them. Therefore the narrative remains, with one exception, as much a product of division as it was at the beginning.

That one exception provides entry into the narrative's thematics of failure. In the last words of his lecture, Stephen suggests that the divided state he has described is true not only of the worldly creator but also of the divine:

The playwright who wrote the folio of this world and wrote it badly (He gave us light first and the sun two days later), the lord of things as they are whom the most Roman of catholics call *dio boia*, hangman god, is doubtless all in all in all of us, ostler and butcher, and would be bawd and cuckold too but that in the economy of heaven, foretold by Hamlet, there are no more marriages, glorified man, an androgynous angel, being a wife unto himself. (*U*, 9.1046–52)

Stephen's return to theology offers a final key for the interpretation of his lecture. Although his last figure is of reconciliation, it is a reconciliation possible only in the realm of ideality, and then only to "glorified" man. The heaven of the passage, normally a source of theological authority, is surprisingly not a place of juncture but the source of earthly oppositions. It is the home of the "*dio boia*" whose authority, like that of Shakespeare, is grounded in the intermixture of creation and death. Yet his last figure registers one important exception to the intractability of oppositions. In heaven the categories of bawd and cuckold cease to exist, for they are eradicated by the androgynous angel, man who has become "a wife unto himself."

This is a curious point on which to close. For after a narrative that calls into question the viability of Platonic totalities, Stephen ends with a vision of sexual containment that clearly evokes, despite its embedding in Shakespearean quotation, the parable of sexual differentiation in *The Symposium*. According to Plato's Aristophanes, man's search for sexual congress is the longing to recapture lost unity, to regain the hermaphroditic state he enjoyed before he was split into individuated sexes. The product of this difference and incompletion is sexual desire, which is an attempt to heal the fissure that divides man from part of himself by rejoining oppositions into wholes. While the achievement of this sexuality in the fallen world remains literally impossible, desire remains the quest for totality. If the original androgynous self could be reclaimed, desire would be simultaneously discharged and dispersed – the self would have no further need to tend towards its opposite for completion.[27]

In this concluding passage Stephen presents a model of successful resolution. Difference is resolved in the working through of desire, which is also the containment of opposites into wholes. Yet Shakespeare knows what Stephen does not. Richard Ellmann has noted that Shakespeare only alludes to Scylla and Charybdis once, and there the monsters take on respectively male and female identities. In *The Merchant of Venice* Launcelot Gobbo says to Jessica "Truly I fear you are damn'd both by father and mother; thus when I shun Scylla, your father, I fall into Charybdis, your mother" (III.v.15–18).[28] This allusion, resonant with the sexual and parental threats that haunt Stephen's contemplations of his own conception in "Proteus," gives further lie to the possibility of ideal union. Scylla and Charybdis may join to produce the artist as male and female, father and mother, but do so destructively. In Stephen's conclusion, "glorified" man exists ironically only in an angelic absence of desire. To be a "wife unto oneself" is to be free of the earthly movement towards marriage, which is the completion of a fragmented self through the resolution of its parts.

The nostalgia for perfect resolution in this conclusion points to the aspect of Stephen's lecture that is most often glossed over in exegesis. Stephen equates Shakespeare not simply with the symbolic father but also with the fragmenting motions of desire itself. Shakespeare's divided self is directly related to the thwarted motions of sexuality and displaced desire. When Shakespeare enacts the ghost, Stephen argues, he is not simply the spirit whose absence informs the presence of the son. He is also the lover betrayed by lust. Gertrude's fictive unfaithfulness in *Hamlet* mirrors Anne Hathaway's adulteries in life, Stephen argues, which drive Shakespeare into the "life of absence" (*U*, 9.1031) that he forces himself to re-enact as the dead king. The bequest of the second best bed and his naming of villains in his plays after his own brothers suggest that *Hamlet* echoes an authentic biographical displacement. Shakespeare, as creator, was victim of the crime he described in art, betrayed by a desire that excluded him from marriage and sent him into a life of exile.

While Shakespeare reproduces and represents that betrayal in art, Stephen argues, he also reproduces sexual betrayal in life. Stephen reads Shakespeare's exile to London as the search to fill an emptied self through erotic displacement. Shakespeare's own adulteries are attempts to reclaim through repetition a marriage that was undone even as it was defined. Shakespeare assumes a "dongiovannism" as cover but discovers that "No later undoing will undo the first undoing" (*U*, 9.458–59), that no degree of erotic involvement can restore the original bond now lost. As he vacillates between his marriage and the adulterous pleasures of London he drives a wedge between self and self-knowledge. Shakespeare's repetitions of Anne's adultery, according to Stephen, "dark[en] even his own understanding of himself" (*U*, 9.463–64).

That self, moreover, becomes identified throughout Stephen's lecture with desire itself. When Stephen reads "Venus and Adonis" as a parable of Shakespeare's seduction by Anne, the "boldfaced Stratford wench who tumbles in a cornfield a lover younger than herself" (*U*, 9.259–60), he discovers there the primal scene of creation. Shakespeare's entry into sexuality becomes, in a powerful metaphorical sense, an incestuous birth – Stephen says that Anne, who seduced and outlived him, "saw him into and out of the world" (*U*, 9.218–19). Stephen therefore names Shakespeare's entry into sexuality as his entry into identity, an equation that informs his entire lecture. He points out that Shakespeare understood this of himself – "He has revealed it in the sonnets where there is Will in overplus" (*U*, 9.923–24).

Most telling, however, is the fractured allusion with which Stephen opens his lecture. Stephen's first narrative words are "A deathsman of the soul Robert Greene called him" (*U*, 9.130). The context suggests that in alluding to Greene's *Groats-Worth of Witte* Stephen calls up the historical Shakespeare, the "him" of the quotation. Yet Greene's phrase, whether the misattribution is ironic or unintentional, has as its subject not Shakespeare but "lust." The famous reference to Shakespeare as "in his owne conceit the onely Shake-scene in the countrie" occurs in Greene's text two paragraphs earlier. Stephen alludes instead to a nearly adjacent paragraph that advises "Flie lust, as the deathsman of the soule, and defile not the Temple of the holie ghost."[29]

Stephen thus initiates his discussion of Shakespeare by covertly defining the artist as desire itself. Yet this symbolic pattern becomes, in the context of the lecture, doubly disunifying. Following the pattern of "Venus and Adonis," Stephen reads Shakespeare's original seduction not only as his birth but also as a wound that leads to his "darkening understanding." Like Odysseus and Adonis before him, Shakespeare is penetrated by the metaphoric tusk of the boar; his entry into selfhood is marked by desire's disfiguration. Shakespeare enabled by sexuality is ironically a Shakespeare emptied of his sense of inviolable selfhood. His seduction means that "Belief in himself has been untimely killed" (*U*, 9.455–56). Moreover, this absence of self-belief and the equation of selfhood with desire undermines the theological metaphors of fatherhood that run concurrently throughout the lecture. The quotation from

Greene establishes a Shakespeare of uncontainable symbolic self-contradiction. Lust is not here, as in the sonnets, merely a waste of shame. It is a defiling of the temple of the Holy Spirit itself, a deathly falling away from the Word. But as Stephen's Shakespeare is himself a version of the Holy Ghost, in the guise of specter and source of language, his identification with desire makes him a self-canceling figure. To flee lust he must flee himself. Desire becomes both sin against the Holy Ghost and symbolic self-betrayal.

The centrifugal forces of Shakespeare's desire, then – the creation of the self and the self's fragmentation, the drive towards both representation and repetition – undermine the possibility of achieving reconciliation within a transcendent selfhood. Even as he is defined by desire he is subject to the categories of division with which Stephen ends his argument:

In *Cymbeline*, in *Othello* he is bawd and cuckold. He acts and is acted on. Lover of an ideal or a perversion, like José he kills the real Carmen. His unremitting intellect is the hornmad Iago ceaselessly willing that the moor in him shall suffer. (*U*, 9.1021–24)

Both tormenter and tormented, Shakespeare emerges as betrayed and betrayer unreconciled. His divisions are the products of desire – to act or be acted upon, to give in to lust, to be at the same time the jealous mind and the body it punishes for its excessive desire. The Shakespeare of this part of Stephen's summation is irreconcilable with the transcendent figure of his conclusion, and Stephen's recantation underlines his own disbelief of the neat closure he provides for his audience. If Shakespeare has indeed "found in the world without as actual what was in his world within as possible" then he could have found in the world only the divisions and self-betrayals Stephen describes him as finding within. As the "lover of an ideal or a perversion," Stephen's Shakespeare emerges not as model Aristotelian, but as the operatic "Don José" desiring too violently to resolve himself with the opposite that could make him whole. It is no surprise that when Shakespeare appears within the mirror in "Circe" he speaks not with his own voice but in "*dignified ventriloquy*" (*U*, 15.3826). Unselfed as he is unmanned, he laughs a "*capon's laugh*" (*U*, 15.3828), and reflects Stephen and Bloom in that archetypal Joycean condition: paralysis.

Not a figure of ideal representation but a symbol of estrangement, Stephen's Shakespeare emerges as a self divided by desire and its linguistic figurations. The implications of this model for the male artist are multiple. As a parable of specifically male creation, Stephen's Shakespeare provides an under-appreciated point of entrance to *Ulysses'* concerns with gender, an understanding of not only the status of masculine identity within Joyce's texts but also the status of female language, a vexed site in recent criticism of Joyce.[30] Stephen has noted that the speech of Shakespeare's own female characters is inauthentic, deriving from male models, historically "spoken" by male actors, the "dignified ventriloquy" that reappears in "Circe." One may extend Stephen's observations about gender, inauthenticity, and theatrical artifice to Molly and the other women of Dublin, such as Gerty MacDowell, whose languages, both public and mental, are mediated not only by male cultural production but by the existential fact of their creation by a male author. As Stephen's lecture suggests, however, the "inauthenticity" of their speech and thought should not be seen as the cultural collusion of an author who buys unthinkingly into myths of the inviolable male artist who creates the malleable female. The male artist, who is the source of voices and scripts, is as divided as the female subject, defined and limited both by his Platonic incompletion and its necessary corollary, sexual and metaphysical desire. In *Finnegans Wake* Joyce notes with clear reference to *Ulysses* that "the penelopean patience of its last paraphe" is "sternly controlled and easily repersuaded by the uniform matteroffactness of a meandering male fist" (*FW*, 123.4–10). Stephen's lecture suggests, that this oppressive and organizing fist is as much a fiction as "matteroffact," suggesting a context for female speech in Joyce: the male creator, despite his ideal self-portrayal, is not free from the divisions and artifice that are inseparable from his creation, or his "lending," of a gendered voice.

More generally, Stephen's lecture, presented under the rubric of dialectical closure, exposes the source of oppositions, including sexual opposition, in desire. Desire becomes the originary and centrifugal force that, as Jacques Lacan has argued, similarly prevents language from remaining in fixed relationship to its signified, always sliding away, like the trope of metonymy in particular, towards "*something else.*"[31] Writing is never far from this equation. Outside his lecture on Shakespeare, Stephen's experience of desire is similarly inseparable from his experience of writing and representation. In "Proteus" Stephen thinks of the "alphabet books [he was] going to write" for the "virgin at Hodges Figgis' window" (*U*, 3.426–27). His remembrance of "keen glances" given to the "lady of letters" (*U*, 3.427, 430) relates the linguistic act with the sexual, as though the act of writing, the alphabet, is an initiation into sexuality not unlike Shakespeare's in Stephen's tale. (The equation is also implicit in Joyce's erotic biographical sketch *Giacomo Joyce*: Stephen's cynical appraisal of women's sexuality in "Proteus," "What about what? What else were they invented for?" [3.135] echoes Joyce's frustrated "What then? Write it, damn you, write it! What else are you good for?"[32]) Even the examples of Stephen's ambiguous relation to writing are strongly tinged by desire. The first riddle to which Stephen alludes in "Nestor" figures writing as dangerously sexual. Although the narrative only registers the first two lines – "*Riddle me, riddle me, randy ro. / My father gave me seed to sow*" (*U*, 2.88–89) – its conclusion posits script as an unambiguous vehicle of desire –

> The seed was black and the ground was white.
> Riddle me that and I'll give you a pipe (or pint).
> Answer: writing a letter.[33]

Here anxieties of sexuality are displaced within anxieties of language. The answer, that the "seed to sow" is "writing," is repressed by Stephen's consciousness. The relationship of writing to sexual dissemination appears only through buried allusion. The most significant equation of "writing" with the dangers of sexual desire appears in Stephen's imitation of Hyde, where the vampire's penetration of the writing "I," "mouth to my mouth," is not only a literalized theft of inspiration but also a disturbing fantasy of sexual violation. Writing, within his own writing, becomes not merely a reflection of the previously written but a full-scale devouring of the self by its own desire to create.

One may read these associations, certainly, as effects of Stephen's psychology, the neurotic working through of the issues that haunt him as an individual. One may attribute this binding of writing and desire to the particularity of Joyce's delineation of Stephen's consciousness.[34] Yet this association of writing with desire obtains more generally in *Ulysses* than can be explained simply by the psychic demands of individual character. If one turns temporarily from Stephen to Bloom, for instance, one can see how readily he too associates writing with the workings of sexuality. The list is extensive. Bloom's intimations of Molly's adultery come from a letter, Boylan's "Bold hand" (*U*, 4.244), while his intimations of his daughter's sexuality spring from the "bad writing" (*U*, 4.413) from Mullingar that comes in the morning's post. He carries on an "adulterous" activity with Martha Clifford entirely through correspondence, and he writes on the beach after masturbating, scrawling "I. AM. A." into the sand in an act of self-definition that is also an act of sexual release (*U*, 13.1258, 1264). Writing's lure is for Bloom a tantalizing secret to be harnessed even for commerce:

> I suggested to him about a transparent showcart with two smart girls sitting inside writing letters, copybooks, envelopes, blottingpaper. I bet that would have caught on. Smart girls writing something catch the eye at once. Everyone dying to know what she's writing. Get twenty of them round you if you stare at nothing. Have a finger in the pie. (*U*, 8.131–36)

The "transparent" cart is a comic reflection of Stephen's "signatures of all things," but the joke has deeper ramifications. Bloom's sign of advertising is a symbol of writing itself as a mode of secrecy and sexual difference. It hides and teases to uncover the hidden. Like Stephen, Bloom searches for an authentic meaning that would put to rest further questioning, the source of desire, what "everyone['s] dying to know" (one notes also the sexual tinge of "finger in the pie"). Yet Bloom's experience of writing differs from Stephen's just as his experience of sexuality differs. Stephen's figurations and fictions suggest an anxiety that writing will endanger the self. Bloom anxiously associates writing with a sexuality that is surreptitious or secretive. Writing stands for the potency that Bloom lacks in marriage and seeks without. When he says "Frailty, thy name is marriage," in Nighttown (*U*, 15.3277), translating *Hamlet*'s "Frailty, thy name is woman!" (I.ii.146) to the relationship between the sexes, he points toward a union that is as without writing as it is without sexuality. When he writes to Martha Clifford he thinks "Folly am I writing? Husbands don't" (*U*, 11.874). And, as if to equate definitively the lamed sexuality of Bloom's marriage with the failure of writing, Joyce emphasizes that Bloom has a "writingtable" at home upon which, as Bello accuses him in "Circe," he "never wrote" (*U*, 15.3173).

An endangering desire, then, a secretive or adulterous yearning toward the other that disunifies bonds while seeking to forge others: so does Joyce thematize writing through Stephen and Bloom, and so does writing appear in the narrative of Shakespeare, in which the linguistic act is inextricable from sexual initiation or adultery, never identified with the unifying bond of marriage or the Platonic recovery of a language that is either at one with itself – voice joining script – or at one with its creator. Language is affiliated with the displacements of desire, rather than the reconciliation of oppositions.

One may read these centrifugal displacements as the metaphoric key to *Ulysses*' linguistic concerns. The master trope of *Ulysses*, ruling both its narrative and its linguistic oppositions, can be understood as "adultery." Adultery, of course, is a literal displacement of desire enacted in the world of social and sexual, rather than representational, concern. It resonates with implications of impurity. When Bloom urges Stephen to eat some "unadulterated maternal nutriment" (*U*, 16.1570) in the cabman's shelter, the periphrasis combines a reference to the freshness of milk with an allusion to both Molly's marital lapse and the adultery of Hamlet's mother. The "soured adulterated milk" in proximity to the "half disrobed" bottle of port in "Ithaca" (*U*, 17.312–13, 306) confirms that adultery and adulteration are correlative for one another. When Ian Watt notes that the styles of "Ithaca" and "Penelope" are "unadulterated examples of the adjustment of narrative manner to the subjective and the objective poles of dualism," his language says more than he may have intended. It suggests that previous style in *Ulysses* may be "adulterated," that it is a mixed and unstable response to dualism and its pressures.[35]

Adultery can be understood generally as the breaking of bonds and the erection of a surreptitious and weakened contract in its place. In betraying a contract the adulterer replaces a ratified and powerful bond with a temporary alliance suspended outside the orders that validate the initial contract. While threatening the stability of an accepted norm, adultery unbinds a unity and erects a false mimetic of unity – a false dialectic – in its place. The adulterer replaces a bond between opposites with a covert or inauthentic repetition of that bond, an external structure that rebels against origin while mockingly replicating it.

Adultery is thus structurally both subversive and parodic, a description that allows for cognate formal and linguistic exploration. A case can be made that the novel itself, a genre historically parodic in origin, has been generated stylistically and thematically by this kind of contract and transgression.[36] But Stephen's tale, by tracing the effect of sexual adultery on the creating self, suggests a larger and analogous conclusion. Writing, the attempted binding of opposites through narrative, is adulterous. In his own narrative Stephen strives to create a dialectical marriage of word and self. He attempts to recapture a lost unity that is the historical certitude of the creative self. He replicates Shakespeare's attempt to recapture the world within by attempting to recapture Shakespeare himself. Yet this replication is insufficient to its model. Instead it exposes the contradictions in its subject, even as it tries to bind the subject's oppositions into a coherent and powerful whole. While using language to avoid the Scylla and Charybdis of false alternatives, both Stephen and Shakespeare are displaced by desire towards unforeseen alliances that replace postulated unities with fragments and imitations of origin: a theory that cannot be endorsed, a self that cannot bind together its erotic life or its dispersed language. Oppositions refuse to be bound dialectically in Stephen's narrative for the same reason that speech and script refuse to be bound in stable opposition in the earlier chapters. Despite his dialectical intentions his own narrative reveals the precarious bonds of all literal and linguistic marriage. The circle cannot be squared in fiction, because language, charged with a desire urging it towards "something else," surreptitiously subverts its own pretenses to join into wholes the self and signified that have generated it.[37]

One may therefore take Stephen's lecture, which appears in a chapter bound by the Joycean emblems of "literature" and "dialectic," as a self-reflexive model for Joyce's own linguistic practice. It confirms the divisions explored in the preceding chapters rather than joining them together, providing them with a psychic rather than a metaphysical basis for their refusal to be bound into unity. After "Scylla and Charybdis" issues of truth and fiction-making become virtually synonymous with the breaking of contractual and sexual bonds,[38] and it is only after Stephen rejects the apparent coherence of his own fiction in favor of an adulterous model of creative language that the stylistic extravagances of the later chapters come to the narrative's fore. Stephen's theory of Shakespeare opens up a fictive space in *Ulysses* for the replacement of the "real" by parody, the hallucinations of desire in Nighttown, and the breakage of mimetic bonds that typify the immediately following chapters. The normative assumptions of realist fiction, that words are married to a series of authentic events to which they correspond, is replaced after Stephen's tale by the recognition that narrative can burst free from dialectical restraints. Language can masquerade as referential while simultaneously undermining its own claims to that bond. Yet at the same time, to identify the adulterous or self-subverting impulse in Joyce's language is not to discard those claims utterly. For this reason it is an oversimplification to consider *Ulysses*, as some recent critics have done, as a workshop where language proliferates without check and narrative contracts no longer apply.[39] Stephen's tale does come to a seemingly coherent, if ambiguous conclusion, while *Ulysses* itself veers into the anti-mimetic, but returns, as the hero to Ithaca, to a closure dependent upon the trust in the transparency of language that the narrative earlier rejects: a referential style as "realist" in its own way as the narrative that preceded "Scylla and Charybdis." While "Ithaca" or "Penelope" are scarcely cut from the same stylistic cloth as "Telemachus," they depend no less on the assumption that there is something actual in the world beyond the word, and that language, however respectively objective or subjective, is in its own terms a trustworthy guide to some mode of representational or psychological truth.[40]

The adulterous relationship, in other words, is not the irrevocable abrogation of an bond, but a threat bound structurally to its opposite. Marriage can be known only as the absence of the adulterous, the adherence to a contract that excludes the alternatives of desire, while adulterous displacement is possible only as the breakage of a pre-existent and potent contract. Neither condition, the establishment nor the breaking of a bond, can be defined without the possibility of its opposite. To break a contract, however arbitrary its context, is to admit the provisional validity of that bond. To erect a parodic or anti-mimetic model in its place is to question, but not necessarily destroy, the realist model whose place it usurps. Such is the issue of *Ulysses* that connects narrative to analogous style: the degree to which the ubiquitous metonymies of desire, bound into language, threaten both the literal marriage of the Blooms and the metaphorical narrative marriage of the word with the world. Perhaps Eugene Jolas, in an early statement of Joyce's contemplation of the "disintegration of the word," most clearly, if unsuspectingly, noted the ambiguously empowering relationship that the destruction of language bears to adultery in Stephen's lecture:

In developing his medium to the fullest, Mr. Joyce is after all doing only what Shakespeare has done in his later plays, such as *The Winter's Tale* and *Cymbeline*, where the playwright obviously embarked on new word sensations before reaching that haven of peacefulness mirrored in the final benediction speech from the latter play which closes the strife of tongues in *Ulysses*.[41]

The final benediction from *Cymbeline* is found at the end of "Scylla and Charybdis." By harking back to Shakespeare Jolas implies that Stephen's lecture is itself about the "strife of tongues" no less than is the pyrotechnic "Oxen of the Sun," from which Jolas takes the phrase (*U*, 14.952). Yet Jolas sees in allusion the reconciliation that Stephen's Platonic model and refusal of his own theory rejects. While contemplating the destruction of language Jolas invokes two plays – *The Winter's Tale* and *Cymbeline* – that focus on reconciliation masquerading as sundering. Both deal with accused adulteries that are ultimately exposed as false, marriages proven faithful after malicious attack from without. The marriages in both plays are revealed as authentically if problematically intact, reconfirmed at the close rather than sundered. Stephen divides Shakespeare into bawd and cuckold by referring to both *Cymbeline* and *Othello*, another play in which adultery is accused rather than authentic, and by ending "Scylla and Charybdis" with an allusion to inviolate marriage, Joyce suggests a final reading of his dialectic. Even as Stephen's narrative itself dismantles the ideal of linguistic unity, neither sundering nor reconciliation is allowed to stand inviolate by the other. Shakespeare, and the Bloom household, become a model for the oscillation between linked opposites, the interpenetration of marriage and adulterousness. If a resolution to the "strife of tongues" is possible, the allusion to *Cymbeline* suggests, it is only through sundering. If sundering is discovered it is only through the possibility of wholeness that it can be known.

While *Ulysses* cannot promise to square the circle of representation, it does provide its own unresolved vision of narrative's dialectical possibilities. At one extreme is a vision of writing fragmented by desire, centrifugal from its referent. This is the vision of Virag, who as he introduces the issue into the text is both a caricature of grasping sexuality and a "*basilicogrammate*," the lord of writing whose "*Egyptian pshent*" and quills over the ears align him with Thoth, god of writing (*U*, 15.2304, 2309). At the other is Stephen's vision of a powerfully external writing, warring against the fragmentation of language implicit in his early meditations and his tale of Shakespeare.

Only the unsynthesized acceptance of both, the implication of one in the other, provide a simulacrum of dialectic: fragmentation chained to the unity that is its irreplaceable alternative.

Yet this dual acceptance is also Dantean. When Stephen thinks explicitly about the powers of linguistic art, contemplating rhyming in "Aeolus," he turns to examples from the *Commedia*:

> . . . . . . . *la tua pace*
> . . . . . *che parlar ti piace*
> *Mentre che il vento, come fa, si tace.*

He saw them three by three, approaching girls, in green, in rose, in russet, entwining, *per l'aer perso*, in mauve, in purple, *quella pacifica orifiamma*, gold of oriflamme, *di rimirar fè più ardenti*. (*U*, 7.717–22)

These first three rhymes come from the tale of Paolo and Francesca in the *Inferno*, the other quotes from the close of *Paradiso*.[42] The fragmented plea of the adulterous lovers for mercy from a silent god stands juxtaposed in Stephen's mind with the poet gazing upon the fullness of ultimate meaning. The two alternatives – adulterous fragmentation and a vision of original plenitude – stand unresolved as examples of linguistic resolution, the alternation of similarity and difference in rhyme. If language emerges in the linguistic texture of *Ulysses* as a mimetic mirror – powerful in its externality, unambiguous in its dialectical power – then it is also incompatibly an agent of adulterousness, the metaphoric razor that cuts away its own grounding in the real, stripping its own pretenses to an authentic marriage or meaning. Stephen's tale of Shakespeare, and *Ulysses* itself, present these paradoxical alternatives, like Buck Mulligan's mirror and razor, as crossed. Language emerges as its own set of undecidable extremes, both Scylla and Charybdis. A powerful instrument of wholeness, it is also the oppositional threat it constantly offers to its own dialectical integrity.

CHAPTER 3

# The cracked lookingglass of the master

'– What exactly is your discourse intended to prove?' '*Not* the desirability of the marriage tie, if that's what you mean, any more than a propaganda for representation and anecdote in art...'

Wyndham Lewis, *Tarr*, 19

[D]oes not all power that is *real* exact that it shall be *visible*...

Wyndham Lewis, *The Apes of God*, 587

The Vortex and the squaring of the circle in *Blast* and *Ulysses* act as the organizing symbols for syntheses postulated and frustrated: emblems of opposition that bear within themselves intimations of unities that are neither achieved nor completely dismissed by the texts that produce them. In *Blast* the manifestoes' claims of contained opposition are balanced by the way *Enemy of the Stars* cancels the rhetoric that surrounds it. Lewis's aesthetic emerges not as the capturing or ratification of the real, but as the formal erection of simulacra that proclaim their power to represent while simultaneously exposing the machinery that turns them, like Bestre's tales, into agents of heroic distortion. In *Ulysses*, similarly, strength in representation is inseparable from weakness. In Stephen's narrative of Shakespeare the forces of desire that lay within narrative language are revealed as divisive to the marriage of sign and object, suggesting that for *Ulysses* adultery and the object itself are bound together as representation's irreconcilable goals and conditions.

At this level of investigation the two authors' aesthetics show remarkable similarities of intent. Lewis's deliberate self-contradiction and ultimate fascination by Bestre's false heroics differs markedly from Joyce's almost rueful treatment of linguistic division, not least in the larger possibilities of containment or dispersal each author offers his potential interpreters.[1] Yet Lewis and Joyce, with their complementary geometrical emblems, create within their works comparable patterns of authority and displacement. In both *Blast* and *Ulysses*, as we have seen, Joyce and Lewis construct narratives that are self-referentially concerned with the validity of aesthetic creation and the author's relationship to that work. Both *Enemy of the Stars* and Stephen's lecture deal with the aesthetic issues that are at stake in their own production: the ability of the creator to exert control over the significance of his creation. Both Arghol and Shakespeare are presented as metaphorical books, selves as texts reading, misinterpreting, and rejecting themselves, and their respective narratives deal comparably with the thematics of failure. In both cases the logic of the fictional argument reveals that the narrating self and his subject – for Lewis the Vorticist and the visual world, for Joyce Stephen and Shakespeare – withdraw authority from their representations even as they seem to grant it. Arghol and Stephen, like Shakespeare, models for their respective author's power, become less sources of revelation than agents of the thematic and stylistic dualities replicated by the narrations that take them as subject.

The two narratives are also linked by affective intent, for they are performances. *Enemy of the Stars* is an act of artistic bravado. Lewis intended that it would change the nature of representational prose through a *coup de théâtre* aimed at fellow artists, its protagonists' actions a masked version of the authentic philosophy of its polyvalent author. Stephen's lecture, whose central Shakespeare is the apotheosis of author as actor, similarly attempts to change the prevailing artistic consensus as represented within *Ulysses*. Stephen is not a newcomer to performance. He enacted the part of a "farcical pedagogue" as an adolescent at Belvedere in *A Portrait of the Artist as a Young Man* (*P*, 73), and the implications of that role haunt the failure of his lecture. In the context of *Hamlet* one may also consider him to be a version of his subject protagonist, directing his own solipsistic "mousetrap" in which to catch the conscience of his artistic opponents. Thus, the common relation of *Enemy of the Stars* and Stephen's lecture to drama as form and subject is that the narratives reveal the dilemma of performative efficacy, the power of narrative to be not simply true to the nature of the world but to affect its conditions.

It is too early to read this desire as political in any larger sense, beyond noting the literary-political context implicit for both narratives. *Enemy of the Stars* and Stephen's lecture take as their primary subjects the psychic construction of subjects and the artistic credos of individuals, rather than the interpellation of those individuals and ideas within social and historical context. For this reason *The Apes of God* is a pivotal document in the relationship of Lewis with Joyce. As its title suggests, *The Apes of God* deals with ideas about artistic mimicry and authenticity; an "ape" of God is an artist who copies the work of a true creator. *The Apes of God* is deeply implicated in Lewis's response to Joyce. In no other work of Lewis is artistic authority such a central and thematized issue; in no other work – *The Childermass* perhaps excluded – are Joyce and *Ulysses* so much at stake as secondary motivation and oppositional subtext. This subtext has been noticed often. Modern critics have tended to foreground the style of *The Apes of God*, and have found it more notable for its intentional differences from Joyce than intrinsic merit, while Lewis's early and overtly partisan critics similarly emphasized the work's thematic distance from Joyce as a self-evident mark of its success.[2] This was indeed how Lewis chose to publicize the book. In the original edition he quoted favorable reviews that made the comparison explicit. An excerpt from Richard Aldington's review in *The Referee* states "that *The Apes of God* is the greatest piece of *writing* since *Ulysses*," while a testimonial from Roy Campbell insists "this book will certainly stand to *Ulysses* as *Candide* does to the *Confessions* and the *Emile* of Rousseau."[3]

For all of these critics *Ulysses* stands as the precursor text which *The Apes of God* follows and revises. Yet while Aldington's praise suggests that *The Apes of God* is a kind of stylistic sequel to

Joyce's work as a work of prose craftsmanship, Campbell's suggests more significantly that *The Apes of God* is engaged with *Ulysses*' ideas as conscious satire. While "Satire" is a central and problematic term in *The Apes of God*, Lewis was atypically reticent about the work's engagement with Joyce. Shortly after publication he admitted to Aldington that his description of the aged Lady Fredigonde in the prologue was an explicit parody of the Joycean subjectivity he had so often railed against in his nonfiction: "The Ulyssean 'thought-stream' method is only appropriate to the depiction of children, morons, and the extremely infirm (Fredigonde), as I have sufficiently demonstrated I think."[4] Yet in identifying this broad critical imitation Lewis omits to mention the many details of the passage that make Fredigonde an explicit parody of Molly Bloom. She is relatively immobile, confined to a chair rather than a bed. We first see her as her hair is combed, while her cap, described as a "*polar ice-cap*" (*AG*, 13), suggests that she is a deadening version of the earth, Molly's symbolic role as Gea-Tellus (*U*, 17.2313). She thunders "Yes" to her servant, which Lewis negates as "*absolute ... in its empty force*" (*AG*, 13), and, like Molly, shows off clothing "*In the manner of an abandoned Andalusian*" (*AG*, 20) while reminiscing about "love's-old-sweet-song" (*AG*, 24).

The ninety-six year-old Fredigonde, who opens Lewis's work as Molly closes Joyce's, suggests that *The Apes of God* is not only a parody but an inversion of Joyce. The details of her characterization imitate essential features of characterization from Joyce and reveal them to be abandoned and unmotivated. Similar parodic imitation is elsewhere in evidence. Lewis's moronic protagonist is Dan Boleyn, an Irish poet who has written only one "most lovely poem" (*AG*, 40). As a "*Dante-young*" (*AG*, 62) who must be kept "safe from the vampires of this earth" (*AG*, 99) he is a portrait of the artist as a young idiot, clearly drawn as a distorted Stephen Dedalus. Lewis announces that Dan arrives in England from the care of a cousin Stephen in Dublin, escaping from relatives who suffer from a Joycean disease: their "speech was abundant and continuous ... they spoke [their thoughts] aloud all the time, with great volubility" (*AG*, 470). The book's larger structures can be similarly read as reflection and undermining. Dan's exploration of the salons of Bloomsbury's false artists under the tutelage of Horace Zagreus, can be read as an anti-Odyssey, a picaresque demolition of Joyce's apparent assumption that knowledge can be gained through either quest or the communion of like souls.

Yet for these elements of technical inversion in Lewis's plan – rejection of interior monologue, replacement of teleologic quest with picaresque, even the placement of Joyce within *The Apes of God* as the subject of an anecdote told by one of Lewis's characters – Joyce's presence in *The Apes of God* is problematic. The second paragraph of the prologue, an introduction to Fredigonde's manor, gives the reader fair if oblique warning of *The Apes of God*'s stance towards *Ulysses*:

> The cat returned, with the state of a sacred dependent, into the gloom. Discreet sounds continually rose from the nether stair-head, a dark whisper of infernal presences. The antlers of the hall suggested that full-busted stags were embedded in its substance. A mighty canvas contained in its bronze shadows an equestrian ghost, who otherwise might have ruffled the empty majesty of the house with confusing posthumous activity. (*AG*, 7)

The painting that contains and controls motion, the emphasis on the stillness of a house ruffled only by motions coincident with "*infernal presences,*" the antlers that synecdochically suggest physical presences fragmented by the inanimate world, all are congruent with the spatial imagery of the Vorticist manifestoes and Lewis's later themes and diction. Yet the cat, entering "*with the state of a sacred dependent,*" the sounds rising from a stairhead, and the juxtaposition of the infernal and sacred around a piece of art that contains a ghost as subject within its shadows, can be read as reflections of the opening of *Ulysses*. As if by allusive fiat even the juxtaposition of "*stags*" and the "*equestrian*" wrench associations of Buck Mulligan and his "equine" face (*U*, 1.15) into Lewis's prose. These echoes serve an ambiguous end. Where Lewis's inversions of character or technique amount to criticism of Joyce's text, the allusions are less clearly oppositional. As fragmentary reflections they bring Joyce's presence into the text without parodic dismissal, providing a partial imitation that does not necessarily hold the imitated text up to revisionist laughter.

This doubleness of approach is compatible with Lewis's Vorticism and the tales of *The Wild Body*. Yet Lewis's narratives of the 1920s cast their nets further than explorations of selfhood, capturing social and historical reality within their purview. *The Apes of God* is no longer the work of the pre-war Vorticist whose painter's eye demanded unambiguous allegiance from the word, but the product of a matured consciousness shaped by the nationalist and European tensions of the First World War. It concerns itself with the nature of fiction, the social and ideological status of narrative and, ultimately, the forces of the world that exceed narrative. Only by examining the issues of authority and inversion embedded in *The Apes of God* can one gauge the distance *The Apes of God* marks both from Joyce and from Lewis's own earlier aesthetic, and enter a region where the themes of *Enemy of the Stars* re-emerge as political analysis.

A minor but telling transposition Lewis performs on Joyce's stairhead and "sacred dependent" is to move them from the top of the Martello tower to the confines of the manor, from the outdoors to an enclosed space. These spaces – primarily rooms – have been central to Lewis's fictions. From the house in Liverpool of *Mrs. Dukes' Million* to the inns and boarding houses of *The Wild Body* stories, enclosed spaces have provided Lewis's characters with a variety of containing frames. In the earlier Lewis narratives, such as the dream of *Enemy of the Stars*, rooms are microcosms of psychological involution, places of contained interaction threatened by the divisions of their inhabitants. They are often places of violence. Arghol's destruction of his books, Kreisler's rape of Bertha in *Tarr*, the frenetic acts of the "Poles" in the Breton pensions, all take place within claustrophobic walls that act as the metaphoric intersection of the social constraints of the external world, with the lack of constraint of the inner. They hide actions from fictive view that are as horrifying and comical as the subordinate clauses within which they are described by the narrators who stumble upon them. In the story "Beau Séjour" in *The Wild Body*, for instance, a kitchen becomes a locus of sexual aggression, laid open to the view of the observer Ker-Orr, who wanders into and withdraws from the scene: "A few days after my conversation in the orchard I entered the kitchen of the Pension, but noticing that Carl was holding Mademoiselle Péronette by the throat, and was banging her head on the kitchen table, I withdrew" (*WB*, 54).

In *Tarr* rooms reflect not simply the partitioning of a violent private from a repressed public arena, but the specific ethos of the individuals who inhabit and create them. Tarr has a particular fetish for space, needing to finish a canvas where he started it, while Bertha and Kreisler are defined by their respective bourgeois apartment and "funerary chamber" (*T*, 75) as definitively, as various critics have shown, as the Balzacian or Dostoyevskian character is implicated in the spaces that become inseparable from their social and psychological concerns.[5] Only Anastasya, the sole authentic avantgardist in *Tarr*, is able to escape definition by space, creating an imagistic violence that exempts her from the impositions of enclosure. She escapes from her bourgeois household by scribbling on the walls – "I inundated my house with troublesome images," she tells Tarr, "They simply *had* to get rid of me" (*T*, 103).[6]

In *The Apes of God* rooms persist in their division of inner from outer. Yet as they mark off psychological space they also stand as signs of the exclusion of what lies without. For Fredigonde what is outside the walls is modernity itself, her interior a space of safety from which she can view the real as shadow:

*She directed her eyes upon the narrow opening in the curtains – where the important thoroughfare, beyond the gates of the private road, was visible. Idly she was watching the bodies of the omnibuses fit themselves into the space and slip out of it, slacking or speeding according to the pulsation of this current of machines. As if they had been shadows upon the ceiling, cast into a darkened room from a sunlit street underneath, she remarked their passage. The window before her shook with the weight of the super-traffic. The amusing skeleton of new skyscraping flats entered into novel combinations with the geometric maze of the patterned curtains.*
(*AG*, 24)

Fredigonde's perceptions neatly reverse Plato's parable of the cave. She faces outward towards the "sunlit street" rather than inward towards its flickering reflections, but the world of forms without – even the emerging skeletons of high-rise flats – are less real than her interior space. Externality is devoid of reality, for it is itself only shadow, described as though it were merely a projection into yet another darkened room. By implication perhaps the effect of an infinite regression of shadows, the external affects Fredigonde only insofar as it alters her visual privileges. It enters the room through the narrow openings that allow the world to amuse and create novel shapes, but little more.

This privileging of interior space over the external is symptomatic of *The Apes of God*. "Here it is different," Zagreus explains to Dan of the world of the Lenten party, "you have to turn this inside-out I should say outside-in" (*AG*, 383). Matthew Plunkett creates with his rows of shells romantic "miniature landscapes" on his table and relegates the outside to an unreal state of indistinct design similar to Fredigonde's – "But aloft the metropolitan sky, contemporary (but for that none the more actual) arranged in indistinct cockades – like the vertex, the tops of the panaches, of a festal procession – traversed the speckled fog of the window-dust" (*AG*, 80). Others treat their interior space as regions defined against the encroachment of others. Lewis describes the house of Lionel and Isabel Kein, the apologists for Proust in the chapter "Chez Lionel Kein Esq.," as though it sentiently seals its inhabitants off from the outside. Their house is "seemingly stone-deaf" to knocking, while the Keins themselves maneuver in a "secret upper-apartment" (*AG*, 237). The Finnian Shaws similarly retreat during their party into an inner sanctum, stationing a guard at the door of their chamber to keep out even their invited guests. Like Lowndes in *Tarr*, Lewis's early bourgeois pseudo-artist, each of the Bloomsburians feels that "people, seemingly, were *always* attempting to get into his room" (*T*, 39).

The room in *The Apes of God* is therefore less an enclosure of psychological and sexual violence, than a space marked off against an externality which its inhabitants perceive as threat and discontinuity.[7] The traffic shakes Fredigonde's windows, and she interprets the jazz played on the streets as a similar harbinger of dislocation and death, the music of the modern that penetrates her room. Its "*daily dancing in the streets*" (*AG*, 16) is an invasion explicitly to be countered by those who control the world of interiors: "*If householders would only combine to prevent that music*" (*AG*, 16) she thinks, all would be well. To allow entrance of any kind is to risk dissolution of the privileged space. The Keins' door intimates entrance as violation. When Dan and Zagreus enter it opens "with a powerful silent caving in," suggesting by way of its adorning Pompeian fresco that the house is itself undergoing a destruction from without (*AG*, 238). When Dick Whittingdon enters Fredigonde's room, similarly, the narrative registers entrance as an unaccounted discontinuity:

he had entirely omitted at first to move forward as he should, out of forgetfulness... Once inside however he had completely overlooked the necessity of closing up the gap made by his entrance, that was it. Ever-absent-minded whimsical personality, a door for it was a puzzling obstacle. (*AG*, 28)

This gap is both literal and metaphorical. The open door is a mark that the balance has changed, that a new personality has entered a previously hermetic environment. But the door also colludes in marking Dick's presence – or non-presence, as "absent minded" suggests – as a lacuna, the interference of the outside upon an inner world that cannot integrate what enters.

The inhabitants of interior spaces in *The Apes of God* thus configure themselves as wholes, more "real" than the outside world, even as they invert perception to protect themselves from that world. This binarism is, of course, rooted in *Blast*. The manifestoes arraign the narcissistic pseudo-artist and support the exiled observer who is the enemy of nature: to look inward, in Lewis's equation, is to adhere to an internality that privileges the flux of "life," while to look outward is to privilege the external, figured in *Tarr* and elsewhere as the "deathliness" necessary for a permanent art. Fredigonde's "thought stream" parodies the "internal method" Lewis contemned in his polemical works of the 1920s, fitting into the latter category of Tarr's often quoted pronouncement, "The armoured hide of the hippopotamus, the shell of the tortoise, feathers and machinery, you may put in one camp; naked pulsing and moving of the soft inside of life – along with elasticity of movement and consciousness – that goes in the opposite camp" (*T*, 312). The room may be read as the successor of the shell and the hide. It is an artificial carapace that marks out the division of authentic from inauthentic representation and locates the arena where that struggle can be played out.[8] This metaphor is active even in Lewis's critical prose. As he advises his readers, one must learn to sequester the work of other modernists within the internal metaphorical "spaces" they have chosen for themselves, as Lewis's fictional pseudo-artists have chosen theirs: "[one must] possess the key to the 'transitional' chaos, which he can then open at will, inform himself at his leisure of the true value of its highly advertised interior, and then close it again, and lock it on the outside" (*TWM*, xi).[9]

The room's transposition of artistic metaphors into narrative devices also carries with it ramifications for social construction. For instance, in the story "The Cornac and his Wife" in *The Wild Body* as Ker-Orr views a theatrical performance in Brittany, the literal confines of walls also become a metaphoric space that divides life from acting:

So the theatre, the people on the stage and the plays they play, is part of the surface of life, and is not troubling. But to get behind the scenes and see these beings out of their parts, would be not merely to be privy to the workings and "dessous" of the theatre, but of life itself. (*WB*, 97)

To act is to take on an additional exteriority. As Ker-Orr notes earlier in the paragraph, the audience at the open-air performance of the Cornac's troupe reacts differently from the audiences that watch inside circus tents – "The absence of the mysterious hush of the interior seems to release them." This externality separates the viewer from the troublesome "dessous" of life, which has become, as with Bestre, less authentic then the trappings of its fictions. For Ker-Orr the Breton troupe is less disturbing when playing in the public squares than when they live their own lives, which are enclosed both literally and metonymically – "the theatre" being both building and abstract institution, a socially constructed space that covers what exists "behind the scenes." A proper performance hides what is internal, forcing an inauthentic life back into inaccessible artistic chambers. Tarr concludes, "good art must have no inside: that is capital" (*T*, 312): performance becomes an additional sign for the division of authenticity from inauthenticity.

Art and society are therefore constrained by homologous economies. Both are performances, and both proceed through imitations that are implicated either in the disturbing interiority of "real life" or in the untroubling surface of externality. Such is true for the pseudo-artists of *The Apes of God*, for whom the line between internal and external, observer and observed, is blurred in social imitation and "art." Pierpoint's "encyclical," a central document in the book's treatment of authority, figures the Apes' salons as theaters of trivial performances, where they act as a "vast array of troublesome 'supers' that swarm all over the stage" (*AG*, 122). Even Dan, anything but insightful, pictures his fellow diners at the Keins' as aspirants to a theater in which they become the performance itself, a line of waiting viewers who become instead their own objects of inquiry – "*The theater-queue had come to life*, now: here, all about him in solid ranks, it chattered and ate... Or the queue had started *acting*" (*AG*, 295–96). They are characters, as Zagreus has pointed out, without an author. Their only referent is their money, with which they conquer space through material rather than artistic means. Like Lowndes, who "had just enough money to be a cubist" (*T*, 39) they create a pseudo-bohemia through their ability to rent the best studios, effectively denying them to the artistic betters whose achievements they can only imitate. Yet this superficiality is itself a false interiority. According to Pierpoint they consider themselves to be "oracles of inside information" (*AG*, 121), with implicit emphasis on the locus of "inside," but are actually the "*un*paying guests of the house of art... who adopt the livery of this noble but now decayed establishment... to mock, in their absence, its masters" (*AG*, 121). Their rooms are the stages of servants, where mimicked roles stand as the social analogue – the adopted livery – of the confusion of money with art.

These liveries come in various fragmenting and mechanizing forms. When Dick enters the narrative, for instance, he is a set of "jolly sprawling fragments" (*AG*, 27) held together by rhetorical functions. Lewis describes him as "a rogue elephant who had perhaps burst into a parish church" (*AG*, 27), while his look is that of a "schoolboy-application to the first steps in scholarship, come into the presence of the form master" (*AG*, 35–36). Dick is clearly no master of forms himself, but only a "pattern of duty" (*AG*, 33). His personality is called into question by quotation marks that mark it off as distant from whatever selfhood might stand in its place: he wears a "happy 'here-I-am' smile" (*AG*, 28) while contemplating the "unquestionable oddity... of being 'Dick'" (*AG*, 29). Other roles are played by Fredigonde, who responds to his pleasantries "impersonating Any-Woman-Flattered" (*AG*, 31), and by others who conceive of themselves in terms of pre-existing models of stereotypical or romantic behavior. The midget Bloggie submerges her personality under an externally determined pattern, modeling herself "upon the asiatic statuette, as seen through the eyes of the Hollywood or West End Producer" (*AG*, 184), while Archie Margolin, the East End Jew, gets ambivalent pleasure from the part in which society casts him, that of Riah in *Our Mutual Friend* – "a myth he freely hated... For his part Arch enjoyed himself in the bitter-sweet of its comic revival – *Positively last appearance!*" (*AG*, 46).

This pervasive mechanizing of character has prompted some to see a disturbing and contradictory break in Lewis's practice: Hugh Kenner writes, "*Time and Western Man* had argued that the behaviorist, in reducing the person to a set of predictable gestures, was insulting the human race. In the same year Lewis was producing a body of fiction on the premise that people were nothing else."[10] Surely self-contradiction is inherent in Lewis's representational procedures. Yet the characters of *The Apes of God* are not mechanized without thematic motivation. Their predictable gestures are congruent with their acceptance of the increasingly deadening social habits that Lewis elsewhere pervasively calls "group rhythms," and as such they fall into the patterns of mechanism that Georg Lukács, following Marx, critiqued as "reification."[11] Perceiving themselves as subjects, the characters are merely objects alienated from authentic art, which is the only valid means of production in Lewis's fictive world. They sacrifice personality for the social exchange-value of status and economic power. Dick takes on his rhetorical roles because he is potential heir to Fredigonde's estate. He becomes, for all intents and purposes, inseparable from his new Bugatti, "regardless-of-cost, left burning in his staring head-lights" (*AG*, 31). Archie, already reduced and hypostatized by his inferior class status as "the militant slum-Jew in excelsis" (*AG*, 46), similarly needs to curry favor. He submerges his own individuality into patterns, such as that of Dickens's "good Jew," which are acceptable to those who hold power over him.

This is not to say that the mechanism of Lewis's characters can be reduced to an economic critique, any more than similar rhetorical levelings in late Dickens can be wholly understood through sociological determinism. The parallel is suggestive, however. In both *Our Mutual Friend* and *The Apes of God* the rhetorical deanimation of characters who hoard or collect – in Dickens corpses and dust, in Lewis cars, art, even whips – becomes a sign not only of economic deadness but of the repression of drives for which hoarding acts as a pathological substitute. These drives are both personal and cultural. Eve Kosofsky Sedgwick has argued that the linguistic fragmentation of bodies, the hoarding and "dust" of *Our Mutual Friend*, disguise a pervasive neurosis of bodily containment, repression of anality, and homoeroticism; these themes are found particularly in the subplot of Bradley Headstone.[12] Sedgwick's analysis is useful for *The Apes of God*. Lewis's hoarding and fragmented characters are overwhelmingly repressed and homosexual. It is unnecessary to claim Lewis's conscious intent to see an implicit connection between fragmentation and eros in the explicit references to *Our Mutual Friend* in *The Apes of God*.[13]

Moreover, repression in late Dickens is not merely erotic but metafictional. Bradley Headstone dies not simply because he cannot control his destructive erotic energies, but because

Dickens's fictional world cannot contain him. There is no room for him – either construed as place to live or space of containment – in the society of which Dickens's novel forms a part. The cultural forces that guarantee his psychological destruction also guarantee his eradication as character from the pages of its fiction. This is fundamentally the critique Horace Zagreus makes of the world of *The Apes of God*. The ethos of collection, fragmentation, and erotic repression has led to an enervated fiction that programmatically excludes or contemns the vital character that once informed the novel and its spaces –

On no account must [the protagonist] be confused with, or even suggest, the "hero" of romantic type. The energy of a Karamazov, or even the successful human type of the order of a balzacian [sic] topdog, would transport him at once into the category of *villains*... It is the neatness with which this is done that assures the success of the "serious" Fiction-writer. (*AG*, 263)

If, as Zagreus claims, fictions are generated by the mythology of the "social Trust" (*AG*, 263) that produces them, the culture of inauthentic performance kills the energy of its fictions as it sacrifices itself. Dan's London hostess Melanie Blackwell lives in a house called the *Villa Saint-Genest* (*AG*, 136). Lewis's implication is that for the Apes (as Sartre reminds us in his own titular allusion to Genest) to be an actor is also to be a martyr.

It is as antidote to this triviality and self-enclosure that Zagreus presents himself to the reader of *The Apes of God*. As the voice of the off-stage sage Pierpoint, whose scathing demolitions of the artistic world Zagreus "broadcasts" into the sitting rooms of the Bloomsburians, Zagreus represents a paradoxically authoritative alternative to the targets of Pierpoint's scorn. Zagreus mingles with the Apes as an invited invader. He is reputed to be half a Follett, therefore related to Fredigonde and privy to the internal world of the Apes, but he is better known for his evasions of external power. A former surveyor and practical joker, he is an expert in space and in the construction of enigmas involving the decentering of authority. He is rumored to have disarmed the sentries at the Royal Palace simply to demonstrate how easy it would be to kidnap the King, while another stunt more trivially represents his interest in the suspension of external control. As Helen reports at Pamela Farnham's, Zagreus once handed the end of a surveying tape to an unsuspecting passer-by, then dashed around the corner and handed the other end to another. He then left the scene and let the victims stand for hours believing that the tape, tautly held by the two, was still under his control (*AG*, 215–16).

As such, Zagreus is a prototypically Lewisian artist, of the pattern already familiar from *Enemy of the Stars*. The suspension of the surveying tape is a Vorticist construction translated into an antisocial prank: an action that exists exclusive of the artist only because of the complementary and arbitrary oppositions that shape its ends. Yet unlike Arghol, whose seclusion and retreat to interior spaces is a prerequisite for creation, Zagreus breaks down the barriers that others erect. He transgresses the Apes' privileged spaces as a power entering from without and eliminating the division of inside and out. When he enters a room, Lewis writes, "the door was burst open" (*AG*, 376) as though registering the pure disruptive force of his presence. He steals doors as practical jokes. Pamela Farnham reports his removal of her front door at her tea-party, and at the climax of *The Apes of God* Zagreus steals a door from the Finnian Shaws so that a ritual satyr dance can be performed upon it at dawn after the Lenten Party (*AG*, 602–04). Zagreus even speculates whether his shadow has the power to pass through doorways, a disruptive and penetrative ability Dan may share:

Mr. Zagreus stared at his imposing shadow moving slightly upon Kein's door ... Dan was there like a shadow too, on and before the door. Were they inside the door as well, in further projections of still less substance – their stationary presences multiplied till they stretched out like a theatre queue? (*AG*, 237)

Zagreus is figured here a Platonic source, throwing his own shadows of "less substance," as though the Apes (and their related image of the theater queue) are merely lesser versions of himself. Social myth renders his powers even more striking. Twice rumors are mentioned – once to be denied by Zagreus himself – that "like Simon Magus" he can walk through walls (*AG*, 329, 377).

Within the circumscribed mythology of the social trust, therefore, Zagreus is the bearer of conventionally mythic energies. His poem of advice to Dan is filled with references to Venus and Adonis, Hippolytus and Phaedra (*AG*, 135), while his disruptions of order are of a self-proclaimed potency with which Lewis's descriptions collude. The costume he wears when performing at the Lenten Party, for instance, is an encyclopedia of mythological emblems that includes the "crown" and "reed and palette of the scribe" Thoth (*AG*, 334–35). Both imply Zagreus's power as a source of authority, the locus of an authentic representational force in a world given over to the mocking imitations of writing and painting. These mythic emblems are joined by Zagreus's own authoritative voice of mimesis, which he offers as corrective strength. His diatribes at the Keins' attack the deficiencies of the fiction produced by the salons, *romans à clef* that are faulty because the individual is unwilling to recognize his representation as his own reflection –

How is it that no one ever sees *himself* in the public mirror – in official Fiction?... Everybody gazes into the public mirror. No one sees himself! What is the use of a mirror then if it reflects a World, always, without the principal person – the Me? (*AG*, 255)

The sentiment has a strongly Irish heritage, blending quotations from Swift and Wilde with Lewis's own idiosyncratic equation of fiction with satire. Swift famously warns in *The Battle of the Books*, "SATYR *is a sort of* Glass, *wherein Beholders do generally discover every body's Face but their Own*," while Wilde observed that nineteenth-century attitudes to Realism and Romanticism depended upon the public's willingness to see its own monstrous reflections, defining the dislike of Realism as "*the rage of Caliban seeing his own face in a glass.*"[14] Both recall in turn Stephen Dedalus's recasting of the two sentiments into his own railing against the "official fiction" of his native country as the "cracked lookingglass of a servant" (*U*, 1.146), in which art suffers both from defects in the mimetic instrument and the viewer's exclusion from the "public mirror" of politics. In this charged allusive context Zagreus's assumed name carries additional literary and mythic weight. As a "Horace," he is a classical satirist, and although none of the characters recognize it, "Zagreus" is another name for Greek mythology's most disruptive and powerful outsider, Dionysus.[15] Thus, when Zagreus storms the Finnian Shaws' inner sanctum, and Phoebus Finnian Shaw stands guard against invasion, the battle between intruder and defender of inviolate space is more than the agon of host and guest. It is a Nietzschean play of mythic and literary energies. The satiric and Dionysiac Zagreus stands against the debased Apollonian of Phoebus, his family, and the Lenten Party, an entropic celebration of sacrifice and incipient resurrection (although not, one notes, self-sacrifice). In the absence of a mimetic world that can engage the consciousness of those reflected, Zagreus nominates himself as the Apes' public mirror. In revealing to the Bloomsburians what they really are, he will, reminiscent of Dionysus revealing his true nature to a recalcitrant Pentheus, both enlighten and destroy.[16]

Like Arghol, however, Zagreus is gradually revealed to be a problematic source of resurrected authority. He describes himself as Pierpoint's "Plato" (*AG*, 316), and Dan sees him as "holy writ" (*AG*, 611). As *The Apes of God* proceeds, however, Lewis makes it clear that Zagreus has been caught up in the same trap of representational inauthenticity as the others. As the literary heritage of his pronouncement on fiction suggests, Zagreus is less original than he claims, nor has he remained innocent of economic collusion in his broadcasts from Pierpoint, the offstage "supreme judge" who is "always absent." Like Simon Magus he pays Pierpoint for his investiture, buying the ideas he presents as his own (*AG*, 453). His writing, moreover, like the magical vanishing act he performs on Dan at the Lenten Party, is false. The "dossier" he has written on Dan is fully tangential to Dan's reality (*AG*, 478–79), while his final report to Pierpoint on Dan's behavior is filled with lies and inversions (*AG*, 607–11). Even his mythological costume suggests the problematic status of his mythic self-presentation. The final emblem that Lewis describes is a heart-shaped locket that Zagreus says contains a phallus, image of eros and creative power. Yet when he opens the locket it is empty (*AG*, 341). If he is Dionysian, then, it is with the provision that his power is no less imitative and potentially empty than the artistic mockery of the painters and writers he criticizes. As J. G. Frazer notes in *The Golden Bough*, Zagreus is particularly the form of Dionysus who apes the predecessor god whose order he would revise – "Scarcely was he born, when the babe mounted the throne of his father Zeus and mimicked the great god by brandishing the lightning in his tiny hand."[17] Frazer's Zagreus meets his downfall through his excessive attentions to himself in the mirror, and when attacked by the Titans is unable to save himself by changing shape. Lewis's Zagreus, as we have seen, is notably fascinated with seeing himself in the metaphoric mirror of representation, and, as shape-changing is implicit in dressing for a costume party, Lewis's use of Frazer may be understood to include Zagreus's implicit parodic "downfall" at the hands of the rather un-Titanic Apes.

Thus, one may read a particular passage of *The Apes of God* as an emblem of these interrelated issues – the internal versus the external, authenticity versus imitation, mythological power versus the debasement of myth into impotence. In the chapter "Chez Leopold Kein Esq." Zagreus and Dan explore their hosts' interior decoration when Zagreus points to a painting:

Dan moved steadily into position before it. He remained some minutes his head tilted up. He thought he could observe Laocoon with his two sons and accompanying serpents, their various limbs and trunks organized into something like galls of the cynips, in chilly colours. A conventionally distorted, antique, floridly-fringed head presided over the congery of tubes, rolling like an ornate primitive ship upon its side, the eyes dilated.
"Chirico!" Horace shouted the name of the Italian master. (*AG*, 240–41)

The painting, like the Keins' score of Schoenberg's *Pierrot Lunaire*, is intended by Lewis to be a self-evident sign of the Keins' hyper-modernist decadence, much as Berg's *Lyric Suite* serves a similar purpose in the description of the Bailiff's party in Lewis's later *Monstre Gai*.[18] But the painting also reduplicates Zagreus's self-eradicating status in his fictive world. The story of Laocoon is a prelude to the treacherous penetration of an enclosed culture, walled Troy, by its enemies. The seer's destruction precedes the overturning of Troy by the Greeks, for whom Zagreus, with his assumed name and mythological costume, stands as a modern representative. Where Zagreus proclaims his mission is to attack falsehood through authority, however, the tale of Laocoon promises the very reverse. It shows instead the successful attack on authority by falsehood, as the oracle or seer is destroyed by emblems of Greek guile and misrepresentation. Assumed by the Trojans to be absent and external to the city, the enemies at the gates are waiting within the Horse, prepared to destroy Troy as a parasite destroys its host.[19]

Lewis's description of the image calls into question the narrative's intimations of the mythic power of misrepresentation. The image is itself a parasite, an outsider which, like the Greeks, attempts to attack and replace a powerful precursor image with its own belated authority. It is a neo-classical copy whose original is barely perceptible through its modernist fragmentations. Dan only "thought he could observe" the figures of the original in its "conventional distortions." Yet because Chirico's "misrepresentation" is weaker than its classical model – more a shipwreck, in Lewis's description, than an authoritative image – this secondary Laocoon belies the power of the narrative for which it can be read as a representational symbol. If the external – the Greeks, representation itself – has the power to overturn the internal or prior – walled Troy, the classical model whose place it usurps – it cannot be through mythology, whose power is lost rather than gained in misrepresentation. The parasite of the image merely debases the past, reducing it to an "antique," a cliché to hang in a salon as a decorative reminder of a power now lapsed.[20]

This critique, moreover, carries additional self-reflexive pressures. "Chez Leopold Kein Esq." is dedicated throughout to Zagreus's opinions of fiction, and, as is implicit throughout Lewis's work, the relationship of linguistic representation to painting. As Zagreus says, with emphasis on the painterly final term, "*Fiction*... is generally an untruthful picture" (*AG*, 262). In this context the Chirico suggests the allusive presence of a related *Laocoon*, Gotthold Lessing's investigation of that very aesthetic issue, inspired by the same classical image and passage in Virgil.[21] Lessing's relevance to Lewis's project is undeniable. Here, for instance, is *Laocoon* on the division of space and time in representation:

> the imitations of painting are effected by means entirely different from those of poetry; the former employing figures and colors in space, and the latter articulate sounds in time. Now, as it is evident that the signs employed must bear a suitable relation to the things represented, it follows that those signs which are arranged in juxta-position with each other, can only express co-existent objects, or an object whose parts are co-existent, while those signs which are consecutive, can only express things which, either of themselves, or in their component parts, are consecutive. (Lessing, 150)

Lessing's conclusions predict Lewis's own discoveries of the necessary failure of a Vorticist prose, and as such are in harmony with Lewis's abandonment of the search for a fully spatialized language after *Enemy of the Stars*. Yet when Lessing further criticizes poets who fail to note the generic differences between poetry and plastic representation, he is even more proleptically damning of Lewis's portrayal of Zagreus:

> In decorating a figure with symbols, the artist elevates it to a higher state of existence; but, when the poet employs these pictorial garnishings, he degrades a superior being to the level of a puppet... All their imaginative beings appear *en masque*, and those who show the greatest ingenuity in these masquerades, are generally least acquainted with what should be their legitimate aim, – namely, to make the creatures of their fancy act, and to characterize them by their actions. (114–15)

These strictures apply programmatically to the techniques of *The Apes of God*. The multiple-page description of Zagreus's mythic costume is a prolonged narrative reduction of a sculptural simultaneity. Zagreus is "like a Mexith's renowned statue bristling with emblems" (*AG*, 334). Yet where Zagreus assumes the costume of his own design as a technique of elevation by association, the prolixity and sequential nature of its description reduces him on the narrative level to the very fragmentation and reification that his mythic emblems are mustered to resolve. Zagreus falls apart into a literalized succession of metonymic objects, his costume diminishing him no less than Lewis's descriptions reduce the Apes to mechanized parts and pieces. As a representative of myth Zagreus in Lessing's terms goes *en masque* to the larger masquerade of the Lenten Party, a character in fiction no less than the other invited guests. Nominally a superior being, his weight of mythological emblems earns him membership, like the other Bloomsburians, in Lewis's "all-puppet cast" (*AG*, 81).

This scenario of self-contradiction and stylistic undermining of the authoritative voice of theory, suggests at first a replaying or reduplication of the structure of *Enemy of the Stars*. Zagreus, like Arghol, lives by an aesthetic theory to which he cannot measure up, and the linguistic temporality and fragmentation of his description compromises his character's integrity. Yet there are strong differences. Arghol's authority is, in a profound sense, guaranteed from without. He is a manifestation of the general figure of the artist established by *Blast*'s manifestoes, outside the play but within the overarching frame of the *Enemy of the Stars*'s original presentation. Zagreus, on the other hand, is entirely self-proclaiming. He appears trustworthy in *The Apes of God* because Lewis establishes him as Dan's guide and, more importantly, because he is for most of the book the only intelligent voice criticizing the obvious inanity of its other characters. Zagreus's voice, therefore, is not grounded on any valid foundation within the frame of his narrative. Pierpoint, the absent philosopher-painter from whom he buys ideas, remains permanently *hors jeu*, both outside the game of the salons and beyond the field of Lewis's narrative.

The problem of Zagreus's defining frame or context is further complicated by the presence of *Ulysses* as a satiric target in the description of Zagreus's mythic costume.[22] When Zagreus exclaims to Ratner "My very fly-buttons are allusive" (*AG*, 337), Lewis takes aim at the polysymbolism in *Ulysses* that allows Leopold Bloom's back trouser button to become a speaking character in "Circe" (*U*, 15.3441). The bulk of the passage, however, suggests a rather different section of *Ulysses*: the lists of pseudo-mythic attributes in "Cyclops." Let us compare representative excerpts from the two, the first from *The Apes of God*:

> The waist was lion-like and ritualistic, resembling that of a Minoan nut (slender and at all events nobiliary) or a kalakhanya.
> Or the wasp-like billowing of the thighs and sylph's flat haunch seemed framed for the stampeding of a Jota.
> The jerkin bristled with coarse black hairs – these were the kaohuang, or famous hair-rays of the Buddha.
> Upon the right side a tortoiseshell was attached to his belt, ready to crack in the fire like the face of an old man ... (*AG*, 335)

> He wore a long unsleeved garment of recently flayed oxhide reaching to the knees in a loose kilt and this was bound about his middle by a girdle of plaited straw and rushes. Beneath this he wore trews of deerskin, roughly stitched with gut. His nether extremities were encased in high Balbriggan buskins dyed in lichen purple, the feet being shod with brogues of salted cowhide laced with the windpipe of the same beast. From his girdle hung a row of seastones which jangled at every movement of his portentous frame and on these were graven with rude yet striking art the tribal images of many Irish heroes and heroines ... (*U*, 12.168–76)

While the styles of both passages are notably distinct they share important similarities. Both are taken from significantly longer mock-epic lists, and sketch imaginative costumes in extreme detail. Both describe their personages from head to foot, emphasize the emblems attached to the belt, and draw attention to the mythic or "tribal" ramifications of the costume's characterizaton. Both serve to position their wearers culturally: the Citizen as "authentic" nationalist Irishman, with his roots in the peasantry and "seastones" of his island nation, Zagreus as the literary aesthete with a taste for cultural esoterica. Yet both also undercut their own pretensions to seriousness through the accumulation of minutiae and absurd attributions. The "famous hair-rays of the Buddha" on Zagreus's costume are, in their own way, as ridiculous as Joyce's inclusion of "Gautama Buddha" as a mock-Irish hero on the Citizen's belt (*U*, 12.197). And if we fail to note the Joycean subtext of Zagreus's satiric costume, Lewis has Dan note at the costume party that among the specifically literary characters in attendance is "the Cyclops, apparently, or Cain and Abel it seemed" (*AG*, 460).

Understanding Lewis's full satiric intent depends upon recognizing the difference between the passages' contexts within their respective works. They are concerned with "frames," the surrounding context in which, in Zagreus's costume, the "stampeding of a Jota" might be comprehended, or in the Citizen's, the degree to which his "portentous frame" is not only his body but the mythic context for his representative emblems: his figure surrounds and contextualizes the objects he wears as a frame contains a picture. The passages' narrative frames within *Ulysses* and *The Apes of God* are radically different. Zagreus's costume is nominally a real object, presented as a garment of mythic potency within the social world of *The Apes of God*. The "portentous frame" for the description of the Citizen, however, is textual fantasy. It is part of the "giganticism" that periodically interferes with the narrative of the "Cyclops" chapter of *Ulysses*, having no narrative "reality" for its characters, but presented to the reader as an act of authorial linguistic invention.

This overstated fantasy acts in part as self-parody within *Ulysses*. It suggests that mythic parallels are limited as promises of revelation – can be inflated and even wrong – even while mythic parallels are active elsewhere as structural technique. The nature of this parody is clinched by Dan's confusion of the Cyclops with Cain and Abel at the party. Mythic meaning for Dan is unclear and trivial; he cannot even determine the proper number of the represented figures, let alone their symbolic value (this confusion also conflates *Ulysses* with the drafts of Joyce's *Work in Progress* then appearing, its motifs of battling brothers providing Lewis with additional critical fodder). And in case we have missed the literary critique, Lewis has his costumed partygoers merge with other figures from modern British literature – the Cyclops joins comparable individuals who range "down to Peter Pan or perhaps Prufrock" (*AG*, 460). By translating Joyce's parody of the "Cyclops" passage into the primary frame of his own narrative, Lewis effectively conflates the ontological realities of Joyce's Bloom with those of the giganticized Citizen, rendering both equally valid – which is to say equally invalid – and equally absurd. If Bloom's trouser button and the parodic figure of "Cyclops" can be ontologically leveled into the "real world," of what value is myth as an authentic mode of representation, particularly where myth can be arrayed against itself in self-parody?

Zagreus's assumption of myth in name and clothing, therefore, raises his theoretical stake in the enterprise of representation. It implies more than direct criticism of Joyce, and is a powerful reappraisal of myth itself. We may understand that reappraisal by considering the modernist reception of myth in general. Claude Lévi-Strauss has argued that myth can be understood as a linguistic system that combines the two registers of Saussurean structural analysis. It is both ground and variation, both *langue*, the set of formulations that allow for a mythic utterance to be articulated, and *parole*, that utterance itself. As an imaginary resolution of real cultural dilemmas, myth acts as a self-perpetuating guarantor of value. Both ideal and manifestation, substance reconstitutable from the juxtaposition of its accidents, myth encloses its own Platonic order, reflective of and yet independent from its cultural materials.[23]

If one can accept this vision of myth as implicit in modernism after *Ulysses* and *The Golden Bough*, then one may read Lewis's reduction of myth to masquerade as not merely an attack on the stylistic propensities of a Joyce or an Eliot, but a generalized attack on myth in narrative. Aspects of Lewis's aesthetic are clearly sympathetic to this approach. In the "Conclusion" of *Men Without Art* Lewis states explicitly:

What should be said, then, it seems to me, first and last, about art ... is that it is a pure game ... [like the life from which it springs] a game in the sense that no value can attach to it *for itself*, but only in so far as it is well-played or badly-played. Art in this respect is in the same class as ritual, as civilized behaviour, and all ceremonial forms and observances – a discipline, a symbolic discipline. (*MWA*, 290–91)

In this context – art as proto-structuralist ritual, game, and symbolic discipline – Lewis's satire of myth becomes a generalized attack on the idea of representational groundedness or authority itself. As a voice without an authenticating ground, Zagreus assumes the garb of a mythology that takes itself as its own substance, much as Frazer described the Greek as "[accustomed] to clothe her naked realities with the gorgeous drapery of a mythic fancy."[24] Yet there are no naked realities here: Zagreus's name mocks the self-generating properties of Frazer's auto-chthonic god while confining him, beyond the reductions of the Joycean costume that it satirizes, to empty reduplications, like the infinite regress of shadows of Fredigonde's geometric purview. He does not recognize his "I" in his own public mirror, because that mirror cannot reflect outside itself. Zagreus's mythological costume and self-presentation use the trappings of myth to point out the absence of any authenticating core of aesthetic or cultural meaning that is external to its own self-contradictory constructions.

This inability is the fundamental source of the "break" in Lewis's work that is articulated by both Kenner and Jameson within different critical contexts. For Kenner, as we have seen, Lewis fell unwarily into a fictional articulation of the very world-view he had earlier criticized as anthropological misinterpretation, while for Jameson the "stupefying and unexpected appearance" of satire in Lewis's work marks a collusive repression of the energy of the individual character (in other words, Zagreus's own critique of "contemporary fiction") in favor of the representation of trans-individual forces in a world whose multinational political reality has become "decisively modified."[25] Yet Lewis's registering of that modified reality in *The Apes of God* is in the first instance ontological rather than political. If in *Blast* Lewis blamed representation for falling short of the fullness of origin and therefore misrepresenting the real, in *The Apes of God* that origin itself has become debased, lost, or invalidated. There is no longer a question of a Bergson misinterpreting the world as fragmented, for reality has become so fragmented that it can no longer support, or differentiate itself from, its own representation. This conclusion is implicit in Zagreus's self-constructed and self-contradictory persona, and in other characters' graspings towards justification. The Keins seek their truth in a projected fictionalization by Proust, and are therefore representative of the characters as a whole, who are Pirandellian "Lies" "*in search of an author*" (*AG*, 246). Moreover, as "real" social beings seek to authenticate themselves by becoming subjects of fiction – or at the Lenten Party coming costumed as them – that fiction is itself ever more based, as Zagreus admits, upon "*a poor reality and so unreal*" (*AG*, 293). A Fredigonde or Osmund Finnian Shaw are all that the world of *The Apes of God* can present as sources of being, the Gnostic "divine Pleroma" (*AG*, 350). The only fiction contained as a part of the text, Ratner's pseudo-Joycean prose, is written by an "eternal imitation-person" (*AG*, 143–44) who substitutes stylistic appropriations of epiphanic origin for authentic belief. Ratner adapts early Joycean stylistic tics into pages of "a *personal* prose" (*AG*, 158): 'A little child picked a forget-me-not. She lifted a chalice. It was there. *Epiphany*. There were three distinct vibrations'" (*AG*, 156). If as Zagreus argues, "*the real* should not compete with creations of Fiction. There should be two worlds, not one" (*AG*, 258) it is unclear, especially given his own ambiguous self-creation as a "public mirror," whether the two can be distinguished. When Matthew Plunkett searches for a cold drink and thinks of "manufactured ice... (now there was no real ice any longer)" (*AG*, 62) he confronts an ontological dilemma of generalized proportions. Where imitation and artificiality have usurped a lost or absent reality, the question of mimetic authority threatens to become meaningless. As Fredigonde thinks with regard to the arbitrariness of names, "*what reference can there be?*" (*AG*, 15)

Here one may re-engage with political interpretation. This ontological dilemma corresponds to a decentering of national identity, a decentering again configured as the fear of the external by the internal. Zagreus's threat is not merely critical but cultural. A homosexual and albino – a painterly commentary upon his own ultimate thematic blankness – he is also an "english exile" (*AG*, 295) whose cultural orientation is no longer British. He has given Fredigonde a "Houssa brooch from Gando" as a talisman and he is said to have spent many years in the Orient, where he became adept at Afghan magic (*AG*, 377). His mythological costume contains as many eastern as western emblems. In his manifold representations of otherness, Zagreus acts as potential representative of a cultural vitality reconverging upon an England that is accustomed to being the center of its empire, rather than the subject of its intrusions. This affects even the spatial realm the Apes attempt to enclose for themselves. Archie Margolin thinks of this contraction of power as he traverses the Folletts' drawing-room, reading its architectural immensities as a reflection of British imperialism:

"The space-mad, the English! – from their spacious days of their great Elizabeth to the Imperial Victoria. But – now that space, itself, has shrunk under their feet, by time contracted – what a race of pygmies!" So the great furniture shouted to his senses the message of its empty scale. (*AG*, 43)

Margolin's observation is historical. Colonial "space" has contracted as time and cultural changes have rolled by. But within Lewis's register of thematic gestures the observation is also metaphysical. Space here has *itself* contracted, forced out by the modern emphasis on temporality, a shift that also includes by implication – remembering the equation of temporality and desire in *Enemy of the Stars* – an anxiety of impotence in the face of an externalized vitality that the center refuses to recognize. When the sexually troubled Matthew Plunkett passes the door of the sexual athlete Zulu Blades, whose marginal exploits provide *The Apes of God*'s narrative with its only erotic potency, Plunkett dismisses him on grounds both sexual and political, as an anxiety-provoking outsider, whose identity as a disindividuated foreigner is inseparable from Plunkett's late-Victorian fears of lost control: "Dirty colonial – they're all the same! Orestylians, Africanders, Kanucks – what an empire!" (*AG*, 79).

Yet, surprisingly, this paranoia of a political center threatened by an external vitality is not confined to England and its empire. Instead *The Apes of God* is pervaded by xenophobia within the British Isles. Sir James, Fredigonde's husband, is obsessed by the idea that the Scottish, in search of a new world hegemony, already run England. His hatred of the Scots, moreover, bleeds into a similarly fanatical distrust of the Irish, blending them together into the indistinguishable category of feared "intruder." As Fredigonde explains to Dick, "It was in vain that I protested that half of the Scotch were now Irish ... owing don't you know to irish immigration ... He would reply that the more mixed they were the worse they became, and indeed the more *scotch.*" While Fredigonde admits this is a "most preposterous paradox and perfectly mad" (*AG*, 32), throughout *The Apes of God* Ireland, Scotland, and Wales coalesce as a nearly indistinguishable source of opposition against England's center. Each of the dissenting voices of *The Apes of God*, apart from Zagreus, whose own origins are mysterious, traces its heritage to the margins of Britain. Dan is of course Irish, while Pierpoint "belongs to a well-known welsh family ... on his mother's side he is irish" (*AG*, 297). Starr-Smith, the invasive blackshirt of the Lenten Party and Pierpoint's "political secretary," proclaims that he "stand[s] outside the anglo-saxon world" (*AG*, 529) because he is Welsh (*AG*, 511), a football player for "Llandudno Wells" (*AG*, 609).[26] Even the whiskey at the Lenten Party, which precipitates Dan's drunkenness and engagement with Zagreus's pseudo-Dionysian performance, colludes with this theme, for it is indifferently "Scotch or Irish" (*AG*, 586). When there are intimations of instability in *The Apes of God*, the British countries other than England are to blame. Zagreus claims that the emblematic satyr dance on the door at the climax of the book is "in the best peasant-tradition" of Ireland (*AG*, 608). Dan thinks throughout of the Easter Rising of 1916, fearing the General Strike that erupts at the end of the book might be a repetition of that violence, while Sir James is equally sure that the "Clydeside Scotch" (*AG*, 621) lie behind it.

Yet those who construct the idea of a national center are no more effective authorities for political structure than is Zagreus for the mythic image. Sir James himself wears an "irish tweed" (*AG*, 38), importing what is marginal into the nominally central, while the Finnian Shaws, whose Lenten Party is the English battleground for Pierpoint's aesthetic and Starr-Smith's political ideas, cannot themselves claim national authority. As Zagreus reveals in his final letter to Dan, Osmund is in fact an "august irish gentleman" (*AG*, 608), while the Finnian Shaws at large trace their heritage from a "Dublin-Scot" (*AG*, 388) – the very national blend Sir James most fears – and claim a false ancestry with "All the boastfulness of a usurper" (*AG*, 389). As the representative nobility of the book constitute themselves a true and inviolable England, they hark back to a national origin that, like Zagreus's world of representation, has no clear demarcation. What they perceive as excluded and dangerous has already entered as the constituency of a center that, in turn, can no longer be constituted as a center. As Starr-Smith exclaims, "there is no longer an English Nation!" (*AG*, 529).

Representational and national process are thus figures for one another. Both are structures organized upon what Zagreus calls "the social trust"; both depend upon the misconstruction of the "I" caught in the public mirror. Defined by their respective authorities as central or oppositional, both are exposed by their narrative as artifices either invaded or inseparable from the forces they would exclude. They are "mythological" in the sense that they depend upon philosophies of mimesis or containment imposed upon them as representational or nationalist fiction. To this degree *The Apes of God* still partakes of what Jameson calls the "national allegory" of *Tarr*, however satirically the multi-national field of the earlier novel may have been reduced to the spectacle of a divided and inherently apolitical Britain turned in against itself.[27]

Yet while *The Apes of God* registers the breaking of national and international politics, it does not in its turn, as Jameson argues of *The Childermass*, suggest a reconstitution of forces under other authoritarian or populist structures. Starr-Smith, whose name and position as Pierpoint's secretary imply that he is Zagreus's ambiguous *doppelgänger*, is not a real Fascist but another literary dabbler who has dressed for the party in the cheapest possible costume.[28] If Marxism exists as a feared externality – the jazz outside Fredigonde's window and inside the party is "marxistic music" (*AG*, 443), accompanied by dreams of museums invaded by a "*Red Sunday-School*" (*AG*, 19) – its institutional power is no less qualified. The Finnian Shaws' servant Mrs. Bosun has a fit while listening to the nightly radio news from the USSR, but this too is no more than part of a ritual charade. "They have this play to do," Zagreus explains of the Finnian Shaws, "it is called BOSUN" (*AG*, 382).

Yet even as both representation and institutional politics in the official social world invalidate their own claims to a power that lies beneath the masquerade of their structures, another conception of groundedness finds its way into *The Apes of God*. During an argument between Zagreus and Ratner, Dan has a vision:

> The struggle raged under the words, the words became beastly. Both used beastly words to each other until he became frightened. Partly it was what they said, partly the way they said – speaking in cipher, or was it a tone-code, of another tongue. – Between the flashes of the speeches this time with great distinctness he had snap-shots of the second scene. Actually he had seemed to catch glimpses of a country that was beneath this land – in which they were locked. – It was something like a glancing landscape, like a dream that was there – he had had that as a schoolboy in Ireland, when the Rebellion was, the night before the arrest of his father, when he had seen through the pavement (as he had dreamed he was walking) scenery beneath his feet. There was a world that ran through things, like pictures in water or in glassy surfaces, where a mob of persons were engaged in hunting to kill other men, in a battle-park, beneath crackling violet stars. Were there trees though – it was a distinct picture and there were parks for fighting? No not trees. Certainly that was treeless also. At both ends there were groves of spikes. A withered world altogether – spike-planted parks it looked like. A needle pricked the skin and there was blood. (*AG*, 416–17)

Here is the first and strongest intimation in *The Apes of God* of a power that is visible and real, yet which eludes, rather than is contained within, representation. It is a "struggle waged under the words" rather than through them, a "scenery beneath" that lies authentically beneath the grounds previously undermined by the characters of *The Apes of God*'s aesthetic and political contradictions. This insight belongs not to Dan but to the narrative itself. Earlier in the book Dan has gone to a production of *The Merchant of Venice* and withdrawn uncomprehendingly to the lavatory (*AG*, 133). At the end of this passage, however, the otherwise arbitrary reference to Shakespeare comes full circle, for it reveals through allusion what the majority of the narrative of *The Apes of God*, including Dan's ignorance, has colluded to hide: that there is in fact a "world that runs through things" beyond the ontologically uprooted image, not simply a world constituted by those images. This world bleeds when it is pricked, and the pricking is done by a return of what has been repressed. It is a resurgence in public manifestation of the violence that earlier Lewis narratives contained as disorders of the individual psyche, relegating to private rooms and metaphorical theaters the impulses that would otherwise burst free of narrative constraints. These impulses are made literal when Dan gets a bloody nose during the Lenten Party magic act. Zagreus attempts to contain Dan within a "vanish" box whose false bottom is supposed to present the illusion of his disappearance, yet reality asserts itself when "The blood came through between the boards" (*AG*, 592).[29]

This "withered" world of public violence connects the images of the Easter Rising, with the yet-to-come General Strike in the "groves of spikes" of Hyde Park. Dan himself is naive. His lack of historical or political insight parodies that of the young Stephen Dedalus in *A Portrait of the Artist as a Young Man*, and like Stephen, Dan associates contemporary Irish politics with his school lessons about the War of the Roses (*AG*, 556). Yet the narrative sees what he, and by Lewis's implication Joyce, either ignores or fails to consider seriously. The "country that was beneath this land" of Dan's vision is not merely the ontological world behind representation, but also the world of contemporary politics. Ireland appears repressed "beneath" England in the etymological sense that "subjection" derives from "thrown beneath" (Lat. *sub*+*jacere*). The connection of a nationalist rebellion, failed, yet by the time of *The Apes of God* successful, with the uprising of a new internal "underclass" signals an intimation within *The Apes of God* of a primitive aggressiveness denied or etiolated by its official narrative world, an anarchy that lies beneath its political and aesthetic structures and threatens their very existence.[30] Sir James Frazer's Zagreus as a vegetation god personifies the fruits of the soil.

Lewis's Zagreus intimates a very different subterranean power, one equally ready to break through the withered earth.

Indeed, the Apes have constantly been concerned about a violence that lies outside their doors. But Dan's vision suggests that the violence lies not without but within. In an early manifesto Lewis blasts England as a "DISMAL SYMBOL, SET round our bodies, of effeminate lout within. VICTORIAN VAMPIRE, the LONDON cloud sucks the TOWN's heart" (B1, 11). The imagery expresses national and political wasting – the emptying out of English identity by the vampire of the *fin de siècle* – as a corollary or "dismal symbol" of what is already inside. This image returns in *The Apes of God* as the Chirico Laocoon, presenting an image of a culture already invaded, and the Pompeian fresco on the Keins' door, which suggests not so much attack from without as a violence bursting upwards from the very earth that was supposed to provide the city a solid foundation. When Dan thinks, "They kept breaking through into something else, as you put your fist through a sheet of paper" (*AG*, 418), Lewis does not merely recast the epiphanic in terms of the whiteness of Melville's whale and the bursting from without through pasteboard masks.[31] Instead the page itself, the physical carrier of the writing that constitutes *The Apes of God*, is figured as both an evasive cover for the real and, more importantly, reality's ultimate victim. It is that which must be broken through from within, "like a fist through a sheet of paper," so that the power it occludes can reveal itself.

Therefore, the upward movement of the General Strike at the end of *The Apes of God* suggests the resurgence of an authentic political power, one that is marked by a falling away of textuality. Earlier in his picaresque travels Dan produced a log of his experiences with the Apes, yet it is an exhausted and inadequate writing. Dan has tired of writing down their descriptions and invents details to please Zagreus (*AG*, 134). The truth only emerges in the log when Dan's script is invaded from within by forces he cannot understand. When Dan's temporary servant Willie Service smuggles an entry in Dan's handwriting into the log that proclaims Zagreus to be an Ape himself, Dan must destroy the writing, burning the page to ignore Service's insights (*AG*, 321–22). Service's name suggests his temporary social role as underling, and his invasion of Dan's realm of "truth" with inflammatory realities adumbrates the larger realm of class unrest of the climactic General Strike. Correspondingly, then, the General Strike coincides with the destruction of textuality. Dan rips apart his letters and the log, which, as a document of his adventures in the Bloomsburian salons, stands as a self-reflexive emblem for *The Apes of God* itself. The destruction is total, even apocalyptic:

> And so he slowly tore that log in pieces. Then after that he tore the letters containing the *Encyclical*, and all those other notes and letters whatsoever, written to him by Horace in good faith, before he had found him out – for he had been found out. His fingers did their sad last work well, and strangled the log and letters. They divided everything – everything in the world – into smaller and smaller pieces – till no sentence at all was intact in all that mass of flattering precept and objurgation. (*AG*, 607)

Unlike Arghol, who unwittingly destroys the book of himself, Dan consciously destroys the book of his world, and is saddened by his lost illusions, as if his shredding of texts is a euthanasia of objects that should be more alive than they are. He "strangles" letters supposedly written, with the full theological authority implicit in the name of Pierpoint's *Encyclical*, in "good faith." Dan re-enacts Arghol's destruction of text with a difference. He does not destroy self, because in this etiolated world there is no "self" to destroy. Yet the thoroughness of his erasure becomes, in Lewis's subordinate clause, a correlative of a much larger destruction. If "no sentence at all was intact" after Dan's labors, the elimination of the sentence is also the annihilation of reality itself, "everything in the world." It is, therefore, no coincidence that as the General Strike emerges and Dan flees to France newspapers cease publication. Texts stop, for political turmoil replaces language's postulated certitude with a maelstrom of "every report of disorder" (*AG*, 618).

The General Strike is a final welling up of chaos, in a world otherwise concerned with representation as a mechanism of order. Dan's log attempts to contain the anomalies of the Bloomsburians in prose. Like *The Apes of God* itself it is a *vade mecum* of artificiality that purports to demonstrate the paucity of a reality that it can nonetheless capture and explain. But throughout Dan's experience representations are signs of not merely textual, but also social, control. Time and again in the narrative of *The Apes of God* Dan loses his way as he travels from salon to salon, and he has two perpetual recourses to regain his proper orientation: maps and the police. Both are omnipresent. When Dan goes to the studio of the lesbian painter "he consulted his pocket-map...He could never have done it without the help of a pocket-atlas of London and his natural map-craft" (*AG*, 221). He is anxious about going beyond the borders defined by his maps, fearing the Tube system that "led straight out into the wilderness right off the map into deserts of country" (*AG*, 114), and makes sure he has his *London Street Guide* firmly in pocket before leaving at the end (*AG*, 613). Even within the Finnian Shaws' house he gets lost in domestic "mazes" until Starr-Smith, whose presence as blackshirt suggests his own authoritarian "mapping" of the political, conveniently provides "a small map scribbled upon an odd and end of notepaper...they might have stepped over the edge of something and never come back, or been involved in a disconcerting cul de sac" (*AG*, 568). Maps are for Dan a guide to a reality that is fully present and ordered only when it can be checked against a representation. Otherwise one risks falling into false spaces, stepping into regions that lie beyond validation by symbolism.

Yet maps are only a surrogate for the police, who are also a source of spatial knowledge. Dan is proud when he can find his destination "without having to ask a policeman" (*AG*, 177) and prefers to use maps only because asking policemen for directions makes him shy (*AG*, 221). The police are a source of anxiety that does not attach to maps. Dan feels under surveillance when "a policeman, with the ominous waddle of The Force, passed him eyeing him up and down" (*AG*, 93), while paranoia about their power leads Melanie to fears that some "great brutes of police" might spirit Dan away to "some place of confinement" (*AG*, 127). Even Lewis's imagery reinforces the status of police as instruments of subliminal order. The masks of faces at Pamela

Farnham's are not simply "Like so many policemen standing in dark doorways at night, alarming the night-passenger" (*AG*, 195-96). They are also the means by which the "heterogenous realities" of the visual image are "held in place" (*AG*, 196). When Dan sees a bus full of policemen during the General Strike and fears being followed, the narrative makes explicit what the recurrent figure of policeman as giver of directions throughout *The Apes of God* implies. Like maps, and the representation in general for which they are a figure, the police are productions of the symbolic order, and are in place not simply to respond to the real, but to regulate it.[32]

Maps and the police therefore join textuality at the end of *The Apes of God* as defective and under assault. Previous to the General Strike Dan realizes that his map of Hyde Park is out of date (*AG*, 574), while popular rumor during the strike reports that a "Police-inspector and two Specials had been kicked to death" (*AG*, 618). Yet the fact that the latter is merely rumor changes the dynamics of the critique. Zagreus has earlier defined the conditions for revolt, and those conditions are contingent not upon the reality of representations but upon their proliferation. "All Revolution is preceded by 'Gossip,'" he states during the Lenten Party (*AG*, 386), and gossip is, from the point of view of the strikers, the sole condition of the strike. The police's response to this gossip is dismissive and insular, supportive of the resurgence of government texts. A constable responds to the Folletts' footman "If you was to believe all wot you was *told*... *I* ain't 'erd nothin' – 'cept wot you see in the Gazette" (*AG*, 619).[33] Yet as gossip, language circulated without traceable roots and with questionable authority, is also the basis of the Bloomsburians' literature and their own social involution; thus, the question of representation comes full circle. The trivial language of the Bloomsburians' social concerns, as Lewis has shown, brings its own destruction, allowing the "world that runs through things" entrance through the cracks of its own institutionalized gossip. Yet according to Zagreus's formulation the strikers are no more grounded or authorized than the social and aesthetic model they presumably attempt to destroy and replace. An ungrounded language remains unauthorized whether the reality in question is of the salons or of the streets. If gossip precedes revolution, in other words, it also contains the seeds of its own disorder or failure.

This failure is borne out by the historical record. The actual General Strike was not the apocalyptic event feared by the characters of *The Apes of God* but a short-lived demonstration of workers' solidarity that had none of the revolutionary repercussions feared by the government. The strikers were unwilling by and large to take over governmental responsibilities.[34] When Archie Margolin flicks matches throughout *The Apes of God* at his social betters, then, it is an adumbration of the failed gesture of incendiary power to come at the novel's end. The General Strike marked not a rupture and reconfiguration of the social world but a recontainment by the *status quo* that produced fears far in excess of its reality. Ultimately it was no challenge to the insular and centerless aesthetic and political model of Zagreus and the Bloomsburians' social world.[35]

If the General Strike itself was a failure, however, its intimations of epiphanic violence for *The Apes of God* is not. And it is at this point that *The Apes of God* most strongly re-engages with *Ulysses*. Earlier scenes prepare the parodic conclusion. The Lenten Party is a mock-"Circean" *Walpurgisnacht* where Dan, like Bloom, changes sex by being dressed as a girl; the escaped apelike Bonassus, echoing the book's title and the mythic conceit of Joyce's Nighttown, reminds us similarly of the contiguity of men with animals. (Joyce described his chapter in a way that equally describes Lewis's: "*The Circe* is a costume episode. Disguises."[36]) After this phantasmagoria, Zagreus retreats to the Follett mansion. There, during the General Strike, he and Fredigonde play out a black parody of the conclusion of Joyce's novel. An albino and homosexual, Zagreus emerges as the mock Bloom suggested by his earlier claim "I thought we Greeks were more jewish than anything else" (*AG*, 243). He accepts the marriage proposal of the ancient Fredigonde, allowing himself to be seduced only so that he may come into the Follett inheritance. Yet as he takes Fredigonde into his arms and she "dropped her lids in token of virgin-rapture"

(*AG*, 624) it is not a token of life, as in Molly's memories, but a token of death. Fredigonde, unlike Molly, is not a woman who reaccepts a returning husband after the deaths of her suitors, as Joyceans of a Homeric mind have suggested.[37] Instead Fredigonde has literally killed her husband, Sir James, to accept Zagreus as her pseudo-Dionysian lover. Upset at the General Strike, he could not ring for his servant because Fredigonde has stolen his bell. Without the ability to return to his own apartments, Sir James dies of rage: "For once he was compelled to listen to what I had to say," Fredigonde explains, "I *intended* him to die!" (*AG*, 622). Within the bounds of the Folletts' impervious drawing room, then, the blunted power of the General Strike is reauthorized, literally with a vengeance. The upsurge of the working classes may not be authentic revolutionary power, but only the historically informed reader of *The Apes of God* knows that, not its characters. And the absence of an analogous underclass in the Folletts' household – servants – reveals the authentic destructive power of language itself. James dies because his servant is not there to protect him from words he would otherwise ignore, from which he would absent himself. In the face of the General Strike he is compelled to listen, and what he hears destroys him.

The room that began in Lewis as a physical containment of psychic energies, thus returns as the aggressive and already invaded site of politics. The Folletts' mansion, no less than E. M. Forster's Howards End, becomes an emblem of England's fate in modernity. The energies of the General Strike are rediscovered in the place of domesticity, and they cause the deaths of both James and ultimately Fredigonde, who succumbs in the final paragraph to the exterior music that *The Apes of God* has configured since its first titled section as "DEATH-THE-DRUMMER" (*AG*, 5, 624). When *The Apes of God* ends with an explicit satire of the close of *Ulysses* there is more at stake than the reassertion or denial of the representational unities for which marriage and adultery act as Joycean figures. For in taking *Ulysses* as an oppositional model, Lewis falls into the dual relationship with his precursor text that *The Apes of God* itself has erected as a problem of representational authority. The aggressive anti-modernism of Lewis's parodies of mythology and subjectivity, the ungrounded and self-contradictory superficies of Zagreus's aesthetic and Lewis's own, the reconfiguration of personal as political concerns, all act as authentic revisions of Joyce's representational project. Yet in so vehemently rejecting internality and the world beyond the image Lewis ends by reasserting what he would deny. Beneath the distortions of his satiric surface and Zagreus's self-consuming aesthetics are anxieties about a reality that is neither reducible to language nor to the role-playing of the false Dionysiac experience: a power that emerges at the end of *The Apes of God* beyond the text and in the world, what Lewis has called elsewhere a "jest too deep for laughter" (*T*, chapter 4).

To this degree *The Apes of God* finds itself engaged with the same representational dialectic as *Ulysses*, if within different terms. As marriage and the threat of adultery co-exist in *Ulysses* as signs of the invasion of fragmentation into an aesthetic concerned with origins and the existence of a noumenality beyond representation, so does Lewis's mirroring of that narrative suggest a reversed invasion, that of an unforeseen noumenality – here the irrepressible energy of violence – rediscovered within an aesthetic nominally concerned with representation's complete independence from the real. Lewis finds himself drawn in by the very terms he subjects to satiric distortion, to a degree that exceeds the persistence of the subject in satire itself. To criticize through imitation – "aping" – one must engage with the ideas one intends to destroy, preserving, if in altered or critical form, what one intends to dismiss – even if one reconstitutes a rejected internality and mythology in terms of the renewed mythology of an apocalyptic "social trust." To this degree Lewis's anti-modernism finds itself trapped within the mirror of modernist, and specifically Joycean, thought. As an oppositional presence it cannot wholly disassociate itself from the target for which it is, like Hanp for Arghol, a destructive *doppelgänger*.

Yet while satire traditionally offers the possibility of moral or aesthetic growth, Lewis's intentionally "non-moral" satire denies the possibility of progress. Its nihilistic treatment of textuality suggests that it embodies Lewis's observation in the later *Men Without Art*: "Art will die, perhaps. It can, however, before doing so, paint us a picture of what life looks like without art" (*MWA*, 225). One ultimately finds in *The Apes of God* the tensions of this unresolved paradox. Lewis's linguistic vision, also carried through in his discursive writing, presages the bleak landscapes of Samuel Beckett. In *The Apes of God* there is no meaningful political language. One must use language at exhaustive length, however, if only to prove language's inability to preserve the conditions that might render it once again meaningful. At the same time the narrative diagnoses political forces whose power is indisputably real, but only destructive. And, in a final turn of the screw, that power itself becomes the target of satire. Lewis's revolutionists are objects of fear, but also of scorn. They are merely other apes, who lash out at holders of social position while wishing to replace them, confusing social performance with political authenticity. The true power of violence and its self-destructive uselessness thus joins the integrity of language and its hopeless collapse in a disastrously double dialectical dance that is exploded rather than resolved by *The Apes of God*'s literally dead end.

One may thus read the final passage of *The Apes of God* as a figure for its own literary and political ambiguities. Archie Margolin strides forward into the "mighty victorian looking-glasses" (*AG*, 625) of the Folletts, an emblem of the future as a grotesque repetition of the past. Yet as a subject Margolin is defined not by his independence, but by his reflection in the very objects of the historical and aesthetic world that he would revise and destroy. The political irony is clear: what cannot be tragedy must be repeated as farce. As satire *The Apes of God* finds itself analogously enclosed. By importing aspects of *Ulysses* into itself as farce, *The Apes of God*, like Margolin, finds itself caught within a mimetic dialectic from which it cannot be entirely free. Advancing in the reflection of historical and literary forces it would revise, it ultimately finds itself subject to a representational power whose authority, like its own epiphanic violence and the *Ulysses* it mocks, can be neither repressed nor nullified. If, as Zagreus suggests, one must always recognize the "I" within the public mirror of fiction, *The Apes of God*, despite its initial denial of the world outside the image, imports within its closed borders the authentic powers of the modernist art, and the modern violence, from which it constitutes its distorted reflections.

CHAPTER 4

# Minds of the anti-collaborators

> [T]he bodily eye sees all objects outside itself but needs a mirror to see itself.
> Giambattista Vico, *The New Science*, paragraph 331

> Such double fables or characters must have been necessary in the heroic state in which the plebeians, having no names of their own, bore those of their heroes; to say nothing of the extreme poverty of speech that must have prevailed in the first times, since, copious as our present languages are, even in them the same word often signifies different and sometimes contrary things.
> Giambattista Vico, *The New Science*, paragraph 581

If Joyce and *Ulysses* are the hidden doubles in *The Apes of God*, the figure of Wyndham Lewis is abundantly evident in the patterns of *Finnegans Wake*. As Adaline Glasheen has noted, the problem with references to Lewis in *Finnegans Wake* is "there is just too bloody much of them."[1] This abundance is programmatic, for Joyce was the first to wish that his counterblast to Lewis's criticisms in *Time and Western Man* be obvious and recognizable. Lewis serves as implicit and explicit subject in no fewer than four of the twelve essays on *Work in Progress* published in 1929 as *Our Exagmination Round His Factification for Incamination of Work in Progress* by friends and supporters under Joyce's supervision. Thomas McGreevy calls upon "the London master of spaces" to attend to the moral of a passage recently published as a pamphlet by Harry Crosby's Black Sun Press:

The author of *Time and Western Man* is a writer of remarkable potentialities but has so much contempt for time that he never takes enough time to finish anything properly. If he would read the story of the Ondt and the Gracehoper, not impatiently, but patiently he might learn from it how to write satire not like a barbarian, ineffectively but like an artist, effectively."[2]

For William Carlos Williams, Lewis poses an even more serious threat. While answering criticism of Joyce in Rebecca West's *The Strange Necessity* he slips into wholesale denunciation of Lewis, calling West's style "A little ill-natured, a little sliding; what might be termed typically British and should be detected as such from the American view, a criticism not quite legitimate, save for England where it may be proper due to national exigencies like the dementia of Wyndham Lewis."[3]

In short, Lewis set out to be "The Enemy" and succeeded for Joyce, provoking intensely defensive reactions both from Joyce's admirers and in the text of *Finnegans Wake* itself. References to Lewis as barbarian and lunatic suggest the strongest reactions to the fact that his critical voice could not simply be sloughed off but demanded response in kind. As Butt, the version of Shem who plays out Buckley's attack on the Russian General, admits in *Finnegans Wake*, alluding to Lewis's suppressed given name, "the enemay the Percy rally got me" (*FW*, 352.10). Other essays in *Our Exagmination* register the power of the voice to which they take umbrage. Marcel Brion appropriates Lewis's criticism of Joyce's temporality as the unspoken rationale for a hyperbolic exultation of Joyce's "time sense." He effectively restates Lewis's opinions in reverse: "Space is nothing," Brion enthuses. Instead time is "perhaps the only reality in the world." It is the "essential factor in a work of art," which Brion, mirroring but not mentioning Lewis, equates with internality: "I imagine that he could write an unprecedented book composed of the simple interior physical existence, of a man...I imagine that Joyce could compose a book of pure time."[4] Only Robert Sage's essay suggests the curious and pervasive status of Lewis's oppositional presence in *Finnegans Wake*:

Figures of the past and present flit through it spectrally as they have through the world's existence and through the mind of Joyce. Finn

MacCool, Adam and Eve, Humpty-Dumpty, Napoleon, Daddy Browning, Lucifer, Wyndham Lewis, the Archangel Michael, Santa Claus, Tristram and Isolde, Noah, St. Patrick, Thor and Dean Swift are a few of the thousands of worthies whose shades pass through the pages of *Work in Progress*.[5]

Caught between Lucifer and the Archangel Michael, Lewis emerges as an archetype larger than his own literary self. Although he might have been pleased by being placed between the prince of darkness and the angel whose name means "who is like God," he is an anomalous figure in Sage's list. Like Swift and Browning (who here blends with "Daddy" Browning, a figure involved in a notorious scandal of the 1920s) Lewis is an author, but he is the only contemporary "worthy" in the pantheon, the sole living figure whose "shade" haunts *Finnegans Wake* not through folkloric or historical strength, but as a presence in Joyce's own literary world. While the original reason for Lewis to appear in *Finnegans Wake* was local and biographical, Sage suggests by implication what would become yet more striking in the finished work. Lewis in *Finnegans Wake* is less an individual than an abstract force, a quasi-mythic construction considerably larger than the feud that earned him initial inclusion in Joyce's drafts.

Attention to Lewis's presence in *Finnegans Wake*, however, has tended to reproduce literary history on the level of local anecdote. Critics have mined Joyce's parodies of Lewis, particularly the two inset fables of "The Mookse and the Gripes" and "The Ondt and the Gracehoper" for allusions to their feud, references that they seldom trace through Lewis's work beyond his immediate essay on Joyce in *Time and Western Man*.[6] These readings have much to do with the contemporary background of *Finnegans Wake*, but little to do with the issues of *Finnegans Wake* itself. By reconstructing the "historical" subtext of narratives that Joyce explicitly presents as "fables" these studies tend to isolate moments in *Finnegans Wake* from their aesthetic context, cordoning off Joyce's argument with Lewis from *Finnegans Wake*'s larger themes of origin and the ambiguities of the literal in a cosmology influenced by the ideas of Vico and Bruno.[7] One must read Lewis's presence in *Finnegans*

*Wake* as a significant strand in the work as a whole, an integral part of Joyce's final fictional meditation on origins and representation.

These subjects, I have been arguing, constitute the fundamental ground of the debate between Lewis and Joyce: the argument over metaphysics and its aesthetic and political ramifications that implicates Joyce and *Ulysses* as the ambivalent doubles of *The Apes of God*. Metaphysics in *Finnegans Wake* thus provides a suitable point of entry for consideration of Lewis's status within the text. That topic is not easily reducible to a single perspective, and was noted as such in the earliest criticism. Samuel Beckett, whose essay "Dante...Bruno. Vico ...Joyce" opens *Our Exagmination*, denied that Joyce's experimental language dealt in metaphysics. The language, to Beckett, concerned itself not with universals but with poetic particulars. There is "little or no attempt at subjectivism or abstraction," Beckett announces, "no attempt at metaphysical generalisation." Yet Beckett also paradoxically suggests that the particularity of Joyce's language represents the "absolute absence of the Absolute."[8] For there to be an absolute lack of an absolute, as Beckett must have been wryly aware, means there is an Absolute after all, a totality based, however curiously, upon the dismantling of its own conceptual grounds. Such dismantling is found throughout *Finnegans Wake*, in which Joyce's punning epistemology offers an interplay between what is absolute and what is negated, what is "whole" and what is "hole":

Now by memory inspired, turn wheel again to the whole of the wall. Where Gyant Blyant fronts Peannlueamoore There was once upon a wall and a hooghoog wall a was and such a wallhole did exist. (*FW*, 69.5–8)

This passage is explicitly about being, demonstrating what "did exist" in terms of a conventional narrative opening, "once upon a time" becoming through Joycean wordplay a Humpty-Dumptian "once upon a wall." But while protesting the existence of the "whole of the wall" the sentence also changes the status of its object. The Vichian "wheel" suggests a casting back into history by memory, while the word "wheel" itself "turns" by homophony into the words "whole" and "wall." These terms replace "wheel" as metaphorical equivalents, playing upon the significance of "turn," as we will later note at greater length, not only as a physical action but also as the movement through which language can stand figuratively for an alien referent: the "trope." The wall becomes rather a "wallhole." It is a wall defined by absence, or a gap in the wall that questions the integrity of the "whole of the wall" itself.[9]

In this small but representative passage "whole" and "hole" coexist under the rubric of narrative convention. The sentence appears to begin a tale that offers "what exists" and demonstrates as it progresses only that it does what it claims imperfectly. Such is typical of *Finnegans Wake*'s treatment of themes of narrative representation, which are dogged by absences and incompletions, "holes" interpenetrating with "wholes." The Norwegian captain in II.iii, for instance, has a "hole in his tale" (*FW*, 323.22–23). ALP's tokens of narrative closure are similarly haunted by loss. When Anna Livia gives gifts to smooth over the rumors of HCE's misdeeds, among them is a gift of narrative absence, a "hole in the ballad for Hosty" (*FW*, 211.19–20). Most importantly, ALP's Letter, *Finnegans Wake*'s most persistent self-reflexive emblem of narrativity, is first described as both the gamut of possibilities and as nonexistence:

> What was it?
> A..........!
> ?.........O!            (*FW*, 94.20–22)

The Letter can be considered both as a "whole," an alphabet that runs from Alpha to Omega, or a "hole," a nullity represented by a series of narrative elisions – the repeated dots – and a zero. When *Finnegans Wake* positions itself as a narrative of the "Hole affair" (*FW*, 535.20), then, it alerts the reader that its relationship to its subject matter is potentially both universal and null, that its completions are disjunct from the narrative closure proffered by "once upon a time." As Jaun asks, "Sure, what is it on the whole only holes tied together...?" (*FW*,

434.21–22). In declaring that "Nought is nulled" (*FW*, 613.14), *Finnegans Wake* implies that within its universe nothingness may be intensified by a further unimaginable negation, but also that everything perdures, that nothingness itself may be nullified as category.

This interplay of "whole" and "hole" suggests a paronomastic replaying of the lessons of Stephen's lecture on Shakespeare writ large. Stephen's lecture, I have suggested, deals with the interrelationship of totality and dispersion, enacted both at the level of linguistic representation and of narrative in terms of marriage and adultery. *Finnegans Wake*'s punning suggests an even more radical and analogous coexistence of a narrative "platinism" (*FW*, 164.11) with a nihilism based upon an "absolute zero" (*FW*, 164.10). As the narrative of a "whole" suggests a language resting Platonically upon an authoritative ground that legitimizes its symbolic project, the narrative of a "hole" suggests the antithetical absence of any essential being, any "pure (what bunkum!) essenesse" (*FW*, 608.4). Just as there is both contradiction and continuity in Stephen's lecture between the theological Word as guarantor of meaning and the adulteries of sexual life and language, the homophony of "whole" and "hole" refuses easy differentiation between apparently incompatible opposites. The word as symbol carries with it the cognate possibility of nothingness, reminding us, as *Finnegans Wake* states in terms of exponential mathematics: "The logos of somewome to that base anything ... comes to nullum in the endth" (*FW*, 298.19–21).

This interrelationship between nihilism and unadulterated theories of being suggests uncertainty about the status of origins, the "base" that might be "anything." As in the lecture on Shakespeare, *Finnegans Wake* establishes its metaphor of origin as the father, who is the producer of language. HCE, whose crime in the Phoenix Park is the cause of *Finnegans Wake*'s narrative, stands for both authorship and parentage. According to "The Ballad of Persse O'Reilly," he is a "Suffoclose! Shikespower! Seudodanto!" (*FW*, 47.19) While retaining the "power" of a Shakespeare, in other words, he is also a muffled Sophocles and a pseudo-Dante. He is also a self-created character. Like the Shakespeare of *Ulysses* he is "a king and no king" (*U*, 9.166), whose appearances throughout as different monarchs suggest his ambiguous status as both tyrannical father and parricidal son. HCE appears as "oddman rex" (*FW*, 61.29) and "adipose rex" (*FW*, 499.16), suggesting in both cases his identity as an exiled Oedipus, product both of Sophocles and Freud: as a "Muster of the Hidden Life" (*FW*, 499.15) he also has an "eatupus complex" (*FW*, 128.36). As "Mr Leer" (*FW*, 65.4) he is both Shakespearean king and nonsense poet Edward, appearing throughout as the Nietzschean "Uberking Leary," (*FW*, 611.33) "High Ober King Leary" (*FW*, 612.4) and "Leary, leary" (*FW*, 582.35), associations that resonate with Irish history and myth, "Lear" blending into "Lir" and "Laoghaire," the king at the time of Patrick's introduction of Catholicism to Ireland.[10]

As this last association with Catholicism suggests, HCE at his most expansive is the source of an apparently authoritative language. He is the "primeum nobilees," both Dantean "prime mover" and winner of the Nobel Prize (in Latin, the "Praemium Nobelium") (*FW*, 356.11). To Shaun he is "the first mover," the referent to whom he owes his own origin as a sign owes its legitimacy to the real from which it springs: HCE is "that father I ascend fromming knows, as I think, caused whom I, a self the sign" (*FW*, 483.27-29). As a hypostatized figure of paternity, moreover, HCE's sexuality may determine what is ultimately real, for the narrative asks "Is dads the thing in such … ?" (*FW*, 528.15-16) The phallus here is nominated as the Kantian *ding an sich*, and, as the confrontation between Patrick and the archdruid towards the end of *Finnegans Wake* suggests, the search for this "true inwardness of reality, the Ding hvad in idself id est" (*FW*, 611.21) is the quest of the historical record of narrative itself, which seeks to establish what is authentically true through the language in which it is named, in "the facts of his nominigentilisation" (*FW*, 31.33-34).

Yet even as this last word conflates the Vichian search for the origins of the gentile languages ("gentilisation") with the origin of naming in sexual or "genital" potency, other phrases suggest that HCE is null. He is an emptiness created "Ex nickylow" (*FW*, 23.16) (Lat. *ex nihilo*) who stands, like Lear, as proof that nothing can be made from nothing. Like Leopold Bloom before him he is as much "Noman" as "Everyman" (*U*, 17.2008). This is reinforced by Homeric references. Like Bloom he is "no man" in his own country, "Nemo in Patria" (*FW*, 229.13). He is affectionately called "Our Outis" (*FW*, 493.24) after the Greek "name" with which Odysseus fools the Cyclops, acting like "nobodyatall with Wholyphamous" (*FW*, 73.9) (Homer's "Polyphemos"). In his ambivalent identification with his son Shem he blends with Bruno of Nolan to become the doubly negative "Nayman of Noland" (*FW*, 187.28), a nay-sayer or "no man" from "no land," while attaining the doubly epistemologically negative status of "Niscemus Nemon" (*FW*, 175.33) (Lat., "We don't know anybody"). The study of HCE as paternal authority threatens to become an act of "Nomomorphemy" (*FW*, 599.18–19), an inquiry into the shape of nothing.

That this Platonic or phallic potency and the negativity of HCE's frequent namings are not simple opposites, however, is suggested by a Vichian tracing of his multiple identities. "First you were Nomad, next you were Namar, now you're Numah and it's soon you'll be Nomon," *Finnegans Wake* warns (*FW*, 374.22–23). The terms of the series suggest HCE's equivocal status. To be a "nomad" is to be without fixed place, a wanderer who cannot be pinned down to a particular location. But one may read the following terms in equally "nomadic" ways. "Namar" suggests both "namer," Adam as source of language, as well as "no more," a marker of loss or falling away.[11] In "Numah," on the other hand, one discerns an echo of the first syllables of "noumenon," a mark of being antithetical to "nomadic," or wandering, significance. The sentence's final term, "Nomon," moreover, contains not only "no man" but also "gnomon." This fourth term, which suggests in its following of three cognate terms a Vichian *ricorso* or return to beginnings, recirculates not only to HCE's identity but also to Joyce's literary beginnings, the mysterious word that fascinates the youthful narrator in the first paragraph of Joyce's "The

Sisters."[12] A parallelogram with an analogous and smaller parallelogram removed from one of its corners, the gnomon in *Finnegans Wake* acts as an allusive correlative both for HCE as character and narrative in general. As a "whole" containing a "hole" that mimics its larger figure, the gnomon figures origins and teleologies (it's "soon you'll be nomon," the sentence suggests, with the gnomon as both temporal end and origin), as a geometrical proof of the implausibility of Platonism. Like the squaring of the circle in *Ulysses*, its potential proof testifies to the impossibility of proof. It provides both an eschatology and a cognate "escapology" (*FW*, 428.22), a means of eluding the centering *telos* that it nominally seeks to establish.

Not surprisingly, the problem of the squaring of the circle also persists in *Finnegans Wake*, as Joyce implied when he wrote to Harriet Shaw Weaver during its writing "I am making an engine with only one wheel ... The wheel is a perfect square."[13] In a text where Shem is accused of "circling the square" (*FW*, 186.12) (reversing the geometrical law as well as idling around Dublin's greens) and the Letter itself contains "blocked rounds" (*FW*, 119.13), HCE embodies a similar contradiction as a comparably impossible narrative and figurative source. Like Stephen's Shakespeare he "emprisoms trues and fauss for us" (*FW*, 127.3–4). If he is a linguistic source his language is threatened both by his divided nature and by his equivocal existence as representative of a fallen reality. *Finnegans Wake* wages his "falsemeaning adamelegy" (*FW*, 77.26), which is both a mocking lament for the fall of the first man (an "Adam elegy") and a cognate double search for linguistic sources, a "falsemeaning etymology" that oxymoronically contradicts its own etymological source (from Greek *etumos*, "true, real," and *logos*). The search for fatherly origins in *Finnegans Wake* is not an inquiry into certainty, for the "sword of certainty which would identifide the body never falls" (*FW*, 51.5–6). This search is rather an exploration into the possible loss or absence of certain sources, "the secrest of their soorcelossness" (*FW*, 23.19).

To the literary critic these arguments are familiar. They have provided the basis not only for valuable recent interpretations of *Finnegans Wake*, but for literary deconstruction, which emphasizes both moments of self-contradictory impasse and the contingencies underlying nominally transcendental standards in what *Finnegans Wake* calls the "radification of interpretation" (*FW*, 369.6–7).[14] Such arguments are not merely linguistic. For if words are legitimized by the possibly noumenal source for which the divided father acts as a pervasive Joycean figure, the relationship of the superficies of the world to that underlying reality becomes similarly problematic. It is an appropriately Joycean paradox that the chapter in *Ulysses* that comes closest to the linguistic extravagance of *Finnegans Wake* also poses this dilemma most lucidly. In the opening paragraph of "Oxen of the Sun," the narrative asks "For who is there who anything of some significance has apprehended but is conscious that that exterior splendour may be the surface of a downwardtending lutulent reality...?" (*U*, 14.17–19) The question is posed in the more optimistic of its two possible articulations. There "may" be some greater reality beneath the surfaces of the world, the "significance" of the "exterior splendour," but that observation retains the skepticism that surfaces may represent nothing at all. At the end of "Oxen," a chapter devoted to language and literature as figures of parentage, the farrago of slang and argot detached from particular speakers suggests the alternative. The phenomenal and linguistic worlds may extend nowhere: they may stand only for themselves, or are at best secondary reflections of previous models, floating free of their articulators and pointing parodically backward to no unitary source.

*Finnegans Wake* registers this emphasis on the insecure grounding of this "funnaminal world" (*FW*, 244.13) with a "carlysle touch" (*FW*, 517.22). As in Carlyle's *Sartor Resartus* (which becomes in *Finnegans Wake* "sartor's risorted" [*FW*, 314.17]) the superficies of the world, and by association writing, become a clothing rather than a revelation of what may lie behind. "We are circumveiloped by obscuritads" (*FW*, 244.15), Joyce notes, as we are surrounded by phenomena in a "veiled world" (*FW*, 139.1). Since we can know no more than the "outer husk" (*FW*, 109.8), we cannot determine whether our conjectures about the real are adequate or, playing upon the name of the founder of the Philosophy of Clothing, Carlyle's Professor Teufelsdröckh, whether they are simply "Tawfulsdreck" (*FW*, 68.21). "[H]ow comes ever a body in our taylorised world," *Finnegans Wake* asks, "to selve out thishis, whither it gives a primeum nobilees for our notomise or naught ... ?" (*FW*, 356.10–12) So while the anatomy of HCE (the already negative "notomise" which is also nakedness, "not a *mise*" [Fr. "manner of dress"]) is "primesigned in the full of your dress" (*FW*, 24.28–29) it remains uncertain whether the clothing of surfaces can be traced to something deeper or simply to "naught," if "by the siege of his trousers there was someone else behind it" (*FW*, 61.25–26).[15] Stories about such clothed realities in *Finnegans Wake* must remain mere "taylor's fablings" (*FW*, 61.28), for they clothe a reality that may not exist at all for "Every old skin in the leather world" (*FW*, 510.16).[16]

For this reason *Finnegans Wake* stands in the same philosophical relation to *Ulysses* as Lewis's *The Apes of God* stands to *Blast*, as both extension and revision. *Ulysses* returns from the linguistic extravagance of "Oxen of the Sun" to the *nostos* of a normative language. "Oxen" remains an experiment in style sympathetic with the anti-epiphanic strain in Stephen's fictive argument, but not a determinant of the work's complete linguistic nature. What was in *Ulysses* a narrative possibility becomes in *Finnegans Wake* a universal dilemma of representation. Here Vico's theory of the origin of languages offers an alternative vision of linguistic authority that intersects with Joyce's revision of Carlyle's transcendentalism. In *The New Science*, the source of the gentile languages – and the qualification is important – is not the spoken Word of the Judeo-Christian tradition, but rather the ruptures of thunder. Primitive man perceives the thunder as a paternal threat and imitates it as a stutter, associating their nascent language with the father's name and rule. Vico explains:

Human words were formed next from interjections, which are sounds articulated under the impetus of violent passions. In all languages these are monosyllables. Thus it is not beyond likelihood that, when wonder had been awakened in men by the first thunderbolts, these interjections of Jove should give birth to one produced by the human voice: "*pa!*"; and that this should then be doubled: "*pape!*" From this interjection of wonder was subsequently derived Jove's title of "father of men and gods," and thus it came about presently that all the gods were called fathers ... "[17]

It is significant that "Oxen of the Sun," with its motifs of birth, paternity, questionable linguistic origin, and observation that "the ends and ultimates of all things accord in some mean and measure with their inceptions and originals" (*U*, 14.387–89), is also the most Vichian chapter in *Ulysses*. The peal of thunder towards the chapter's end acts as a revision of the "utterance of the word" (*U*, 14.1390), the paternal voice that ushers in an era of historical and linguistic fragmentation. Through the mediating figure of Blake's threatening "Nobodaddy" (*U*, 14.419) the *logos* becomes literalized as the external rupture that Stephen has earlier presented to Mr Deasy as his sardonic and now Vichian God, the "shout in the street" (*U*, 2.386).

Thus, Vico provides a parable of disunified paternal origin that coexists in *Finnegans Wake* with the Judeo-Christian theology from which it specifically exempts itself. This exemption is a kind of disingenuous slight of hand, for Vico claims that his theory applies to the gentile languages only. If he claims "every gentile nation had its Jove" (*NS*, par. 380), as John Bishop notes, he could not or would not include the Christian tradition among those who found their speech through the threats of a thundering barbarian father, for what was acceptable to eighteenth-century Italy as a vision of Greek and Roman origin no doubt courted charges of blasphemy as a revision of Christianity.[18] *Finnegans Wake* tellingly places the thunder source, "Jove bolt, at his rude word" (*FW*, 80.28), as an unassimilated counter-mythology to the central dispersion of authenticity of the "propaganda fidies" (*FW*, 80.20) of the *logos*, which as the papal source of Catholic expansion represents a universal symbol of speech as pervasive religious origin, the "Allhighest sprack for krischnians" (both Christians and, in this context, followers of Krishna) (*FW*, 80.20–21).[19] Like the "whole" and the "hole," these Vichian and Christian visions of paternal origin are superimposed as aspects of each other's equivocal power. Blake's revisionist Christian Nobodaddy turns into the childish Wakean "Noodynaady," whose "actual ingrate tootle" (*FW*, 253.16–17) is also the voice of the Vichian "Him Which Thundereth From On High" (*FW*, 62.14), while the Christian "paternoster" is undercut as the father who produces only comic atmospheric ruptures in place of the divine word, the Vichian "farternoiser" (*FW*, 530.36) who, like Blake's Nobodaddy, "Farted & belched & coughd."[20]

*Finnegans Wake*'s originating father is thus no "monomyth" (*FW*, 581.24) (either phallic monolith or singular tale of origin), but rather the oxymoronic conflation of competing mythologies. The creation dependent upon him is divided against itself, like the earwig from which HCE, as "Humphrey Chimpden Earwicker" takes his own entomological and etymological origin or "buginning."[21] *Finnegans Wake* revises the biblical *fiat lux* as the principle of creation by recasting it as "Let there be fight" (*FW*, 90.12), or, in a paraphrase of the Gospel of John, "In the buginning is the woid" (*FW*, 378.29) (the "word" also being the "void"). For if the Word is on one hand made flesh it is also the Vichian source of rupture, where "The war is in words" (*FW*, 98.34–35). The question of linguistic or thematic stability becomes an issue of "platoonic leave" (*FW*, 348.8). The possibility of unification ("Platonic love") is subordinated linguistically and thematically to the vocabulary of battling oppositions ("platoonic") and surcease ("leave").

To this degree Beckett is right to reject the presence of a singular metaphysics in *Finnegans Wake*. As the "reporterage on Der Fall Adams" (*FW*, 70.5) Joyce's narrative presents itself as a compendium of Wittgensteinian import. As the "fall" of the patriarch is also the "case" of the father (Ger. *Fall*, "case") its world is the totality of what is the case, a document of its manifold "falls" or, as *Finnegans Wake* describes itself, the "book of that which is" (*FW*, 570.8–9).[22] This has powerful implications not only for the idea of philosophic origin in *Finnegans Wake* but also for the symbolizing that can be based upon its postulated unities. For if one may have access only to the perceptible "cases" of phenomena, the multifarious "supperfishies" (*FW*, 524.31) of the "audible-visible-gnosible-edible world" (*FW*, 88.6), all that can be knowable ("gnosible") are surfaces, those pointers that allow us to perceive the world and make it part of ourselves (in the sense that "superficies," which Joyce punningly combines with a hint of the biblical parable of proliferating loaves and fishes, can be "edible"). *Finnegans Wake* replaces the idea of symbolic knowledge as a "panepistemion" (*FW*, 116.31) (Gr. "universal knowledge") with a more contingent knowledge that is based upon accidents, a knowing that remains necessarily figurative. Epistemology becomes an "Epistlemadethemology" (*FW*, 374.17). Its "themes" lie not in transcendental theories but in the "case" or *fall* of the Letter – the "epistle" that is both *Finnegans Wake*'s central emblem for the historical transmission of symbolic meaning and for language itself.

This aspect of *Finnegans Wake* seems to embrace Lewis's insights in *Blast*. By accepting the surfaces of the world and its consequent symbols, Joyce seems to accept what he calls the "coat of homoid icing which is in reality only a done by chance" (*FW*, 149.26–27). He valorizes the Aristotelian "accident" ("chance") of the Carlylean "coat" over the Platonic cause that is never fully eradicated from *Ulysses*. Yet in *Blast*, unlike in *Finnegans Wake*, the accidental has ontological value: for Lewis what is visible is what is indisputably real. In *Finnegans Wake*, on the other hand, even the accidental is inaccessible except as figuration. There is no simple set of reducible "surfaces" to its narrative or to the style through which that narrative emerges. This aspect of *Finnegans Wake* may be usefully apprehended in terms of its status as dream.[23] As Freud argues, dream materials are always submerged by the machinations of the dream work. Rhetorical operations called condensation and substitution translate the dream's raw psychic materials into the images of the manifest surface, presenting to analysis only compressed and metonymic figurations that stand in for the "actual" content that is inaccessible directly.[24]

The analytic possibilities of Freud's argument for the linguistic and narrative form of *Finnegans Wake* are many. For our purposes, we may contrast Freud's system of symbolic narrative substitution with the substitutions implicit in systems of painting. In Lewis's representational aesthetic the real object is replaced on the canvas, if despite itself, by an iconic or representational substitute. In Freud's schema, and in Joyce's, the "real" object is replaced by a more abstract system of tropes, in which "original" meanings are subjected to chains of metaphors and metonymies. I use the term "trope" to mean a rhetorical turn here advisedly, for it is Joyce's own consistent usage within *Finnegans Wake* for the processes of narrative and familial replacement. Linguistic representation, for instance, is a matter of "mistletropes" (*FW*, 9.19), warring figures ("missiles") erected in the place of the prelapsarian garden, the father's "prefall paradise peace" (*FW*, 30.15). Just as Shaun and Shem battle to replace the father's occluded authority – to become metaphors for the father – so does troping become inseparable from the nature of being a son. Shaun makes this "affliction" of figuration explicit. Defending his own creative lapses, he declares he is ill with "A bad attack of maggot it feels like. 'Tis trope" (*FW*, 410.5). While warning Shem away from creativity, moreover, Shaun taunts him "Turn about, skeezy Sammy, out of metaphor, till we feel are you still tropeful of popetry" (*FW*, 466.9–11). To be "tropeful of popetry," Shaun implies, is not only to be filled with the figurations or linguistic turns of poetry, but also to use metaphor as a turning about the authority of the father, "popetry" subsuming the manipulative authority of the church ("popery" blended with "puppetry"), as well as the attempt ("try") to *be* the father ("pope"). The most important identification of troping or "turning" with sonship, however, occurs in the riddle game of II.i. Here the rainbow girls spin around Shaun and represent "a guarded figure of speech" (*FW*, 237.5–6) which Shem must guess to resolve the uncertainty of the game. The answer, which Shem does not guess, is "heliotrope." In other words, the answer that stands in for the absent motivation, is not merely a color or flower that means "turning of the sun." "Heliotrope," given both the girls' ringing around Shaun and *Finnegans Wake*'s abundant dependence upon homophonic associations, suggests not merely the cyclical action of time – the "sun" "turning" – but also the "turning" or "troping" of the "son."[25]

*Finnegans Wake* most explicitly engages with Lewis around this issue. The identification of Shem with Joyce and Shaun with Lewis has long been recognized. Shem's parabolic writing of *Ulysses* in 1.vii, and Shaun's identity as "mein goot enemy" (*FW*, 155.19), author of a "postvortex piece" (*FW*, 150.7) and "irony of the stars" (*FW*, 160.22) in 1.vi, point unequivocally to the characters' biographical origins; Lewis is as clearly the didactic Professor Jones as the Shem who "writ[es] the mystery of himsel in furniture" (*FW*, 184.9–10), echoing *Blast*'s strictures that artists should not allow too much of themselves into their printed work, is the overly "personal" artist arraigned by Lewis.[26] The biographical squibs, echoing *Time and Western Man* and parodying Lewis's and Joyce's personal interactions, are too numerous to trace in detail; examples must suffice. When the critic of the Letter complains of the "Aludin's Cove of our cagacity" (*FW*, 108.27–28), and Shaun addresses Shem as "aladdin, amobus" (*FW*, 407.27), one hears unmistakable echoes of Lewis's complaint that interior monologue in *Ulysses* "lands the reader inside an Aladdin's cave of incredible bric-à-brac" (*TWM*, 91) and produces a shapeless "monument like a record diarrhoea" (*TWM*, 92) ("cagacity" from It. "*cagare*," "to shit"). The former reference echoes throughout *Finnegans Wake* in Shaun's objection to the technique of interior monologue, "innerman monophone" (*FW*, 462.16) changing into "moanolothe inturned" (*FW*, 254.14), introjected complaint and self-hatred. The reference to "diarrhoea" leads both to Shaun's examining Shem's "diarrhio" (*FW*, 467.19) (a "diary," like *Ulysses*, is a book of the day) and, more importantly, to all of 1.vii. There Shem's inscriptions upon his body with excremental ink fuse Lewis's complaint with accusations of Joyce's solipsism, transforming both into a scene of confrontation, rendered literal as if by Freudian dream work.

Shaun mimics Lewis's aesthetic accusations. He complains that because Shem fails to appreciate visuality his art suffers ("he's been failing of that kink in his arts over sense" [*FW*, 490.5], aesthetic criticism also containing a "kick in the arse") He complains of Shem's "craft ebbing" and of his "Grindings of Nash" (*FW*, 290.28), blending Lewis's declaration that the drafts of *Work in Progress* represented a faltering of technique, critics' complaints about Joyce's sexual perversity, and Lewis's derivation of Joyce's prose style from the Elizabethan Thomas Nashe.[27] When Joyce writes that HCE "set the living a fire" (*FW*, 131.13–14) and has Shaun accuse that Shem "would endeavour to set ever annyma roner moother of mine on fire" (*FW*, 426.3–4) he echoes Lewis's observation that Joyce's *Chamber Music* "would hardly even have set the Liffey on fire for five minutes" (*TWM*, 75).[28] Shaun speaks in Lewis's chosen idiolect. Borrowing the antimonies of *Blast*, he declares "I'm blessed but you'd feel him a blasting rod" (*FW*, 250.24). He calls Shem an "Annamite Aper of Atroxity" (*FW*, 179.14–15) and a "blethering ape" (*FW*, 192.4) in the rhetoric of *The Apes of God*, describing also the previous occupant of Shem's inkbottle house as a Lewisian "split-man," "one's half hypothesis of that jabberjaw ape" (*FW*, 125.19). The Shaun who draws ALP's genitals as a geometrical diagram in II.ii is the Lewis who promises "no bones without flech" (*FW*, 149.5) in his angular portraiture, and who spent much of the 1920s working "underground" on a massive project called *The Man of the World* (in *Finnegans Wake*, like the Letter, things are "met with misfortune while all underground" [*FW*, 113.31–32]).

The accusations are personal on both sides. Professor Jones's allusion to a book called in part "*Why am I not born like a Gentleman*" (*FW*, 150.26) echoes Lewis's insistence that Joyce was excessively concerned with being a "gentleman" (*TWM*, 108), while his accusation that Shem is "trying to copy the stage Englesemen" (*FW*, 181.1) reproduces Lewis's accusation, also addressed by Frank Budgen, that Bloom is less a character than a "stage Jew" who is "not even a Jew most of the time, but his talented irish author" (*TWM*, 101). Joyce, in his turn, portrays Lewis as an elitist sermonizer. Professor Jones announces "my explanations here are probably above your understandings" and objects to lecturing to "muddlecrass pupils" (*FW*, 152.4–5, 8). He believes he is the superior artist, claiming "I am a mouth's more deserving case by genius" (*FW*, 159.26), but he is actually as socially conscious as his competitor – "this soldier-author-batman for all his commontoryism is just another of those souftsiezed bubbles who never quite got the sandhurst out of his eyes so that the champaign he draws for us is as flop as a plankrieg" (*FW*, 162.5–9). Lewis, who lists his military and artistic credentials seriatim in the introduction to his autobiography *Blasting and Bombadiering*,[29] is a failed campaigner who attempts champagne-like wit in his "drawings" but falls flat, his garden-variety conservatism ("comonmtoryism") edged by *resentissment* at his failure to be educated at an elite British military academy such as Sandhurst. In further deflation Joyce associates Shaun throughout *Finnegans Wake* with footwear. When Lewis and Joyce first met in 1920, Lewis claims, he helped T. S. Eliot deliver a package to Joyce containing used shoes, a gift from Ezra Pound.[30] Shem's complaints multiply. "You gave me a boot ... and I ate the wind" (*FW*, 19.33–34), associates "Wyndham" with "wind," and suggests that Lewis crammed his own suggestions down Joyce's gullet, while "A true friend is known much more easily, and better into the bargain, by his personal touch, ... response to appeals for charity than by his footwear, say" (*FW*, 115.8–11) seems, in the normalcy of its language, to ask circumspectly for personal consideration from his colleague.[31] Shaun as Jaun is lauded for "his humane treatment of any kind of abused footgear" (*FW*, 429.7–8), and appears with "Worndown shoes upon his feet ... In his hands a boot!" (*FW*, 489.22–23). In a final indignity, Shaun the Post appears even as deliverer of shoes worn beyond their time. The name "Shuhorn the posth" (*FW*, 556.36) relegates Shaun to the status of mere expediter, the "shoehorn," and blames him with posthumousness, turning his visit into the delivery of a dead letter.

This list of allusions is scarcely comprehensive. However, it is easy to see how the undeniable value of these puns and counterattacks for readerly amusement have masked their theoretical enmeshment with *Finnegans Wake*'s serious concerns. They point to the fact that the two characters who correspond to the possibilities of representation or troping – linguistic and iconic – are cast by Joyce as Lewis and himself in the guise of HCE's twin sons. As representation in *Finnegans Wake* is subsumed by the larger figure of the Letter, issues of literality and reference blend with psychically charged issues of sonship and replacement, and particularly with the various forms of replacement offered by different aesthetics. Accordingly the Letter's attributes as both language and carrier of language appear in the guise of the sons, no doubt with a nod towards Vico's observation that language and letters developed contemporaneously, that they were "born twins" (*NS*, par. 33). "Shem the Penman" (*FW*, 125.23) and "Shaun the Post" (*FW*, 206.11) stand not only for Joyce and Lewis but respectively for language itself, the "penman" who produces the word, and the "postman," who carries the written message – the "post" of "postman" implying Shaun's function as deliverer of what has already been written. This twinning of author and post is superimposed over a series of oppositions familiar from *Ulysses* and post-structuralism's roots in Joyce: early versus late, spirit versus embodiment, speech versus script. For instance, when Shaun as the Ondt accuses Shem as the Gracehoper of "writing off his phoney" (*FW*, 418.3, echoed 464.22) his accusation is not only that Shem creates a "phony" or inauthentic script, but that he does so by transforming a prior speech or sound (Gr., *phoné*) into a debased "writing." In all cases, the paired roles of the sons suggest an analogous linguistic and more generally "semiological" (*FW*, 465.12) question ("sem" here also equals "Shem") about the value of metaphor. In the absence of a certain center, which trope can most adequately represent its implicitly self-canceling and paternal subject?

What needs to be stressed in identifying Lewis as a model for the oppositional son in *Finnegans Wake* is the degree to which Shaun is not simply a parody of Lewis as an historic individual, but rather an abstracted or allegorical model of the Lewisian representational tradition *per se*. For although Shaun and Shem, as author and deliverer of the Letter, are on one hand figures for language, their representational status further subdivides into the oppositions that underlie the larger opposition of speech and script. They stand respectively for the visual and the audible, the eye, like that of Lewis's Bestre (who appears in *Finnegans Wake* as the "bester of redpublicans" [*FW*, 53.28]) arrayed against the ear. When Shaun as Professor Jones announces

"Every admirer has seen my goulache of Marge... which I titled *The Very Picture of a Needlesswoman*" (*FW*, 165.13–16) and refers to "The hatboxes which composed Rhomba, lady Trabezond" (*FW*, 165.21–22), Joyce goes beyond simply needling Lewis's 1913 Vorticist canvas "Portrait of an Englishwoman."[32] He more generally identifies Shaun with visuality as a metaphysical or tropological choice. This identification is emphasized even in the introduction of Shaun's name and "title," which appears first as a pun on his status as painter (or "Pinter" [*FW*, 92.7]). As a Lewisian "tarr" with a "telltale tall of his pitcher on a wall with his photure in the papers" (*FW*, 232.36, 233.1–2), Shaun stands for visual representation and aesthetic misrepresentation ("telling tall tales" about painting while reveling in visual publicity of his person). The first mention of "Shaun the Post," accordingly, puns on his identity as Lewisian artist, one whose job is to "Show'm the Posed" (*FW*, 92.13).

As representative of visuality Shaun stands for a questionable tradition that recapitulates and satirizes Lewis's art criticism. Joyce's prolonged description of his apparel at the beginning of III.i suggests that he is, like Carlyle's Teufelsdröckh, a philosopher of surfaces, a thinker with faith in the transcendental. But Shaun himself appears only as a "picture primitive" (*FW*, 405.2), one of a series of associations with primitivism throughout *Finnegans Wake*. One of the first references to Shaun as Kevin describes him, in contradiction to Shem's intensely private writing, "chalking oghres on walls" (*FW*, 27.5–6). He produces public art that is also childish vandalism, creating monsters ("ogres") while also preserving a primitive system of symbols (the archaic Irish Ogham alphabet). Shaun's sidenote in II.ii "URGES AND WIDERURGES IN A PRIMITIVE SEPT" (*FW*, 267.R1), in block letters that recall the typography of *Blast*, evokes Lewis's satiric painting "The Cept" (1921) and alludes both to his claims in *Blast* that Vorticists are "Primitive Mercenaries in the Modern World" (*B*1, 30), and to his comment that "The Art-instinct is permanently primitive." (*B*1, 33)[33] Visuality, the word "primitive" suggests, belongs to the past, for, as other allusions suggest, visual artifacts are signs of connection with what no longer exists. Paintings, *pace* Rembrandt, are "rerembrandtsers... to date link these heirs to here" (*FW*, 54.2–3). Moreover, the iconic tradition attracts questers towards an ideal materiality that eludes even the finest artists – "[T]he space question," Shaun as Professor Jones admits, is a place where "even michelangelines have fooled to dread" (*FW*, 160.36–161.1). In promising a unity, visuality forgets that there are "two sights for ever a picture" (*FW*, 11.36). Therefore, to represent spatially is to fall into the fallacy of confusing phenomenal appearance with scientific fact. As Jaun, Shaun warns the girls of St. Brides against "hogarths like Bottisilly and Titteretto and Vergognese and Coraggio with their extrahand Mazzaccio, plus the usual bilker's dozen of dowdycameramen" (*FW*, 435.7–9). If one wishes for "the ungainly musicianlessness so painted in sculpting" (*FW*, 121.25–26) one may as well turn to the photography of "cameramen" as to the masters of the past. For as Taff (another version of Shaun) notes in II.ii, blending Bosquet's remark on the charge of the Light Brigade with a reference to "graphic man" and the inventor of the photograph: "Say mangraphique, may say nay por daguerre" (*FW*, 339.23) (Fr. *C'est magnifique, mais ce n'est pas la guerre* roughly transformed into "It may be art, but it's not a daguerreotype").

The photograph in *Finnegans Wake*, with its scientific pedigree, is a similarly suspect register. Like the "rerembrandtsers" of painting it creates only a "fadograph of a yestern scene" (*FW*, 7.15), while raising false expectations of the intrinsic reality of the thing seen. When contemplating the survival of the Letter *Finnegans Wake* notes:

Well, almost any photoist worth his chemicots will tip anyone asking him the teaser that if a negative of a horse happens to melt enough while drying, well, what you do get is, well, a positively grotesquely distorted macromass of all sorts of horsehappy values and masses of meltwhile horse. (*FW*, 111.26–30)

At first glance the passage seems to present the photograph as an ideal or permanent register of form, one that offers, as do the Floras in II.i, "Then shalt thou see, seeing, the sight. No more hoaxities!" (*FW*, 239.12–13) The melted negative offers a concrete emblem of the *quidditas* or "whatness" of Stephen's aesthetic in *A Portrait of the Artist as a Young Man*. As a closed system of the ideal and its infinitely reproducible manifestation, the photograph guarantees that values persist in representation as its image adheres in its negative. Yet the passage's recasting of Stephen's sardonic thought in *Ulysses* "Horseness is the whatness of allhorse" (*U*, 9.84–85) as an inquiry into "horsehappy values" suggests that parody has taken over philosophy. The two interposed "well"s in the passage offer hesitation rather than certitude about an image reduced in transformation to the "grotesquely distorted." In other words, if the "masses of meltwhile horse" maintain a "horseness" it is unclear that the horse itself could be reconstituted as image. What begins as "horseness" can end up, as it is variously distorted throughout *Finnegans Wake*, as the Trojan mockery of a "*horsegift*" (*FW*, 418.20), the visual clarity of the "innwhite horse" (*FW*, 510.30) giving way to the obscurity of the "darkest horse" (*FW*, 487.32) as an equine analog to Stephen's concern in *Ulysses* for the "darkness shining in brightness which brightness could not comprehend" (*U*, 2.160). What promises quiddity may, in short, leave one graphically "horseless" (*FW*, 446.24). For if there is no visual first mover or "first horsepower" (*FW*, 459.33) when the "horseshow magnete draws his field" (*FW*, 246.23) (as a horseshoe magnet "draws" a visible magnetic field in iron filings) then we are "a whit the whorse" (*FW*, 84.27) for trying to postulate one. We try to find whatness in the prostitution of the image, where "horse" and "whore" blend, and therefore become "theosophagusted over the whorse proceedings" (*FW*, 610.1–2).[34] As Shaun represents both Lewis and the ambiguous reality of the seen, then, Shem stands in the guise of Joyce – from Shaun's point of view – against the visible in favor of the audible. As Shaun notes disapprovingly, he is both "camera shy" (*FW*, 171.33–34) and "all ears" (*FW*, 169.15). To this degree he shares an identity with HCE. If HCE is a mere "spoof of visibility" (*FW*, 48.1) he can still "talk earish with his eyes shut" (*FW*, 130.19), "Irish" become a purely audible phenomenon. Shaun objects loudly to Shem's championship of the audible, shouting "Down among the dustbins let him lie! Ear! Ear!" (*FW*, 409.2–3), transforming a general cry of group agreement ("hear! hear!) into the agent of hearing itself. For Shem is not, in Shaun's opinion, a positive force. He is "Not ay! Eye! Eye!" (*FW*, 409.3), not only non-visual and negative, but also simply not Shaun (the speaking "I") – and therefore subjectively suspect.

Yet the ear, like the eye, is also an objectively problematic source of value. On one hand *Finnegans Wake* notes "for while the ear, be we mikealls or nicholists, may sometimes be inclined to believe others the eye, whether browned or nolensed, find it devilish hard now and again even to believe itself" (*FW*, 113.26–29). After all, whether angelic or devilish ("michael" as the punningly visual "michelangeline" juxtaposed against old "nick" the "nihilist") the ear is more trustworthy than the eye, which is itself "devilish," Bruno of Nolan darkened ("browned") and blindly dysfunctional ("nolensed"). Yet on the other hand the ear can itself be weak. As a scrambled passage from the Psalms suggests, adherence to the ear may lead to a one-sided rejection of the other senses, much as Shaun refuses to acknowledge the audible – "*Habes aures et num videbis?* (*FW*, 113.29–30) (Lat. "Have you ears and will not see?").[35] For "inclined to believe others," the ear can be fooled. As Earwicker HCE is also "Ear! Ear! Weakear!" (*FW*, 568.26), sometimes under attack by "soundwaves" that "trompe him with their trompes" (*FW*, 23.26–27), audibility becoming a force of deception (Fr. *tromper*, to deceive). Even as the audible suggests the primal Vichian force of the father's thundering voice (and we are reminded that the modern science of "telephony" is simply a contemporary "stealing his thunder" [*FW*, 52.18,31]) its reverberation throughout *Finnegans Wake* as radio transmission reminds one more of the obscure source of broadcasts than of an originating presence. As *Finnegans Wake* wonders, the search for the empty father converges with the struggle towards apprehension of the audible, "why is limbo where is he and what are the sound waves saying ... [?]" (*FW*, 256.23–24).[36]

In formal terms, then, *Finnegans Wake* stages a search for an adequate language that mirrors the struggle between Lewisian visuality and Joycean audibility, played out in the work itself. The struggle is evident by the opposed ways in which *Finnegans Wake* describes its own style. On one hand the tissue of multilingual puns from which the work is built is a "sound seemetery" (*FW*, 17.35–36) where audible meanings are buried in a "cemetary" of punning associations and visual misdirections. On the other the puns create a set of visual obstacles that disclose meaning through verbalization, where one can "singsigns to soundsense" (*FW*, 138.7). In this oscillation lies the possibility of a dialectic in which meaning depends equally upon eye and ear. "What can't be coded can be decorded if an ear aye sieze what no eye ere grieved for" (*FW*, 482.34–36) *Finnegans Wake* states, and the motto cunningly conceals its own ambivalences. "To code" is to conceal meaning, "to decord" to untangle threads or cut knots, as much a solving of problems as its cognate "decode." If the "ear aye seize" what "no eye ere grieved for" the ear or the audible may discern or untangle what the eye alone did not even suspect. But at the same time, the sensory opposite lies embedded in its alternative. "The ear aye sieze" includes both "ear" and "eye" in its status as validation ("aye"), while "eye ere grieved" includes both "eye" and "ear" in its status as temporal permanence ("ere"). The eye and ear, in other words, blend as puns within the very language that replicates their conjunctions and oppositions.

The phenomenal status of Shem and Shaun as sensory tropes, therefore, offers *Finnegans Wake* the only potentially balanced metaphysic that can underlie the "cases" of the world. For when Joyce notes towards the beginning "They will be tuggling foriver," referring implicitly to the brothers, he also declares "'Tis optophone which ontophanes" (*FW*, 13.15–16). Only the combination of the visual and the audible (Gr. *optos* and *phonos*) can allow what is real to shine forth or appear (Gr. *ontos*, "really, truly" and *-phanes*, from *phainesthai*, "to appear"). At this level of investigation *Finnegans Wake* stages a dramatic enactment of the philosophical dilemmas of "Proteus" in *Ulysses*, taking Lewis as one of its dialectical poles. Stephen's Aristotelian distinctions between *diaphane* and *adiaphane*, his balancing of the *Nacheinander* and *Nebeneinander*, are recast as the potentially epiphanic fusion of the relative ineluctabilities of the visible and audible (*U*, 3.1, 3.7–8, 3.13–15).

For this reason, and surprisingly, *Finnegans Wake*'s internal formal emblem for an authentically dialectical mimetic is the modern technology of the film. Unlike the static picture or the bodiless Vichian voice of the wireless transmitter, the aesthetic and technological feat of the "soundpicture" (*FW*, 570.14) pulls together sight and hearing into a fusion that can, like *Finnegans Wake*'s oneiric structure, both "roll away the reel world" (*FW*, 64.25) (both the "real world" and the "reel" of the film) and constitute it symbolically as "Longshots, upcloses" and "Shadows by the film folk" (*FW*, 221.21–22). Presented paratactically with religion as an access to transcendent reality, film is the grail for "searchers for tabernacles and the celluloid art!" (*FW*, 534.25). When the waking world seems to interpose itself towards the end of *Finnegans Wake* and the Porter's bedroom appears as so much "Footage" (*FW*, 559.31), it reminds us not only that HCE is the "projector" (*FW*, 576.18) of the filmic dream that is the whole of *Finnegans Wake* but also that the dialectical fusion of eye and ear constitutes a general ontology that extends beyond the dream's exceptional suspension of phenomenal laws into an authentic mimesis of waking experience. If Shaun as Lewis cannot alone trope the father adequately, his blending with Shem in the dream's filmic language suggests a formal reconstitution of the subject – the father who is absent, as John Bishop has argued, because he is asleep.[37]

While the film as medium offers *Finnegans Wake* a formal analog for the proposed dialectics of its language this "complex matter of pure form" (*FW*, 581.29–30) is not necessarily reflected by *Finnegans Wake*'s narrative content. The fables of "The Mookse and the Gripes" and "The Ondt and the Gracehoper" offer alternative versions of this sensory and brotherly dialectic precisely where references to Lewis become most dense. The identifications here are overtly biographical. Shaun as the Mookse is filled with a Lewisian appetite for phenomena, having dined on "gammon and spittish" (*FW*, 152.22). He objects to the non-visual aspects even of the stream, which is verbal and scarcely graphically deep – it "talked showshallow" (*FW*, 153.6). He is concerned with the "dresser's desdaign on the flyleaf of his frons" (*FW*, 153.15) (combining the title of Lewis's book *The Caliph's Design* with the "disdain" of the Carlylean dresser) and thunders "Blast yourself" (*FW*, 154.10) at the Gripes, who as Joyce (the "grapes" that the "fox" of the fable tries to devour but cannot) has tried to make a "silken nouse out of a hoarse oar" (*FW*, 154.10). This "hoarse oar" is not simply the "sow's ear" of the old saying. For a "silken nouse" is not only a silk purse but a soft method of hanging oneself ("nouse" as "noose") as well as a seductive theory of the mind (Gr. *noos*). One can easily seduce or hang oneself, the Mookse implies, on the philosophic propulsion (the "oar" of the "ear") provided by a theory of audibility that is imperfect ("hoarse") and related to a belief in *quidditas* (the "horse" present in *Finnegans Wake* as ontological exemplum). The Mookse has therefore "vacticanated his ears" (*FW*, 152.23) for protection, retreating behind a papal web of self-justifying visual "ipsofacts" (*FW*, 156.9).[38] The Mookse, however, is as flawed as the Gripes, and just as single-minded. He has "sound eyes right but he could not all hear" just as the Gripes has "light ears left yet he could but ill see" (*FW*, 158.12–13). Yet even as the synesthesia of "light ears" and "sound eyes" suggests the achieved blending of the senses elsewhere figured as filmic, the narrative denies the Mookse and the Gripes the right to resolve themselves in fact rather than language. They are carried away into invisibility before the narrative conclusion, with the only resolution or unity provided by the cloud Nuvoletta, who cries a "singult tear" (*FW*, 159.13), an emblem of oneness offered under the sign of theological despair ("singult" includes both "single" and "sin guilt;" the latter is *Finnegans Wake*'s theological response to the fall of unities of "wholes").

"The Ondt and the Gracehoper" reflects opposition still more quizzically. The relationship of Shaun and Shem has changed from that of hungry eater and inaccessible food to hoarder and wastrel, ant and grasshopper. This struggle is played out against an explicitly metaphysical background, which contains references to "spinooze" (*FW*, 414.16), "akkant" (*FW*, 414.22), "schoppinhour" (*FW*, 414.33) "aristotaller" (*FW*, 417.16) and the volumes of "hegelstomes" (*FW*, 416.33), all of which reflect the Ondt's "phullupsuppy" (*FW*, 417.15) the phallic assurances of philosophy blended with the Lewisian appetite ("full up with supper"). The Ondt, like Lewis (for he is a "windhame" [*FW*, 415.29], both "Wyndham," and a "wind home," a windbag of Aeolian proportions), passes judgements based upon his all-encompassing and negative nature.[39] As a "weltall fellow" (*FW*, 416.3) he is not only physically imposing but is also a self-nominated totality (Ger., *Weltall*, "universe"). His pride in his "eyeforsight" (*FW*, 417.23) contrasts boldly with the Gracehoper, who is "blind as batflea" (*FW*, 417.3) and creates only audible sounds, "jingled" (*FW*, 416.8–9) "of his joyicity" (*FW*, 414.23).[40] To the Ondt the Gracehoper is barbaric, his behavior both "Libelulous!" and "Inzanzarity!" (*FW*, 415.26)[41] and he declares that the Gracehoper must translate his temporality into visuality, for he is a "zeit for the goths" (Ger. *Zeit*, "time" becoming Eng. "sight") (*FW*, 415.26–27). Yet as a "true and perfect host" (*FW*, 417.24) (both welcomer and military hoard) the Ondt is not entirely separate from his opposite. In a final song of uncertain narrative origin, the Gracehoper as Joyce forgives the Ondt their differences, noting that they are, like Dante's spendthrifts and hoarders in the *Inferno*, "*Wastenot with Want, precondamned, two and true*" (*FW*, 418.30). They are in a sense eternally unified despite the unwillingness of both participants. (When the Gracehoper adds "*Till Nolans go volants and Bruneyes come blue*" [*FW*, 418.31] it is with the sense, through Bruno of Nolan, that the seeing eye remains immutably as it is, "Brown eyes" never becoming "blue".) If the Ondt deals in "spacest sublime" but has no "song sense" with which to "beat time" (either to conquer time or to create music) (*FW*, 419.6–8), the Gracehoper suggests there is still the possibility of an "artsaccord" (*FW*, 415.18) between them. Although they are "mouschical umsummables" (*FW*, 417.9) (unable to be added together audibly or "musically," which is also implied by the instrumental pun of "artsaccord" ["harpsichord"]) they are at the same time "not a world of differents" (*FW*, 417.10).

The two tales suggest a double fable of equivocal tropological resolution, a dialectic rendered notably problematic as it is enacted under the rubric of "hegelstomes." The tales are in Shaun's words a "fable one, feeble too" (*FW*, 414.17–18). For if the conclusion or "moral" of "The Mookse and the Gripes" suggests a reinforcement of difference, the persistence of a "harpsdischord" (*FW*, 13.18) between Lewis's and Joyce's competing theories of representation and art, the conclusion of "The Ondt and the Gracehoper" conversely suggests a kind of resolution of dualities through a Dantean yoking of opposites. The latter's "artsaccord" opposes the "singult tear" of "The Mookse and the Gripes." It replaces a sign of remorse and absence (insofar as sin and guilt are the theological aftermath of expulsion) with reconciliation, dualities conjoined into equivocal wholes, Lewis's negative "ondtology" joining the Joycean ontology for which it is a pun.

The fables thus recognize Lewis as both narrative other and ambiguous reflection. As parallel narratives of equal authority they envision Lewis alternately as an utterly oppositional figure incapable of integration within the Joycean project and as an essential, if inverted, component of his Wakean brother, the Don Quixote in need of his confessional "Sin Showpanza" (*FW*, 234.6) (both Cervantes's Sancho Panza and one who reveals every sin, Gr. *pan*, "all"). In his role as visuality, certainly, Lewis can be contained within Joyce's project, for *Finnegans Wake* seeks a linguistic style that would be both visible and audible. Yet Lewis's relevance in these tales exceeds the sensory, and the authority of his presence cuts in a number of contradictory ways. In a sense the fables are not Joyce's at all. Both narratives appear not in Shem's voice, which would suggest the author's unambiguous imprimatur, but in the invasive voice of Shaun. The fables are already filtered through a mock Lewisian, rather than an explicitly Joycean, consciousness. Moreover, in its lack of ambiguity the fable is more formally ambiguous than the other narrative modes in *Finnegans Wake*. As a genre the fable offers neither the strong vision of doubleness explicit in other narrative forms in *Finnegans Wake* (the dualities of questions and answers of the radio talk show of I.vi or the sequence of unanswered riddles throughout) nor the unambiguously conciliatory perspective offered by *Finnegans Wake*'s filmic moments (most notably the "television show" in which Shem and Shaun as Butt and Taff become "*now one and the same person*" [*FW*, 354.8]). Fables are associated with moralism, didacticism, and closure. As the only fables in a work encyclopedically concerned with varieties of narrative, their status as narrative and as representations of Shaun's voice raises issues that are both formal and narratological. In recognizing Lewis as both opposite and associate why does Joyce use the fable, in Lewis's voice, as a vehicle of parodic insight?

To answer this question effectively one must move beyond *Finnegans Wake*'s portrayal of Lewis as representative of space and vision, and re-engage with Vico's *New Science*. Fables are bound up with *Finnegans Wake*'s issues of language and history. Shaun introduces the second fable as one of his "grimm gests" (*FW*, 414.17), which suggests not only that it is cognate with one of Lewis's "jests too deep for laughter," but also that it is one of the "grimm grimm tale[s]" (*FW*, 335.5) of folkloric history, particularly as the Brothers Grimm appear elsewhere in *Finnegans Wake* as historical theoreticians of the letter. ("Grimm's Law," which formulated the phonetic shifts that occur in the development of Western languages, becomes "Gramm's laws" [*FW*, 378.28], from Gr. *gramma*, "letter.") If it is "grimm," and therefore of serious import, the fable is also a "gest." This points strongly to Vico, who believed that the "gest" or mimetic movement, was the origin of symbolic language itself.[42] Derived from the "gest" in *The New Science*, the fable plays a specific developmental and narrative role. Like the myth, from which Vico does not fully distinguish it, fable is a figure for an "ideal truth" (*NS*, par. 205). Vico fancifully derives its etymology from "logic," which he further glosses as "from *logos*, whose first and proper meaning was *fabula*, fable, carried over into Italian as *favella*, speech" (*NS*, par. 401). As part of the etymological family that binds speech to the *logos*, then, fable is privileged as rationality and the origin of truth itself. As form, moreover, it bridges the gap between the poetic speech of a people, which becomes embodied in myth, and the individual narrative, which emerges in the classical world as the moral tale or exemplum.

Yet this individual narrative, the "single fable of the sort invented by Aesop" (*NS*, par. 424), developed in response to particular historical pressures. Vico quotes from one of the prologues to Phaedrus' *Fables*:

> *Nunc fabularum cur sit inventum genus,*
> *Brevi docebo. Servitus obnoxia,*
> *Quia, quae volebat, non audebat dicere,*
> *Affectus proprios in fabellas transtulit*
> *Aesopi illius semita feci viam ...*
>
> (Attend me briefly while I now disclose
> How art of fable telling first arose.
> Unhappy slaves, in servitude confined,
> Dared not to their harsh masters show their mind,
> But under the veiling of the fable's dress
> Contrived their thoughts and feelings to express,
> Escaping still their lords' affronted wrath.
> So Aesop did; I widen out his path)       (*NS*, par. 425)

The fable, in other words, is political allegory. It marks the surreptitious entrance of an oppositional voice into the master's manse, representing at one remove issues of social power. For instance, Vico reads Aesop's fable of the lions' partnership as a parable of the unequal distribution of political power between the plebeians and the heroes during the Grecian wars (*NS*, par. 425, 559). Under the surface narrative of interactions of beasts, lie disguised truths that challenge authority. In the sheep's clothing of the enslaved narrative the fable smuggles ideological messages into the social and linguistic worlds that would otherwise reject it.

This Vichian parallel suggests that the Shaunian or Lewisian fables, as integral parts of a structure based upon *The New Science*, are in and of themselves political. Their very appearance within *Finnegans Wake* confirms their status as carriers of allegorical truth. They smuggle the victim's gesture against ideological or narrative closure into an oppositional context.[43] That context, as we have seen, is largely aesthetic. The fables can be read as Joyce's parody of Lewis's complaining voice, which asserts mastery over its brother while playing the comic role of the oppressed even as it oppresses. Yet as motifs elsewhere in *Finnegans Wake* confirm, the context is also explicitly political. Throughout *Finnegans Wake* there is continuity between Shaun's representational and political identity. His eye has been not merely the dispassionate Lewisian observer of the subject, but its aggressive Lewisian attacker. One recalls Lewis's painter Vokt, for instance, who in *Tarr* "flung a man or woman on to nine feet of canvas and pummelled them on it for a couple of hours, until they promised to remain there or were incapable of moving, so to speak" (*T*, 82) and is unsurprised to find this trait translated into Shaun. When HCE is threatened by a "heckler with the Peter the Painter [who] wanted to hole him" (*FW*, 85.5–6), the phrase suggests aesthetic danger, describing a Lewisian painter as one who turns his subject through aggressive attack into the nihilism of the "hole." Yet it also evokes contemporary political history through layered associations with visuality. Peter the Painter was an English anarchist whose involvement in an incident known as the "Siege of Sidney Street" alerted the London of 1910 – and the young Mussolini – to the lures and dangers of the overthrow of social order.[44] His name in this context becomes synonymous with a gun used to shoot a literal "hole" through his subject. The eye is figured as a potentially destructive instrument of social upheaval, which for Shaun becomes a violent visuality that can be harnessed for reactionary ends as well. When Shaun condemns Shem, he combines the camera with the gun, describing how "for the very fourth snap the Tulloch-Turnbull girl with her coldblood kodak shotted the as yet unremuneranded national apostate" (*FW*, 171.31–34). The camera's gaze suggests that for Shaun the eye has become an aggressive instrument of centralized power. It not only can decenter the social order, but with a "coldblood kodak" can rid the social order of its opponents.

Shaun's criticisms of Shem are therefore as nationalistic as they are representational. If he is upset with Shem's status as hearing and audibility, Shaun is yet more upset with Shem's independent and anti-nationalist politics. He insists that Shem take on his responsibilities to the *polis*, explaining that "all nationists must, and do a certain office" (*FW*, 190.13), alluding, as Dominic Manganiello has noted, to Thomas Kettle's home-rule Irish paper *The Nationist*.[45] In the guise of Justius he becomes explicitly fascist, condemning Shem (who bears the name of Noah's son) as a "semisemitic serendipitist" (*FW*, 191.2–3) and shouting "heal helper!" ("Heil Hitler!") (*FW*, 191.7), becoming a "teetootomtotalitarian" (*FW*, 260.2) (the "teetotum" a child's top named from the Latin "*totum*," "all," short for a game in which the winner "takes all").[46] Indeed the similarity of Lewis's actual given name "Percy" to that of Patrick Pearse, one of leaders of the Easter Rising of 1916, suggest a confluence between the strategies of the fascistic European expansionism of the 1930s and the Irish struggles of the previous decades. Lewis as "Shaun the Post" is not merely a twentieth-century version of "Sean the Post" from Dion Boucicault's *Arrah-na-Pogue*, but is also the nationalist child of the abortive rebellion at the Dublin General Post Office. His "pearse orations" (*FW*, 620.24), like those of Patrick Pearse, underline the confluence between the authoritarianism of militaristic expansionism and the equal but opposite stridency of an egoistic nationalism.

Shaun presents his eye as not merely visual but as the "I" of the controlling subject, whose gaze attempts to define and establish mastery over the other. As "Toffeethief" the "lipoleum" he spies on the Willingdone, using his eye as a surreptitious political weapon (*FW*, 10.1), while in II.iii he links vision and history by noting the role the eye plays in preserving political power. When he evinces interest in "DYNASTIC CONTINUITY" (*FW*, 275.R1) and "THE INFLUENCE OF COLLECTIVE TRADITION UPON THE INDIVIDUAL" (*FW*, 268.R1), in the block typography of *Blast*, he declares his allegiance to the "PANOPTICAL PURVIEW OF POLITICAL PROGRESS" (*FW*, 272.R1). Like Jeremy Bentham with his Panopticon, a structure in which a single central observer can inspect a large number of imprisoned subjects arrayed around him, Shaun makes his own vision of the "I" not only figuratively, but literally, central. The existent social order is therefore insufficient to his zeal for power. Although he notes he "Want[s] to join the police" (*FW*, 300.1) and Shem quickly registers the inordinate success of his will to power, exclaiming "ENTER THE COP AND HOW" (*FW*, 306.R1), Shaun demands to participate in a more absolute system of regulation. His "autocratic writings" (*FW*, 303.19) are the external signs of a desire for complete rule by the "I," the establishment of an "eggoarchicism" (*FW*, 525.10) or complete rule by the ego, a phrase that suggests not only the Lewisian food motif ("egg"), but also the "archaic fixity of the ego" of Lewis's *The Childermass* ("ego archaicism").[47] And since his politics are both conservative and totalitarian, "anterevolitionary" (*FW*, 234.11) and concerned with what Lewis called "the art of being ruled" (and which Joyce satirizes as the "art of being rude" [*FW*, 167.3]), Joyce presents that ego as the agent of a power not merely visual and political but also linguistic. As Shaun exclaims, "My unchanging Word is sacred" (*FW*, 167.28).

These parodies of Lewis's painterly and political persona are patent and perhaps seemingly extrinsic to the workings of *Finnegans Wake* itself. Yet the confluence of Wyndham Lewis's given name with that of both Patrick Pearse and the Wakean father (Percy and "Perse O'Reilly") reminds us that the Shaunian ego's attempt to impose its own laws upon the body politic is already implicit in the heritage of the father, whose favorite son, not surprisingly, is Shaun.[48] This heritage is both linguistic and historical. The movement from the prehistorical to the historic in *Finnegans Wake* is the Vichian shift from linguistic and political chaos towards a culture organized by the father's word and law. Prehistory is both prelinguistic, "toofarback for messuages," and prior to the enumeration of social codes by cultural arbiters, "before joshuan judges had given us numbers" (*FW*, 4.19–20). HCE's appearance in the world, therefore, represents the entrance of founder, enforcer, and judge. He is the "establisher of the world by law" (*FW*,

55.8–9), the "Holy policeman" himself (*FW*, 562.17–18). Ironically, in a move made familiar by French psychoanalysis, the father's entry into the world initiates both the social order and the consequently necessary repressions by which his own crimes are judged. As *Finnegans Wake* jeers towards its opening, "Hahahaha, Mister Funn, you're going to be fined again" (*FW*, 5.11–12), deviations from a central norm are punished by societal penalty (the "fine"), and that crime is defined as pleasure beyond the bounds of the Father's Law, the "fun" made possible, but also repressed, by the Word. The entry of the father's Word as Law both enables communication and limits the range of acceptable reference. As the divided foundation of language the paternal utterance is also the "polisignstunter" (*FW*, 370.30), the regulatory force that delimits the proliferation of the signifier (the "police" of the "*polis*" who stunts linguistic multiplicity, from Gr. *poly-*, many, and Eng. "signs"). As the self-destroying delimitor of the signifier, HCE is also the seemingly freedom-loving but repressive voice of Irish nationalism. His cognomen "Herenow chuck english" (*FW*, 579.20–21) connects him also to Pearse, whose wish to eliminate English from Ireland joins him with Lewis as a figure who would adjudge what constitutes appropriate language for aesthetic and political ends.

As the oppressive usurper who wishes to replace tropologically the "unchanging Word" of the father, then, it is ironic that Shaun is a teller of fables. He claims for himself the fable's political power, presenting "The Ondt and the Gracehoper" as part of a stump speech to the people of Ireland, and he uses fables to present favorable images of his own ability to hold opposition at arm's length, or to resolve oppositions within his own "welltall" selfhood. That his "unchanging Word" is inauthentic, however, is suggested both by genre and presentation. A political victimizer, Shaun presents himself as victim, co-opting the Vichian rhetoric of the slave. (Again, one thinks of Lewis: Tarr tells Anastasya, "It is the artist's fate almost always to be exiled among the slaves" [*T*, 241].) Yet in the context of Shaun's oppression the actual enslaved is Shem, and the "Lewis" who speaks fables in *Finnegans Wake* is actually speaking in the language he claims to reject, which is Joyce's. This is both an existential (insofar as Shaun is created through Joyce's language) and thematic dilemma. When Shaun describes himself as "obsoletely unadulterous" (*FW*, 161.17) he is not only boasting of his "wedding" to his limited conception of the Word, but is recapitulating the Joycean figure, familiar from *Ulysses*, of adultery and faithfulness as figures of representation. "The word is my Wife," Shaun exclaims (*FW*, 167.29), and accuses Shem of behavior translated from sexuality into language. In a world where one can be "married to reading and writing" (*FW*, 146.22) he claims that Shem is "covetous of his neighbour's word" (*FW*, 172.30). Yet by insisting upon "Putting Allspace in a Notshall" (*FW*, 455.29), or reducing the universe to repressive rules ("shall not"), Shaun falls into the very Hamlet-like solipsism of which he has accused his brother. If Shem in his inkbottle house is, according to Shaun, a "self exiled in upon his ego" (*FW*, 184.6–7), then Shaun, who describes himself as "my own most spacious immensity as my ownhouse and microbemost cosm" (*FW*, 150.36–151.1), mistakes his powers of prohibition for a similarly inward or internal control of the nutshell of "infinite space." When Joyce ultimately reveals that Shaun has actually stolen his language from Shem in the role of Thoth, "Words taken in triumph ... from the sufferant pen of our jocosus inkerman militant of the reed behind the ear" (*FW*, 433.7–9), he not only satirizes Lewis's unwilling fall into a Joycean modernism but brings forth from Lewis's rhetoric the divisions that have always been implicit within it. By creating the criteria against which they themselves trespass, HCE and Shaun provoke the other to call them to account (in HCE's case the authors of the satirical broadside "The Ballad of Persse O'Reilly," in Lewis's case Joyce).

To this degree Joyce indicts Lewis within his text of the *de facto* textual sin of *The Apes of God*. Lewis's repressions of the language of the other, like Shaun's, disguise his reflection of that rhetoric from without. As Joyce's fictive creation Shaun-as-Lewis is necessarily "Persse transluding from the Otherman" (*FW*, 419.24–25), Lewis as "Percy" discovered within the

Joycean text as parasite, translating in a deluded manner ("transluding") from the voice of the other into the voice of an overweening self. As the bearer of a centralized authority and aesthetics, then, Lewis enters *Finnegans Wake* as a version of his own self-contradicting protagonists. Joyce submits Lewis within *Finnegans Wake* to the narrative fate of self-mutilation and contradiction that has typified Lewis's own fictive protagonists. Shaun emerges as the prototypical Lewisian hero, the self who marks his distance from the other yet is caught up by its own, in this case Vichian and Joycean, rhetoric.

While revealing Shaun as self-defeating, however, *Finnegans Wake* does not reject him utterly. Although the fables of "The Mookse and the Gripes" and "The Ondt and the Gracehoper" are parodically constructed through Lewis's voice they retain a doubleness of their own, an authority guaranteed by the Gracehoper's and the Ondt's presence within them, the adherence of the authentically Joycean within the Shaunian or Lewisian voice. The fables retain the integrity of the relationship between the brothers: it is impossible to read Shem's unmasking of Shaun as a pure vanquishing or defeat, any more than *Finnegans Wake* provides an easy choice between the oppositions of the "whole" and the "hole." Not only Shaun but also Shem is an expert forger, not only "one who makes" in the sense that Stephen Dedalus wishes to "forge" the consciousness of his race, but also one who illegally copies, who takes on an illicit identity. To this degree the relation between brothers, opposed yet compensatory, can be justified through *Finnegans Wake*'s often cited pattern of the valorization of oppositions, explained through *Finnegans Wake*'s quotations of Bruno's dictum about the coincidence and re-establishment of contraries.[49] In this reading Shem and Shaun are "equals of opposites ... and polarised for reunion by the symphysis of their antipathies" (*FW*, 92.8–11), models of a universal metaphysics that understands binarisms as the alternation of a unity with an opposition to which it is intrinsically linked. The forger Shaun stands dialectically with the forger Shem, and the ownership of language – the question of ultimate authority as writerly originality and the power to speak – becomes metaphysically moot. The Shakespearean "lending" of language in *Ulysses* reappears in new guise as the need to "repurchas[e] his pawned word" (*FW*, 596.30–31), to reclaim an originality lost or bartered away.

Yet as Stephen's grappling with dialectic in *Ulysses* has shown, the Joycean relationship of thesis and antithesis is not necessarily recuperable within a conventional model of the reconciliation of contraries. This observation is rendered yet more striking by Lewis's embodiment in *Finnegans Wake* of the intertwining of politics within representation, an identification that expands well beyond the local context of Pearse's nationalism. As Shaun, Lewis becomes a ready-made oppositional myth for the confluence of social and aesthetic meaning. His presence in the book emphasizes the degree to which the the resolution of opposites is crucial not only to metaphysics but also to issues of social organization. This is evident both in the fables and without. The Mookse, who "harped on his crown" (*FW*, 152.25) and gathers behind him his "satraps" (*FW*, 154.13), is a figure for rule and social control achieved through writing. As the only English Pope, Adrian IV, he presents the Gripes (who is also Ireland and "raskolly" [*FW*, 156.10] or schismatic, from the Russian *raskol*) with the papal bull *laudibiliter* (*FW*, 154.22) that would cede Ireland over to the control of the Roman church.[50] Mookse versus Gripes becomes a political struggle over language, therefore, not only sight versus audibility (contained within "*laudibiliter*") but also a battle between parties, the Gripes become Whig (he cheeps in a "whiggy" voice [*FW*, 153.36]), the Mookse become Tory (he sits in his fullest "justotoryum" [*FW*, 153.26]). Shaun emphasizes this confluence of politics and representation in his introduction. When he addresses "The Mookse and the Gripes" to the "Gentes and laitymen, fullstoppers and semicolonials" (*FW*, 152.16) he blends the physical marks of writing (full stops, semicolons) not only with issues of empire (semicolons become "semicolonials") but with a recognition of his audience as the core of social organization itself, Vico's "gentes."[51]

The political ramifications of writing appear throughout *Finnegans Wake*. The "*Word made Warre*" (*FW*, 175.12–13)

Joyce reminds us, and notes that "scribicide," the killing of or through writing, is merely an offshoot "of military and civil engagements" (*FW*, 14.21–25). Kevin's "chalking oghres on walls" (*FW*, 27.5–6) is an act of Pearsean revolution construed as inscription, the resurgence of a public and nationally charged writing (the Ogham alphabet), while Shaun's accusation that Shem is "writing off his phoney" (*FW*, 418.3, echoed 464.22) aligns Shem with the equally revolutionary politics of "Yankee Doodle" (who goes "ariding on his pony" in a song from the American Revolution). Puns reveal deeper affiliations between authorship and civil disruption. "When men want to write a letter" changes to "hun men wend to raze a leader" (*FW*, 278.18–21), the linguistic desire that typified *Ulysses* changed paronomastically into the political desire for incipient regicide. Even reading and writing, which are ordinarily paradigmatically private tasks, become subsumed within the invasive political act of "raiding" (*FW*, 482.32). When Butt merges with Taff in the filmic television show within the tavern, their resolution is not a merely formal merging of opposites. Shaun as Taff (and Lewis) dissolves his personality into the search for political authority; he "*in an effort towards autosotorisation, effaces himself in favour of the idiology alwise behounding*" (*FW*, 352.18–20). His resolution with Butt is not merely a metaphysical conjunction but a Hegelian or Marxist moment of economic and class dialectic, master and feudal enemy temporarily suspended in synthesis – "BUTT and TAFF (*desprot slave wager and foeman feodal unsheckled, now one and the same person*[)]" (*FW*, 354.7–8).[52]

The ambiguous linguistic dialectic of *Ulysses* therefore returns in *Finnegans Wake* as a no less problematic political dialectic of oppressor and oppressed, master and slave. Joyce's undercutting of Shaun's authoritarian voice is a political as well as a representational gesture in both content and style, a demonstration that he, not Shem, is the "doctator" (*FW*, 170.22), the dictator self-disguised as healer. It reveals the self-contradictions within the totalitarian voice, while replacing the assumed monolithic speech of pseudo-fascism with linguistic multiplicity. However, this is not to claim that Joyce's linguistic experimentation marks a genuinely radical political vision, although it is no doubt this aspect of the "revolution of the word" that appealed to the editors of *transition* and to the radical European intellectuals of the 1960s for whom *Finnegans Wake* became a paradigmatic theoretical text. *Finnegans Wake* satirizes forms of revolutionary politics as abundantly as it does totalitarianism.[53] The failed unities of the Mookse and the Gripes are transformed into the struggle of "Marx and their Groups" (*FW*, 365.20), while part of the trumped up case against HCE is that he is "a plain pink joint reformee in private life" (*FW*, 59.27–28) and "an engles to the teeth" (*FW*, 75.19–20), a "Red theatrocrat" with the "pinkprophets cohalething" (*FW*, 29.15–16) (Communist prophets "coalescing" and forming cooperatively a healthy ["hale"] government [from Old English *thing*, "assembly"]). Parlor revolutionaries are simply "remarxing in languidoily" (*FW*, 83.15), while Butt refers in passing to "reptrograd leanins" (*FW*, 351.27–28), presumably those with "leanings" toward the new Russian republic, whose following of Lenin leads them to excessive dependence ("leaning in") and retrogressive ideas ("retro" found within an anagram of Petrograd). References throughout to the "Nazi Priers" (*FW*, 375), the Gestapo ("Gestapose to parry off cheekars" [*FW*, 332.7–8], the Gestapo versus the Russian CheKa, the Russian secret police of 1917), and the "red time of the white terror" (*FW*, 116.7–8) (the "Red Terror" of Communist repression in Hungary in 1919 and the "White Terror" of its anti-Communist backlash) guarantee that *Finnegans Wake*, despite its hermetic writerly surface, disturbingly refracts the political struggles of its century. Communism and fascism, however imbricated with Vico's theories of recurrence, retain the urgency of their contemporaneity even as Joyce withholds engagement, in a Sartrean sense, with either.[54]

Yet this consistent inflection of representation by non-partisan (or multi-partisan) politics suggests a rationale for Lewis's inherence within a text that owes its intellectual structure to Vico, despite Lewis's satire in *The Childermass* of Vico's cyclical vision of history.[55] Lewis, I have argued, worked from the assumption that language is not only a symbolic system but the mechanism by which man ambiguously regulates and decenters social order. This insight, rather than Vico's cyclical vision of history, is also *Finnegans Wake*'s largest debt to *The New Science*. When Shaun accuses Shem of involvement in a "conversazione commoted in the nation's interest" (*FW*, 172.31–32) the Italian of "conversazione" directs us to *The New Science*, whose own discourse ("conversation") is deployed towards the consideration of language's role in the formation and maintenance of states. Where Vico's cyclical "theory none too rectiline of the evolution of human society" (*FW*, 73.31–32) attempts to account for the origins of language, it also attempts to define the larger structural similarities that bind all social structures. It views the state as a "socially organic entity of a millenary military maritory monetary morphological circumformation" (*FW*, 599.15–17) in which language is the master trope of all the interrelated structures by which man deals with fellow man. Marriage (the "maritory"), the military, and economics (the "monetory") all reflect and are contained by the morphology of language's birth and collapse, as manifestations of history already implicit in the "sameold gamebold adomic structure" (*FW*, 615.6), the "atomic," "Adamic," and "etymic" structure, of the Word.[56]

By importing Lewis's voice into his text Joyce performs an act of textual criticism that is also an ambiguous acceptance, through Vico, of the Lewisian archetype. His parodies of Lewis are, as *Finnegans Wake* puts it, both "sibicidal" (*FW*, 40.31) and "paridicynical" (*FW*, 610.14–15). They are both "cynical parodies" of a brother artist and attacks on Lewis's attempt to take on the father's voice as his own. But Shaun's "taylor's fablings" (*FW*, 61.28) are not merely proof that as bearer of Carlylean phenomena Lewis is "sew wrong, welsher" (*FW*, 322.8). They are also implicitly carriers of Vichian and Brunonian truth. Lewis's own work, as early as the Vortex's double vision of reconciliation and lack of reconciliation between sign and object, has stood self-destructively upon the paradox of opposites joining and not joining. This activity of achieved and denied dialectic, becomes in his later work an explicitly ideological denial of the dialectical workings of

Marxism that attempts to preserve in the realm of aesthetics the inviolable oppositions of the viewer and the viewed. His presence in *Finnegans Wake* acts as a reminder of the processes of history that both he, and Joyce, explicitly reject: the Marxian *telos* that depends upon the reproduction rather than the synthesis of oppositions, and which *Finnegans Wake* subsumes within the cyclical history of *The New Science*.[57] Therefore, if Lewis rediscovered what Shaun calls the "political secret" (*FW*, 150.20) of ideology's inherence within the language of the private – the artist's studio, the salon, the home – Joyce accepts and revises that observation by recasting it in Vichian terms. According to *The New Science* families, the very core of domesticity, begin in fear of the thunder father's Word. By dramatizing history as the dream of the family (which is also the nightmare from which Stephen Dedalus claimed he wished to awake), Joyce takes on a quintessentially Lewisian task. With their roles divided and multiply reassigned among the players of a universal family romance, the "nightly redistribution of parts and players by the puppetry producer" (*FW*, 219.7–8), Joyce's characters go *en masque* to the costume party of history as resolutely as the "all-puppet cast" of *The Apes of God*. The language through which they are created emerges not as an endless proliferation of signs, as post-structuralism has sometimes reduced it, but as the medium of psychic and ideological division by which the self, through history, attempts to progress towards both individual and – insofar as the family is the model of community – social identity.

Joyce therefore partially answers and inverts Lewis's objections to modernist solipsism (which was also, significantly, the classical Marxist objection to modernism in general)[58] by finding within the intensified subjectivity of language and dream the patterns of the social structures that Lewis, in *The Apes of God*, depicted as centerless and self-subverting. By exploring the dream state and its language Joyce does not entirely deny the external or "reel world" in favor of an illusory internality, any more than he valorizes the "hole" over the "whole." The internal world stands paradoxically intertwined with the workings of the external, the political structure of the family discovered in the workings of the very psyche that ideological criticism has typically viewed as antithetical or the dangerous counter-example to achieved collectivity. Vico's claim "the world of civil society has certainly been made by men, and ... its principles are therefore to be found within the modifications of our own human mind" (*NS*, par. 331) is thus the guiding political vision of *Finnegans Wake*. Joyce discovers in the mind of the father not only the locus of a Shaunian repressive authority, but also the site where, as in Lewis's Vortex, dialectic and the rejection of dialectic can coexist. Here, where "our social something bowls along bumpily" (*FW*, 107.32–33), is where the public world adheres in the private, and where linguistic profusion – which is Joyce's figure for a universal and multi-national fusion, a "landleague of many nations" (*FW*, 540.2) – can be contained within the mind's simultaneously singular and self-undermining Word.

Satirized as totalitarian artist and political thinker, then, Lewis becomes both an emblem of inhibition and of a paradoxically liberating universality for *Finnegans Wake*. He confirms that everyman is not simply subjectivity but is the public animal without whom there would be no "politico-ecomedy" (*FW*, 540.26–27), no counterbalance for familial and historical struggle. This identification is also a matter of representation. For "representation" is not merely an iconic concern but is also a democratic one, referring also to that human troping by which a member of a community is synecdochically invested with the power of the whole through election. As "representative man," HCE takes his cognomen from an actual political "representative" "Here Comes Everybody," (*FW*, 32.18–19) the nickname of H. C. E. (Hugh Culling Eardley) Childers, a nineteenth-century Parlimentarian.[59] HCE's rumored "parliamentary honours" (*FW*, 59.29) equate his universal body with the "body politic" (*FW*, 165.27), particularly in Dublin, where the city motto, much punned-upon in *Finnegans Wake*, proclaims the health of the city in proportion to the propriety of its individual members: "*Obedientia civium urbis felicitas*," "The Citizen's Obedience is The City's Happiness."[60] The Wakean question "*Are We Fairlys*

Represented?" (*FW*, 176.7–8) juxtaposed with "Do you Approve of our Existing Parliamentary System?" (*FW*, 306.28–30) suggests that for Joyce as well as for Lewis, representation concerns the organization of political rule as well as the proprieties of artistic portrayal. The marginal comment to the later question, "*Alcibiades*" (*FW*, 306. L4), the honorable soldier and statesman from Lewis's favorite Shakespeare play *Timon of Athens*, clinches the association. That Joyce particularly nods towards Lewis for insight into this "politicoecomedy" is further suggested by the line that nearly follows the term, "Thank you, besters!" ("Bestre") (*FW*, 540.28–29). And for this reason, while dubious of Lewis's anti-democratic conclusions and satirically inhabiting and exaggerating his voice, Joyce cedes Lewis a place, as the Gracehoper does the Ondt, as his artistic other and twin.

Suitably, Joyce places this concession in Shaun's voice. When Shaun calls Shem "my shemblable! My freer!" (*FW*, 489.28) the allusion echoes Baudelaire's cry to the *hypocrite lecteur*, but states his accusations of an unwilling and guilty likeness in terms of his indebtedness to Joyce's linguistic experimentation (his "Shem babble") and his own freedom thereof (*frère* become "one who frees"). At the same time Joyce implies that the relationship is reciprocal. Joyce as Shem is also a watcher, one whose "gazework" (*FW*, 224.26) shares in Shaun's values, a co-performer of fables whose warring opposites and *doppelgängers* bear more relationship to the paradigmatic Lewisian relationship of Arghol and Hanp, Tarr and Kreisler, or Zagreus and Starr-Smith, than to Joyce's own Stephen and Bloom. Writerly identities thus fuse. When Issy notes that she is "so keen on that New Free Woman with novel inside" (*FW*, 145.29) the object of her readerly desire may be either *A Portrait of the Artist as a Young Man* or *Tarr*, both of which appeared in serialization in *The Egoist*, originally called *The New Freewoman*. And when Shem goes "in for scribenery with the satiety of arthurs" (*FW*, 229.7), he is simultaneously Joyce, who received a subsidy from the Society of Authors, and the insatiable Lewis, who published *The Apes of God* with his own Arthur Press, a press named, appropriately given *Finnegans Wake*'s caricature of Lewis as insisting upon monovocality, for its the supposed universality in all language. The "freer" who is also the *semblable* must be freed even as he frees, by his implication with the brotherly likeness for whom he is both mirror image and inextricable identity.

Joyce's treatment of Lewis in *Finnegans Wake* is thus considerably more than the blocking of critical blows. Merely to "parrylewis" (*FW*, 352.14), to counter Lewis's thrusts without appropriate counterblasts, would be to fall punningly into "paralysis," to concede the impossibility of action or artistic progression. Joyce admits in *Finnegans Wake* that if the other is a partner in the troping of the absent cause – even if that other is repressive – it is through the reflection of the other that one defines one's own identity: by the mimetic echoing which is both parody and acceptance, the establishment of similarity and aesthetic difference. Joyce demonstrates that Lewis's ideas can be incorporated within a whole that nonetheless refuses to yield to its declared negation, to deny as strenuously as possible that "*Percy Wynns*" (*FW*, 440.9) on the battleground of art. As a "heterotropic" book (a book of many tropes), *Finnegans Wake* subsumes but knowingly does not eliminate its most "artthoudux" (*FW*, 252.20–21) critic, providing at best an equivocally dual answer to the implied question hidden within "orthodox," "art thou the leader?" (Lat. *dux*).

We may read the Letter, which is both language and *Finnegans Wake* itself, as the product of "the continually more and less intermisunderstanding minds of the anticollaborators" (*FW*, 118.24–26). Lewis stands within the text as the most prominent of Joyce's anti-collaborative voices. He is the "besterwhole [Bestre] ... operating the subliminal of his invaded personality" (*FW*, 247.7–9), a quasi-mythic force of inauthentic and authentic artistic and political speech who is both "more and less" than his parodic and "intermisunderstanding" portrayal, an integral part of the partially Lewisian "*Vortex*" (*FW*, 293.L2) that is *Finnegans Wake* itself. He stands as the mode by which, as *Finnegans Wake* states, "*quodlibet sese ipsum per aliudpiam agnoscere contrarium*" (*FW*, 287.26–27) ("everything recognizes itself through something opposite"). As a "quodlibet" is a musical form in which a composer weaves new themes together contrapuntally with pre-existent melodies, so does *Finnegans Wake* take Lewis's ideas as prominent themes for its "ten canons in skelterfugue" (*FW*, 121.28). Like his Bestre, Lewis emerges as an emblem of the aggressive "I," a carrier of dialectical and anti-dialectical energies. He is a figure for his own, but also for Joyce's, vision of an art determined not simply by its exclusion of opposition, but by its recognition of the other as the canonical echo – at times literal, at times inverted – of its aesthetic and political procedures.

# Conclusion

> The prouts who will invent a writing there ultimately is the poeta, still more learned, who discovered the raiding there originally. That's the point of eschatology our book of kills reaches for now in soandso many counterpoint words.
>
> James Joyce, *Finnegans Wake*, 482.31–34

> This is an old dilemma. Combatants infect each other, whereas non-combatants remain relatively immune.
>
> Wyndham Lewis, *Men Without Art*, 131

Conflict in the works of Joyce and Lewis is inseparable from questions about authority in origin and ideology, combat emerging as both cause and effect of the authors' "counterpoint words" and the metaphysical and political attacks of their "books of kills." These questions emerge from Lewis's and Joyce's fictional treatments of the dualities of self and sign, of signs and the referents that ground and exceed them, and ultimately of the relationship of artist with oppositional artist. Joyce's and Lewis's expulsion and acceptance of the other as part of the artistic self is rooted in and paradoxically reflects the oppositions within their works. Lewis appears in *Finnegans Wake* explicitly, as Joyce and *Ulysses* appear implicitly in *The Apes of God*, as both parodic object and authoritative subject.

We have seen that this dual conflation is adumbrated by the metaphysics of Joyce's and Lewis's earlier work, which prepare the terms for the aesthetics of dubious origin in *The Apes of God* and *Finnegans Wake*, what Joyce calls the "raiding there originally" of the authorial voice. In *Enemy of the Stars* Arghol enacts and subverts his own rhetoric. As he lives up to the ideas of the philosopher Stirner he also parodies Stirner, becoming a mocking copy of his announced original self, at the same time as Lewis enacts and subverts a Romanticism that he can neither claim nor elude. Stephen and his Shakespeare inhabit similarly ambivalent roles. As artists who attempt to create themselves, they prefigure Shem's and Shaun's attempts to replace the father with their own created selves, attempts called into question by Shakespeare's equivocal selfhood and Stephen's recantation of his own arguments. Representation emerges as inseparable from distortion, authentic mimesis juxtaposed with mimesis's crippling failure.

These problems of metaphysics find their public analogues at the point where Joyce and Lewis most clearly concur politically. Their works demonstrate a shared disbelief in the efficacy of violence as a mode of political progress. Lewis's fear of the levelling effects of mass violence is matched in Joyce by the containment of mass politics within history's cycles. Revolutionary movements and civil wars appear in *Finnegans Wake* as swings of a pendulum that is destined ever to give way to its counter-balancing political opposite. That Lewis's and Joyce's diagnoses ultimately cut in opposed directions – Lewis towards a pragmatic pessimism, Joyce towards an inclusiveness based on the longest possible view of history – does not invalidate the analogous intent of their critiques. Lewis's embrace of authoritarianism after the First World War and Joyce's subsumption of history within Vico proceed from similarly perceived relations between aesthetics and ideology. Both are attempts to reclaim historical authority for a world where conventional teleologies have become suspect. Mr Deasy's vision of history in *Ulysses*, in which all things move towards one great end, is denied by Lewis in favor of the seizure of historical process by fiat, while Joyce writes with the poetic certainty that straight lines are illusions, that all events are subject to circular processes that sublate but can never eradicate them. *The Apes of God* and *Finnegans Wake* are both responses to the shouts in the street of contemporary history, and their treatment of philosophic dualities is matched by the interdependence of their political gestures. Lewis built his artistic and political edifices on what he perceived as the failures of a West taken over by theories of multiplicity, which he linked in *Time and Western Man* with Joyce as exemplar, through communism and democracy to the ur-source of temporality. Joyce, in turn, subsumes artistic and authoritarian singularity in *Finnegans Wake*, drawing the ideological visions made available to him by Lewis into his own ambivalent philosophical totality.

Further, we have seen that the nature of the individual within Joyce's and Lewis's fictions suffers a sea change. The chamber dramas of *Blast* and *Ulysses* give way to historical stages in *The Apes of God* and *Finnegans Wake*, where psychological inwardness is dispersed into larger social forces. The desire that in their earlier works is bound up in psychic autonomy is subsumed in the latter works by public concerns. In *The Apes of God* and *Finnegans Wake* desire is redirected inward, away from societal manifestation, towards the "inversions" represented respectively by homosexuality and incest. The historical and external worlds take center stage as the source of renewed and displaced conflicts, and their portrayals of sexuality become more and more private, inhabiting the regions which Joyce describes in "Scylla and Charybdis" as the opposites of adulterousness, incest and homosexuality being the extreme joining of like with like.[1] Lewis's and Joyce's later characters (if such is an appropriate term for *Finnegans Wake*) act within realms of desire that are newly constrained and subordinated – the father's desire for the daughter in *Finnegans Wake*, for instance, becomes of secondary interest to the ever-present historical struggle of the brothers. As they treat both public and private experience, then, *The Apes of God* and *Finnegans Wake* attempt to redefine man's nature within a public sphere that is ever more threatened by the subversive impulses of the body politic and the individual psyche. This treatment, in turn, finds its roots in the world's shifting sense of itself between the World Wars, where individual experience seemed for the first time to be overcome by the terrors of collective history. Joyce and Lewis note the involutions of their subjects, even as they close them off from further fictional consideration.

We may argue, therefore, that however much Jameson claims

that "national allegory" coexists in *Tarr* with what he calls, after Jean-François Lyotard, the "libidinal apparatus," *Tarr* represents an exception in Lewis's works rather than the rule.² My analysis has shown that political concerns in Joyce and Lewis are marked not by ideology's strategic recontainment by figurations of desire, but by the absence, destruction, or etiolation of "normal" sexuality, which in Lewis is heterosexuality, in Joyce the married sexuality that has in his works no satisfactory manifestation. Yet we may note further that this movement from private to public makes manifest what has been always latent in Lewis's and Joyce's earlier work. In *Blast*, for instance, political statement is inseparable from ideolectic wit. When Lewis suggests that the King could be converted to Vorticism (*B*1, 8) the gesture is merely a squib that redounds to the cleverness of the author. But when Lewis includes Charlotte Corday in the list of the "Blessed" (*B*1, 28) his gesture hints at the larger theaters of societal change. It seems indirectly to endorse the sexual politics of the contemporary suffragette movement, qualified support for which appears in *Blast*'s last pages.³ Yet it also points forward to the counter-revolutionary fervor of his mature writings. Similarly, when *Blast* promises that Vorticism will "Stir up Civil War among peaceful apes" (*B*1, 31), one cannot but hear a proleptic echo of the threatened civil war at the end of *The Apes of God*, radical artistic desire turned to reactive political fear. Lewis's personal quest for artistic revolution gives birth to its opposite in the world, as the years between *Blast*'s and *The Apes of God*'s publications transformed radical potential into manifest destruction.

Lewis does not stand alone among English writers in reacting strongly to modern politics and transforming them into fiction. In *Finnegans Wake*, HCE, in Shaunian mode, claims "I will westerneyes those poor sunuppers" (*FW*, 537.11), a comment whose ramifications are worth unraveling. In Joycean context "sunuppers" are the Irish nationalists who wait for the rising of what *Ulysses* calls Arthur Griffith's "homerule sun" (*U*, 4.102). To "westernize" them is to contain anarchy, related to the East through Russia and its revolution, by a centralized Western rule. The pun suggests that to "westernize" is to see through "western eyes," the visual politics of Lewis, author of *Time and Western Man*. But by connecting West and East, and the threat of nationalism with the fear of revolution, Joyce also juxtaposes Lewis with Joseph Conrad. Before *The Apes of God* was written, Conrad's *Under Western Eyes* exposed the failures of a nascent socialism, its hypocrisies revealed by a writer disillusioned by the maelstrom of history. Joyce's glancing connection is worth taking seriously. Conrad, whose major fictions deal with the problems of history, truth-telling, and political rule, is Lewis's clearest thematic forerunner. Together, despite their manifest differences as writers, they are the pre-eminent English political modernists. The Polish refugee whose skeptical and pessimistic fiction grew from his experience of political exile presages the English soldier, whose experiences in the First World War forever altered the philosophic substance of his fiction.

Joyce's status as political writer is harder to define. His political nature is most clear when he insists on the necessary relation of public history to personal experience. Such relations obtain throughout his works. Certainly by the time of *Finnegans Wake* the two are equated. An "act of union" (*FW*, 585.25) is both the merging of the Irish and British Parliaments and sexual intercourse; "Withdraw your member!" (*FW*, 585.26) becomes both Parliamentary cry and prophylactic command. The very buildings of Dublin become inseparable from private experience. The Four Courts of Dublin, seats of public judgement, become the "four divorce courts" (*FW*, 422.4–5), places where personal bonds are mediated and dissolved. And when *Finnegans Wake* laments "the levelling of all customs by blazes" (*FW*, 189.36), the phrase itself levels a historical reference, the burning of the Dublin Custom House during the civil war of 1922, with a comparable disaster in marriage in *Ulysses*, the destruction of Victorian customs of fidelity by "Blazes" Boylan.

Yet as early as *A Portrait of the Artist as a Young Man* the child Stephen equates politics with metaphysical concern and personal need. He feels pain "that he did not know well what politics meant and that he did not know where the universe ended" (*P*, 17). We may ultimately read Joyce's work as a whole as a response to Stephen's fears. In *Ulysses,* where Parnell and his adultery is synonymous with lost Irish unity, or in "The Dead," where a failure of marital desire coincides with the decay of Irish nationalist culture, politics and private desire are inextricably entangled. We may take one instance as exemplary of Joyce's pervasive interrelation of private and public. When Gabriel Conroy in "The Dead" taps on the windowpanes and wishes to be at the snow-capped Wellington Monument in the Phoenix Park, the reader who knows *Finnegans Wake* should feel a Vichian moment of recognition, end returning to source. Here, far earlier than *Finnegans Wake,* Joyce merges crippled phallic power, marital alienation, and the threats of colonialism, into a single monolithic correlative: the Wellington Monument, covered with tableaus that praise the British empire yet is capped by chilling snow, becomes a nexus of sexual, artistic, and nationalist inertia. The equation demonstrates that for Joyce, as for young Stephen, the universe, which is the sum total of personal knowledge and experience, ends precisely where politics begins. History is shaped by individual desire, and man builds society in his own macrocosmic shape. His monoliths – which include *Finnegans Wake* – stand testament to the frustrations, but also the necessity, of political and artistic multiplicity.

To perceive Lewis's and Joyce's interconnectedness is thus to revise our sense of modernism. To recognize that Joyce's art is mediated by Lewis is to affirm that Joyce's response to authoritarianism is central to his last work, a response with aesthetic and metaphysical as well as political import. More generally, because Lewis's and Joyce's work show connections that can be called neither simply differences or similarities, we can no longer comfortably relegate Lewis to his chosen role as antithesis to modernism, the "Enemy" whose ideas merely "corrected" his peers through an idiosyncratic and comic negation. We need to recognize Lewis as an essential writer within a modernism that for both aesthetic and political reasons can no longer be easily divided into the categories of "mainstream" and "marginal." The considerable originality of his prose, the recognition of his achievement by his peers, as well as the influence of his ideas on Joyce, suggest his central importance to the construction of early twentieth-century literature. We can no longer ignore Lewis's work because of its stylistic roughness, and its gruff and satiric inhumanity. To do so is to cripple our understanding of modernism's full range and complexity, and to impede our understanding of the contemporary works that Lewis took as his sources and satiric targets.

Thus, in apprehending Lewis's and Joyce's "anti-collaboration," we may reinstall them within literary history as an unusual case of the dual thinking that was typical of modernism, from the collaboration of Joseph Conrad and Ford Madox Ford to the collaboration of Ezra Pound and T. S. Eliot. *Finnegans Wake* proves that Joyce recognized the parallel. When *Finnegans Wake* says "Thank you, besters!" (*FW*, 540.29) ("Thank you, Bestre!") Joyce takes Eliot's dedication of *The Waste Land* to Ezra Pound as "*il miglior fabbro,*" and transposes it onto Lewis, "the better maker" of "Bestre."[4] And when Shaun calls Shem "my shemblable! My freer!" (*FW*, 489.28) Joyce alludes not simply to the "*Mon semblable, – Mon frère!*" of Baudelaire's *Les Fleurs du Mal* but again to *The Waste Land*, where Eliot includes Pound within his voluminous address. In naming Lewis as the Arnaut Daniel to his Dante, Joyce also nominates Lewis as the Pound to his Eliot. Lewis for Joyce, as Pound for Eliot, is the literary predecessor and competitor, the thinker against whom one must struggle in the search for self-definition as artist.

The collaborative oscillation of self and other is thus the larger movement of Joyce's and Lewis's fictions, whose treatments of authority and representation are grounded upon the attractions of psychological and political division made available, in part, by one another's work. And here, after asserting interdependence, we may distinguish difference. For Lewis these divisions are both tragic and comic. His protagonists are caught, as he describes Shakespeare's heroes, "in a *real* action; whereas they come from, and naturally inhabit, an ideal world," but his theories suggest that representation itself takes the Nietzschean step from *incipit tragoedia* to *incipit parodia*.[5] Lewis's equations of fiction with satire and representation with misrepresentation, taken together with his attention to the ideological ramifications of all representation, make him a particularly astute, if politically paradoxical, forerunner of much Marxist criticism, particularly of post-modern criticism that relates the image to social production.[6] Yet unlike Marx, Lewis posits no social or historical space (the hero's "ideal world") wherein contradiction can be finally contained. His work shows no moment where the shifting of oppositions and paradox can be safely grasped as a final or teleological structure – this nowhere more strongly than in *The Childermass*, where history's dead-end becomes a final denial of signification or progress. And if the confluence of tragedy and parody or the valorization of surfaces in his major works are generally associated not with the canonical modernists, but with the schools of fiction that followed thereafter – of American novelists such as William Gaddis or Thomas Pynchon, say, or the practitioners of the *nouveau roman* – then that is a mark of Lewis's success in authentically breaking free of that modernism, of opening up for fiction what T. E. Hulme called "the re-establishment of the temper or disposition of mind which can look at a *gap* or chasm without shuddering."[7]

That these gaps and chasms are also everywhere present in Joyce needs no special stress. Yet where Lewis's claims for unity and duality turn against one another in strict and self-consuming paradox, Joyce foregrounds the gap or chasm as only one pole of a pair of representational possibilities that allows unity and duality to have a truly simultaneous presence, reconciliation interlocked with, rather than subverted by, its own denial.[8] In theological terms Joyce presents this simultaneity as a doubt that acts as paradoxical guarantor of wholeness. Yet if the Church in *Ulysses* is, according to Stephen, "founded irremovably because founded, like the world, macro and microcosm, upon the void" (*U*, 9.841–42), when Shaun borrows the metaphor wholeness gives way to an equivalent division. He accuses Shem "you have reared your disunited kingdom on the vacuum of your own most intensely doubtful soul" (*FW*, 188.16–17). As these differing quotations suggest, the coexistence of opposites in Joyce is not, as in Lewis, a problematic and unforeseen paradox that exceeds the limit of paradox proposed by its issuing aesthetic. By founding representation upon the doublenesses of mimesis and anti-mimesis, unity and duality, both authority and the dismantling of the authoritative voice, Joyce finds a source of positive, but also negative, value in the divided origin that Lewis sees only as the source of a comic despair. Joyce fatalistically accepts "a loaded Hobson's which left only twin alternatives" (*FW*, 63.2–3), because duality is a Hobson's choice – no choice at all. Yet if *Finnegans Wake*'s cyclicality seems to offer no more ultimate hope for human progress than Lewis's pessimism, Joyce also intimates that archetypal fragments can be shored against history's ruin. This unwillingness to separate integration from disintegration is the source of the divisions that have typified Joycean criticism from its source. If opposites in Joyce are simultaneously conciliatory and oppositional, one erects artificial divisions by arguing that Joyce embodies only realism or symbolism, only containment versus dispersal, only a pure concern with language or a pure concern for the political world in which language is embedded. A complete criticism of Joyce must take into account the issues raised by Lewis's structural presence in his work – that is, the degree to which Joyce's works render problematic the division of opposite from opposite, presenting unity and diversity as necessary if paradoxical components of the same aesthetic and ideological processes, which are not only self-subverting but also self-establishing.

To discover Lewis and Joyce within each other's texts is thus to discover two visions of modernity inhering within one another. The philosophic and theological oppositions of Joyce's early work become charged in his latter work with a vision of reconciliation and difference that intertwines language with politics. While for Lewis political language becomes charged with a nihilistic force of difference that, in a final Joycean irony, in his later works becomes explicitly theological.[9] That their interrelationship can be read in larger terms as the inherence of a strongly Nietzschean "post-modernism" within a skeptically theological "modernism" (and vice versa) may be taken as a corollary of my observations. For one must understand Lewis and Joyce not simply as the reified force of difference nor, as they appear in *Finnegans Wake*, as twins. They are rather powerful opponents whose mirroring of one another admits within their aesthetic bounds elements of their own subversion. Their disagreements are subsumed within their fictions as the sign of a paradoxical influence, and an authorial authority, that they express as difference but incorporate within their own representing selves. We as readers must consider their writing jointly. Their body of work is a crucial document of modernism, a set of compelling fictions whose textual antagonisms, in the words of *Blast*, are for "neither side or both sides" (*B*1, 30) – and ours.

# Notes

## INTRODUCTION: OPPOSITION AND REPRESENTATION

1 Frank Budgen, "Further Recollections of James Joyce," *Partisan Review*, vol. 23, no. 4 (Fall, 1956), 539; reprinted in *James Joyce and the Making of "Ulysses"* (Bloomington and London: Indiana University Press, 1960), pp. 314–28.
2 See Ezra Pound, "Wyndham Lewis," *The Egoist*, 1: 12 (June 15, 1914), 233, and T. S. Eliot, "A Note on *Monstre Gai*," *Hudson Review*, 7: 4 (Winter, 1955), 526. Eliot did not confine his praise to style alone. He referred to Lewis's story "Cantleman's Spring Mate" as "one of the finest pieces of prose in the language" (See Eliot, "Literature and the American Courts," *The Egoist*, 5: 3 [March 1918], 39).
3 Wyndham Lewis, *Paleface: The Philosophy of the Melting Pot* (London: Chatto and Windus, 1929), p. 98.
4 Wyndham Lewis, *Blasting and Bombardiering* (Berkeley: University of California Press, 1967), p. 35.
5 Aristotle, *Metaphysics*, in *Works of Aristotle*, vol. VIII, trans. under the editorship of W. D. Ross (Oxford: Clarendon Press, 1972), paragraph 986a.
6 James Joyce, *Selected Letters*, ed. Richard Ellmann (New York: Viking Press, 1966), p. 306, from a letter to Harriet Shaw Weaver dated 27 January 1925. For a detailed discussion of the philosophic argument between Aristotle and Bruno see Theoharis Constantine Theoharis, *Joyce's "Ulysses:" An Anatomy of the Soul* (Chapel Hill: University of North Carolina Press, 1988), chapters 1 and 2.
7 Hugh Gordon Porteus, *Wyndham Lewis: A Discursive Exposition* (London: Desmond Harmsworth, 1932), p. 19.
8 Arnold Goldman has argued acutely that Lewis's aesthetic problems and those presented by Stephen Dedalus in *A Portrait of the Artist as a Young Man* are identical, turning merely in opposite directions. See Arnold Goldman, *The Joyce Paradox: Form and*

*Freedom in His Fiction* (Evanston: Northwestern University Press, 1966), p. 58.
9 Lewis, *The Childermass* (London: John Calder, 1965), pp. 26, 99.
10 Ezra Pound, *The Literary Essays of Ezra Pound*, ed. T. S. Eliot (New York: New Directions, 1968), p. 424.
11 See, for instance, Julian Symons, *Makers of the New: The Revolution in Literature, 1912–1939* (New York: Random House, 1987) and Timothy Materer, *Vortex: Pound, Eliot, and Lewis* (Ithaca: Cornell University Press, 1979). Materer refers to Lewis's and Joyce's "lifelong rivalry" as a matter of course, but stands on less certain ground when he attempts to place Joyce within Lewis's camp through Pound, claiming "Joyce was potentially a force within the Vortex" (pp. 11, 164).
12 See Richard Aldington, "The Influence of Mr. James Joyce" (*English Review* 32, April 1921, 333–41), and Eliot, "*Ulysses*, Order and Myth," (*Dial*, 75, November 1923), reprinted in Bernard Benstock, ed. *Critical Essays on James Joyce* (Boston: G. K. Hall and Co., 1985), pp. 25–27.
13 Budgen, *James Joyce and the Making of "Ulysses,"* pp. 13, 273. Page references in the following paragraphs will appear in the text. Lewis calls Bloom a "stage Jew" in the context of complaining about *Ulysses*' cultural clichés in general, including also "a stage Irishman (Mulligan), or a stage Anglo-Saxon (Haines)" and later the "wooden figure" of Stephen Dedalus (*TWM*, 96–97).
14 Rebecca West, "'Tarr.'" Reprinted *Agenda*, 7: 3 and 8: 1 (Autumn – Winter 1969–70), 67.
15 Harry Levin, *James Joyce: A Critical Introduction*, revised and augmented edition (New York: New Directions, 1960; originally published 1941), p. 92.
16 Levin, pp. 165–66 and 112. Lewis compares Joyce's prose style in *Work in Progress* to that of Nashe at some length in *Time and Western Man* directly after the discussion of Bloom and Mr. Jingle (pp. 106–09). SueEllen Campbell has seen further echoes of Lewis's concepts of character and technique in Levin's book (See *The Enemy Opposite: The Outlaw Criticism of Wyndham Lewis* [Athens: Ohio University Press, 1988], pp. 154–55).
17 See Richard M. Kain, *Fabulous Voyager: James Joyce's "Ulysses"* (The University of Chicago Press, 1947), pp. 3, 17, 240.
18 Hugh Kenner, *Dublin's Joyce* (Bloomington: Indiana University Press, 1956), p. 362.
19 Kenner notes that Joyce's descriptions are often inflected by the narrative idioms that would be used by the character described, which he calls "The Uncle Charles Principle" (See *Joyce's Voices*,

[Berkeley: University of California Press, 1978], pp. 69–71). For Lewis's complaint, see *Time and Western Man*, p. 109.
20 See, respectively, *Dublin's Joyce*, p. 136 and *Joyce's Voices*, p. 8; *Dublin's Joyce*, pp. 79, 170; *Dublin's Joyce*, p. 83. "Ernest Hemingway, The 'Dumb Ox'" is the title of chapter 1 of Lewis's *Men Without Art* (1934). "Split-man" and "ape of God," both typical locutions of *The Apes of God*, appear also throughout much of Lewis's cultural criticism. In *The Pound Era* Kenner claims a connection between the synchronism of Lewis's criticism and the later developments of the New Criticism, all the while spinning a performance in the tradition of *Time and Western Man*: massive, assertive, and idiosyncratic. No less than Lewis, Kenner attempts to define the *Zeitgeist* through a series of intercultural investigations spun around a central idea and held together largely by the rhetorical brilliance of its author. See *The Pound Era* (Berkeley and Los Angeles: University of California Press, 1971), p. 30.
21 Derek Attridge and Daniel Ferrer, eds., *Post-Structuralist Joyce: Essays from the French* (Cambridge University Press, 1984), pp. 5–6.
22 Arnold Goldman's *The Joyce Paradox*, for instance, however valuably it opens "paradox" as a consideration in Joyce, depends upon a Kirkegaardian model that is extrinsic to Joyce's work itself. More recently Vicki Mahaffey has revivified the idea of paradox in Joyce by arguing that one should understand *Ulysses* as embodying "two opposing possibilities," including, among others, "the referentiality of language and its materiality," and that "betrayal is not only inevitable, but implicit in the very decision to pledge fidelity to only half of an arbitrarily partitioned reality" (*Reauthorizing Joyce* [Cambridge University Press, 1988], pp. 3–4). Even a single critic's work can demonstrate this tension towards dichotomous analysis. Margot Norris, who began her investigations of *Finnegans Wake* from an ahistorical and linguistic perspective, has recently defended Joyce against Peter Bürger's aestheticist vision of modernism by finding throughout his work the historical and social density that Bürger attributes to a politically charged avant-garde. See Norris, *The Decentered Universe of "Finnegans Wake"* (Baltimore: Johns Hopkins University Press, 1976) and *Joyce's Web: The Social Unraveling of Modernism* (Austin: University of Texas Press, 1992).
23 See Robert T. Chapman, *Wyndham Lewis: Fictions and Satires* (London: The Vision Press, 1973) and Timothy Materer, *Wyndham Lewis the Novelist* (Detroit: Wayne State University Press, 1976).
24 See Hugh Kenner, *Wyndham Lewis* (Norfolk: New Directions Books, 1954), and Fredric Jameson, *Fables of Aggression: Wyndham Lewis, The Modernist as Fascist* (Berkeley: University of California

Press, 1979). More recent interpretations reproduce equivalent disagreements. Daniel Schenker in *Wyndham Lewis: Religion and Modernism* (Tuscaloosa and London: The University of Alabama Press, 1992) for instance, treats Lewis as a religious author, defined largely by his interest in Being outside the confines of self, while David Ayers in *Wyndham Lewis and Western Man* (New York: St. Martin's Press, 1992) finds in him a destructive anatomist of western man whose literary works are irredeemably marred by pervasive anti-Semitism and fellow-traveling with Nazi ideology.

25 For fine work on Lewis and Pound see Reed Way Dasenbrock, *The Literary Vorticism of Ezra Pound and Wyndham Lewis* (Baltimore: Johns Hopkins University Press, 1985) and Vincent Sherry, *Ezra Pound, Wyndham Lewis, and Radical Modernism* (New York and Oxford: Oxford University Press, 1993). Michael Levenson's *Modernism and the Fate of Individuality: Character and Novelistic Form from Conrad to Woolf* (Cambridge University Press, 1991) is a valuable exception to the general practice of cordoning Lewis off from the other modernists.

26 See Trilling, "The Leavis-Snow Controversy," in *Beyond Culture: Essays on Literature and Learning* (New York: The Viking Press, 1965), p. 167.

27 See respectively Richard Ellmann *The Consciousness of Joyce* (London: Faber and Faber, 1977), Dominic Manganiello, *Joyce's Politics* (London: Routledge and Kegan Paul, 1980), Colin MacCabe, *James Joyce and the Revolution of the Word* (London: Macmillan, 1978), Cheryl Herr, *Joyce's Anatomy of Culture* (Urbana and Chicago: University of Illinois Press, 1986), and Margot Norris, *Joyce's Web*.

28 Edward Said makes the point in passing in "Swift as Intellectual," in *The World, the Text, and the Critic* (Cambridge: Harvard University Press, 1983), p. 76.

29 See Vincent Sherry, *Radical Modernism*, who explicates Lewis's affiliations with Pound against the tradition of the French *idéologue*, and Tom Normand, *Wyndham Lewis the Artist: Holding the Mirror up to Politics* (Cambridge University Press, 1992), whose work on Lewis's painting convincingly synthesizes his stylistic evolution with his changing political vision.

30 See "Literary History and Literary Modernity" in Paul de Man, *Blindness and Insight: Essays in the Rhetoric of Contemporary Criticism*, second edition, revised (Minneapolis: University of Minnesota Press, 1981), p. 143.

31 See Joseph Conrad, "[W]ords also belong to the sheltering conception of light and order which is our refuge" (*Lord Jim* [Middlesex: Penguin Books, 1986], p. 274), and D. H. Lawrence,

"She knew, as well as he knew, that words themselves do not convey meaning, that they are but a gesture we make, a dumb show like any other" (*Women in Love* [Middlesex: Penguin Books, 1976], p. 178).

32 John Millington Synge, preface to *The Playboy of the Western World* (Random House: New York, 1935), p. 3.
33 T. S. Eliot, "*Ulysses*, Order and Myth," p. 27.
34 See Susan Eilenberg, *Strange Power of Speech: Wordsworth, Coleridge, and Literary Possession* (New York and Oxford: Oxford University Press, 1992).
35 See respectively John Paul Riquelme, *Teller and Tale in Joyce's Fiction: Oscillating Perspectives* (Baltimore: Johns Hopkins University Press, 1983), Mahaffey, *Reauthorizing Joyce*, and Frances L. Restuccia, *Joyce and the Law of the Father* (New Haven, Yale University Press, 1989), who examines Joyce's paradoxical rebellion and submission, via a psychological model derived from Deleuze, as a masochistic textual relationship with cultural and patristic authorities.
36 He claimed "*The Enemy of the Stars*, a play written and published by me in 1914, obliterated by the War, turned up, I suspect, in Zurich, and was responsible for the manner here and there of Joyce's book [*Ulysses*]" (*TWM*, 110). The radical discrepancy between Lewis's and Joyce's styles indeed provides Fredric Jameson's *Fables of Aggression* with its strongest case for Lewis's antithetical relation to mainstream modernism. Attempts to demonstrate the influence of Vorticist prose style upon Joyce, on the contrary, largely fail to convince. See, for instance, Dennis Brown, *Intertextual Dynamics within the Literary Group – Joyce, Lewis, Pound and Eliot: The Men of 1914* (New York: St. Martin's Press, 1991), pp. 89–93.
37 See letter dated 5 May 1906 to Grant Richards, *Letters of James Joyce*, II, ed. Richard Ellmann (New York: The Viking Press, 1966), p. 134. Leavis dismissed Lewis as "brutal and boring" in his Richmond Lecture, "Two Cultures? The Significance of C. P. Snow," reprinted as "Two Cultures? The Significance of Lord Snow" in *Nor Shall My Sword: Discourses On Pluralism, Compassion, and Social Hope* (London: Chatto and Windus, 1972), p. 53.
38 "Super-Nature versus Super-Real" (1939) in *Wyndham Lewis on Art: Collected Writings, 1913–1956*, ed. Walter Michel and C. J. Fox (London: Thames and Hudson, 1969), p. 330.
39 Jameson calls *The Apes of God* "virtually unreadable for any sustained period of time," (p. 5). Dasenbrock states, reconfiguring effect as theme, "The premise of *The Apes of God* seems to be that

it can have no readers" (*Literary Vorticism*, p. 178). Nearly alone among modern critics, Sherry devotes some thoughtful pages to detailed analysis of its style (*Radical Modernism*, pp. 105–13).

## 1 THE TELL-TALE EYE

1 Edgar Allan Poe, "The Tell-Tale Heart," in *Poetry and Tales* (New York, Library of America, 1984), p. 555.
2 Wyndham Lewis, "Tyronic Dialogues – X. and F.," in *The Tyro* no. 1 (April 1921), p. 7. Reprinted in *The Complete Wild Body*, pp. 361–70.
3 Wyndham Lewis, *Mrs. Dukes' Million* (Toronto: The Coach House Press, 1977), p. 365.
4 Robert Currie's suggestion that *Tarr* takes its name from E. T. A. Hoffmann's novel *Murr* seems less likely, despite the unquestionable allusion to Hoffmann in the name of Tarr's rival Otto Kreisler. Lewis's pronouncements on modern society in *Blast* ("Human insanity has never flowered more colossally" [*B*1, 145]) and later works ("we live in a sort of lunatic asylum," [*MWA*, 14]) are consistent with Poe's tale. In either case, however, the title's relationship to the work of an author who worked in the tradition of German Romance is suggestive. See Currie, *Genius: An Ideology in Literature* (London: Chatto and Windus, 1974).
5 Fredric Jameson, *The Prison-House of Language: A Critical Account of Structuralism and Russian Formalism* (Princeton University Press, 1972), p. 74.
6 Wyndham Lewis, *Rude Assignment: A Narrative of My Career Up-to-date* (London: Hutchinson and Company, 1950), p. 120.
7 Wyndham Lewis, "Tyros and Portraits," in *Wyndham Lewis on Art*, ed. Walter Michel and C. J. Fox, p. 187.
8 Wyndham Lewis, "Essay on the Objective of Plastic Art in Our Time," in *Wyndham Lewis on Art*, p. 201.
9 In the tradition of British painting, see for instance John Constable, who said: "Painting is a science and should be pursued as an inquiry into the laws of nature" (quoted by E. H. Gombrich, *Art and Illusion: A Study in the Psychology of Pictorial Representation* [New York: Pantheon Books, 1960], p. 175).
10 See William C. Wees, *Vorticism and the English Avant-Garde* (University of Toronto Press, 1972), Richard Cork, *Vorticism and Abstract Art in the First Machine Age* (Berkeley and Los Angeles, University of California Press, 1976), and Timothy Materer in *Vortex: Pound, Eliot, and Lewis*.
11 Wyndham Lewis, introduction to the catalog of *Wyndham Lewis and*

*Vorticism*, reprinted as "The 1956 Retrospective at the Tate Gallery," in *Wyndham Lewis on Art*, p. 452.
12 See Reed Way Dasenbrock, *The Literary Vorticism of Ezra Pound and Wyndham Lewis*, p. 65.
13 See also Pound's *Gaudier-Brzeska*, chapter XI, in which he expands upon his conception of the Vortex as a "radiant node or cluster" (New York: New Directions, 1970), p. 92.
14 Lewis would later appeal to "death" rather than a separate "life" as the necessary condition of art. Tarr's "deadness is the first condition of art" (*T*, 312) is much echoed by Lewis's in later writings, and is often taken as an unequivocal key to Vorticist thought. Yet the manifestoes' struggle to shift and provisionally redefine the terms of "life" and "nature" betray a vitalism that stands opposed to the "*nature morte*" of the naturalist, even if Lewis would later recast that opposition in different terms.
15 Wyndham Lewis, "Prevalent Design," in *Wyndham Lewis on Art*, p. 123.
16 For this reason I disagree with Daniel O'Connell, who claims that Lewis's aesthetic is antithetical to the Kantian-Coleridgean concept of the mind as "the prime constituent and even producer of the world of experience" (*The Opposition Critics: The Antisymbolist Reaction in the Modern Period* [De Proprietatibus Litterarrum, Series Minor, 14] [The Hague and Paris: Mouton, 1974], p. 109). So to conclude is to take at face value Lewis's later and often revisionist claims for his earlier intent, trusting the retrospective teller over the manifestoes' tale.
17 John Ruskin, *The Stones of Venice*, vol. 2 (Boston: Dana Estes and Company, undated), p. 165.
18 T. E. Hulme, "Bergson's Theory of Art," in *Speculations: Essays on Humanism and the Philosophy of Art*, ed. Herbert Read (New York: Harcourt, Brace and Company, Inc., 1924), p. 146.
19 Henri Bergson, *Time and Free Will*, trans. F. L. Pogson (London: George Allen and Unwin Ltd, 1950), p. 128.
20 This passage may also have a directly *ad hominem* subtext. Lewis called Roger Fry a "Pecksniff-shark" in a "Round Robin" sent to supporters of Fry's Omega workshop and to the press in October 1913, after Fry allegedly stole an important commission from Lewis (see *The Letters of Wyndham Lewis*, ed. W. K. Rose [Norfolk: New Directions, 1963], p. 50). The break with Fry and Lewis's subsequent establishment of the Rebel Art Center were the first steps towards Vorticism, as well as the initiation of the feud with the Bloomsbury group that would later lead to the writing of *The Apes of God*.

21 See the *American Dictionary of Printing and Bookmaking* (New York: Howard Lockwood and Co., 1894), pp. 218–20. I am grateful to John Paul Riquelme for bringing its relevance to my attention.
22 Julien Benda, *Belphégor*, quoted by Lewis without more detailed reference in *The Art of Being Ruled* (London: Chatto and Windus, 1926), p. 260. Reed Way Dasenbrock notes that this is Lewis's own translation of the last paragraph of the foreword, a passage found on pp. xxiii–xxiv of the contemporary English version, trans. S. J. I. Lawson (London: Faber and Faber, 1929). See Dasenbrock, notes to the critical edition of *Art of Being Ruled* (Santa Barbara: Black Sparrow Press, 1989), p. 415.
23 Lewis renders the relationship between Romanticism and sexuality explicit in "Cantleman's Spring Mate" (1917), where Cantleman reads Hardy as "a morbid intercourse with a romantic abstraction." See "Cantleman's Spring Mate," in *Blasting and Bombardiering*, p. 308.
24 See, for instance, Dasenbrock in chapter 4 of *Literary Vorticism*, or Daniel Schenker, who refers to *Enemy of the Stars* in passing as a "squib" (*Wyndham Lewis: Religion and Modernism*, p. 44). Hugh Kenner has noted in *Wyndham Lewis*, however, that the play's narrative is a determining model for Lewis's later fiction, and Wendy Stallard Flory has called the play "a serious, eloquent and complex piece of self-analysis" ("*Enemy of the Stars*," in *Wyndham Lewis: A Revaluation*, ed. Jeffrey Meyers [London: Athlone Press, 1980], p. 92). Lewis's most astute recent critic, Fredric Jameson, however, leaves Lewis's Vorticist period, including *Enemy of the Stars*, largely undiscussed.
25 Lewis makes this description explicit in a 1932 revision. He adds "*Nature and he pursue opposite paths, in a hostile polarity.*" See Wyndham Lewis, *Collected Poems and Plays*, ed. Alan Munton (Manchester: Carcanet New Press, 1979), p. 148.
26 Lewis misquotes the book's correct title, *Der Einzige und Sein Eigentum*. Alan Munton suggests that Lewis was working from the memory of reading the German original when he was himself a student (*Collected Poems and Plays*, p. 221). For Stirner's currency among the early moderns see Michael Levenson, *A Genealogy of Modernism* (Cambridge University Press, 1984), pp. 63–68.
27 See "Max Stirner and the Enemy of the Stars," *Lewisletter* no. 1, (Publication of the Wyndham Lewis Society, December 1974), pp. 5–6. Kinnimont notes that Stirner embodies "a triumphant egoism [with] which Lewis, or at least Arghol, must have been in some sympathy" (p. 5). He concludes that the altercation is an "obscure" example of Vorticism's inexplicable contradictions.

For a somewhat different understanding of Stirner's presence in *Enemy*, drawing upon Lewis's concept of the "not-self," see Toby Avard Foshay, *Wyndham Lewis and the Avant-Garde: The Politics of the Intellect* (Montreal and Kingston: McGill-Queen's University Press, 1992), pp. 30–33.

28 Max Stirner, *The Ego and His Own*, trans. Steven T. Byington, ed. John Caroll (London: Jonathan Cape, 1971), p. 112. Further references will appear in the text.

29 Lewis's repetition of this scene late in his career – the rejection of a revelatory text as the symbolic prelude to a protagonist's self-destruction – may be taken as an indication of its centrality to the issues raised by his work. In his last important novel, *Self Condemned* (1954), Lewis's protagonist René Harding throws the copy of *Middlemarch* he has tried to read over the side of a ship. Unwilling to recognize that his intellectuality and emotional frigidity will drive his wife to suicide and reduce him to a "glacial shell of a man," Harding refuses to read Eliot because he is unwilling to recognize himself in Eliot's Casaubon, much as Arghol is unwilling to recognize himself in Stirner, with results made clear by the novel's title.

30 Lewis, *Rude Assignment*, p. 129.

31 See, for example, "Plan of War," and "Slow Attack," which are reproduced in *Blast* 1 between the title and the text of *Enemy of the Stars*, between pp. 55, 57.

32 "Super-Nature versus Super-Real" (1939) in *Wyndham Lewis on Art*, p. 333.

33 Lewis, *Rude Assignment*, p. 129.

34 The image of the soldier doubled against himself recurs in Lewis's drawings. See "Two Soldiers" from "Timon of Athens," 1912 (plate 104) and "Anti-War Design" from the jacket of *Count Your Dead: They are Alive!*, 1937 (plate 884) in *Wyndham Lewis: Paintings and Drawings*, ed. Walter Michel (Berkeley: University of California Press, 1971).

35 See introduction to Alan Richardson, *A Mental Theater: Poetic Drama and Consciousness in the Romantic Age* (University Park: Pennsylvania State University Press, 1988). Richardson bases his argument upon analysis of Wordsworth's *The Borderers*, Byron's *Manfred*, *Cain*, and *Heaven and Earth*, Shelley's *The Cenci* and *Prometheus Unbound*, and Beddoes's *Death's Jest-Book*.

36 For comments on Seneca, closet drama, and the avant-garde, see Michael Evenden, "Inter-Mediate Stages: Reconsidering the Body in 'Closet Drama'" (in Catherine B. Burroughs and Jeffrey David Ehrenreich, eds., *Reading the Social Body* [University of Iowa

Press, 1993]), pp. 246–48. Lewis was always attracted to the Senecan side of Shakespeare, which emphasizes the fate of the tragic individualist. *Blast* includes a reproduction within the pages of *Enemy of the Stars* of a drawing from his 1912 portfolio based on *Timon of Athens*, while his book on Shakespeare and Machiavelli, *The Lion and the Fox*, deals largely with Timon and Coriolanus, two "egoists" whose apparent self-sufficiency leads, like Arghol's, to self-destruction.

37 Richardson, *A Mental Theater*, p. 5.
38 Lewis, *Collected Poems and Plays*, p. 175.
39 Otto Rank, *The Double*, trans. and ed. Harry Tucker, Jr. (Chapel Hill: University of North Carolina Press, 1971), p. 48.
40 My use of Freud and Rank here may be taken as an endorsement of Renato Poggioli's observation that "in the spirit of avant-garde art, ideology and psychology are quite as important as poetics and aesthetics" (*The Theory of the Avant-Garde*, trans. Gerald Fitzgerald [Cambridge: The Belknap Press of Harvard University Press, 1968], p. 63). In Poggioli's terms, Lewis's destructive self combines the categories typical of the avant-garde: nihilism, antagonism against others (here represented by tradition and the public), and "agonism," "an hyperbolic passion, a bow bent towards the impossible, a paradoxical and positive form of spiritual defeatism" (p. 66).

## 2 'THE MIRROR AND THE RAZOR

1 Dante, *Inferno*, XXXIV, line 139.
2 Dante, *Paradiso*, XXXIII, lines 133–36. English translations are from John D. Sinclair, *Dante's "Paradiso"* (New York: Oxford University Press, 1977).
3 Dante defines "fantasia" in the *Convivio* as "the power by which the intellect represents what it sees" (Sinclair's note, *Paradiso*, p. 486).
4 William T. Noon, *Joyce and Aquinas* (New Haven: Yale University Press, 1957), pp. 44 and 79. Noon cites in particular "*Voces autem quae sunt praecipua inter signa, ... non significant naturaliter sed ad placitum*" from the *Summa Theologiae* (II–II, q. 85, a.1, obj. 3).
5 See particularly Jacques Derrida, "Plato's Pharmacy," in *Dissemination*, trans. Barbara Johnson (University of Chicago Press, 1981), pp. 63–172. Joyce is a constant philosophic presence in much post-structural theory. See, for instance, Derrida's use of an epigram from *A Portrait of the Artist as a Young Man* to introduce part III of the above essay; the epigram to "Cogito and the History of

Madness," and his quotation from Joyce, whom he problematically calls "perhaps the most Hegelian of modern novelists" as the final line of "Violence and Metaphysics" (both in *Writing and Difference*, trans. Alan Bass, University of Chicago Press, 1978). Recently Derrida has stated explicitly "*chaque fois que j'écris, et même dans les choses de l'académie, un fantôme de Joyce est à l'abordage*" ("Every time I write, even in the most academic pieces, Joyce's ghost comes aboard") ("*Deux Mots pour Joyce*" in *Ulysses gramophone* [Paris: Éditions Galilée, 1987], p. 27. For a useful summary of Derrida's allusions to Joyce see Geert Lernout, *The French Joyce* (Ann Arbor: University of Michigan Press, 1990), pp. 56–71.

6 This has become the *locus classicus* for discussions of Stephen and language, which are often categorized in terms exclusively metaphysical or phonological. Edward W. Said in *The World, the Text, and the Critic* ([Cambridge: Harvard University Press, 1983], p. 48) and Jules David Law have presented the case for an overtly political interpretation of this passage. Law's readings of this passage of various figurations in "Nestor" are similar to my own. See "Joyce's 'Delicate Siamese' Equation: The Dialectic of Home in *Ulysses*" (*PMLA*, 102: 2, March 1987, 197–205).

7 See Law, "Joyce's 'Delicate Siamese' Equation," p. 197.

8 For discussions of figurations of war in "Nestor" see Robert E. Spoo, "'Nestor' and the Nightmare of History: The Presence of the Great War in *Ulysses*" (*Twentieth Century Literature*, 32: 2, Summer 1986, 137–54), and E. L. Epstein, "Nestor," in Clive Hart and David Hayman, eds., *James Joyce's "Ulysses": Critical Essays* (Berkeley: University of California Press, 1974), pp. 17–28.

9 James Joyce, *Dubliners* (New York: The Viking Press, 1961), p. 108.

10 Joyce claimed "In writing the 'Mass for Pope Marcellus'... Palestrina did more than surpass himself as a musician. With that great effort, consciously made, he saved music for the Church" (Frank Budgen, *James Joyce and the Making of Ulysses* [Bloomington and London: Indiana University Press, 1960], p. 182). Margot Norris considers at some length a comparable controlling of voice, the Pope's ban on female singers in church choirs, in "'Who Killed Julia Morkan?': The Gender Politics of Art in 'The Dead,'" chapter 5 of *Joyce's Web: The Social Unraveling of Modernism* (Austin: University of Texas Press, 1992), pp. 97–118.

11 Within the very first few pages of the first chapter Mulligan takes on "a preacher's tone" (*U*, 1.20), "a Cockney accent" (*U*, 1.299), "an old woman's wheedling voice" (*U*, 1.355–56), "a fine puzzled voice" (*U*, 1.368), "A finical sweet voice" (*U*, 1.378), "a

hoarsened rasping voice" (*U*, 1.381) and a "quiet happy foolish voice" (*U*, 1.583).

12 Karen Lawrence has usefully described *Ulysses* as "deliberately antirevelatory" (*The Odyssey of Style in "Ulysses"* [Princeton University Press, 1981], p. 7).

13 See Cecil J. Sharp and Herbert C. Macilwaine, *The Morris Book, with A Description of Dances as Performed by the Morris Men of England*, Part 1. (London: Novello and Company, Ltd., 1912). This allusion may entail a slight warping of *Ulysses*' diagetic frame. Sharp and Macilwaine note that the original edition of their book appeared in July, 1906, two years after the date of *Ulysses*' narrative, "when the movement for the revival of folk-dancing was in its infancy, within, to be precise, three months of the first exhibition of Morris-dancing given in London under our direction" (p.7). It is difficult to determine from this work if London's co-opting of the Morris as picturesque ritual lagged behind or inspired the revival of the Morris in its places of origin.

14 The poem begins "Who will drive with Fergus now, / And pierce the deep wood's woven shade, / And dance upon the level shore?," lines that appear in fragmented form at the climax of "Circe." (*The Collected Poems of W. B. Yeats* [New York: Macmillan Publishing Co., Inc., 1979]).

15 Don Gifford with Robert J. Seidman, *"Ulysses" Annotated: Notes for James Joyce's "Ulysses,"* second edition (Berkeley: University of California Press, 1988), p. 62.

16 Richard Ellmann, *James Joyce, New and Revised Edition* (New York: Oxford University Press, 1982), p. 442f.

17 Schema to Gilbert, reprinted in Gilbert, *James Joyce's "Ulysses"* (New York: Vintage Books, 1955), p. 30, and Kenner, *Dublin's Joyce* (Bloomington: Indiana University Press, 1956), p. 226. The earlier Italian schema sent to Carlo Linati differs in many respects, listing the "technic" of the chapter as "*Gorghi*" ("Whirlpools"), the sense as "*Dilemma Bitagliente*" ("Two-edged dilemma"). Ellmann reprints this schema with translation in *Ulysses on the Liffey* (New York: Oxford University Press, 1972), unnumbered pages between pp. 188–89.

18 See Gilbert, *James Joyce's "Ulysses,"* pp. 211–26, and Noon, *Joyce and Aquinas*, pp. 105–25.

19 S. L. Goldberg, *The Classical Temper: A Study of James Joyce's "Ulysses"* (London: Chatto and Windus, 1963), pp. 35, 66.

20 Richard Ellmann, *Ulysses on the Liffey*, and introduction to *Ulysses*, p. xiv. Clive Hart corroborates, noting "*Ulysses* and *Finnegans Wake* are studies not in universal break-up but in universal

reconstitution" (*Structure and Motif in "Finnegans Wake"* [Chicago: Northwestern University Press, 1962], p. 45).

21 See Kellogg, "Scylla and Charybdis," in *James Joyce's "Ulysses,"* ed. Hart and Hayman, p. 151, and John Paul Riquelme, *Teller and Tale in Joyce's Fiction*, p. 204.

22 Kenner, *Dublin's Joyce*, p. 243, and David Hayman, "*Ulysses*": *The Mechanics of Meaning*, revised and expanded edition (Madison: University of Wisconsin Press, 1982), pp. 65–66.

23 William Schutte, *Joyce and Shakespeare: A Study in the Meaning of "Ulysses"* (New Haven: Yale University Press, 1957), pp. 95, 67. Clive Hart similarly refers in passing to the "partially serious theory of *Hamlet*," but makes no attempt to further differentiate what is serious – on Joyce's or Stephen's parts – from what is not (*Structure and Motif*, p. 25).

24 Ellmann, *Ulysses on the Liffey*, p. 85.

25 See Joyce, *Stephen Hero* (New York: New Directions, 1963), particularly chapter 19, where Stephen imagines the artist "standing in the position of mediator between the world of his experience and the world of his dreams" (p. 77).

26 Stuart Gilbert, for instance, reads the whole chapter as a "long Platonic dialogue," or "quasi-Platonic dialogue" in which "Stephen plays the rôle of a Socrates... [he] leads his reluctant elders along a dialectic tightrope" (*James Joyce's "Ulysses,"* pp. 212, 216) while Kellogg finds in "Scylla and Charybdis" a "mock-Socratic dialogue," not the "formal dialectic of the philosophy course but the living dialectic of the library steps and offices" ("Scylla and Charybdis," in *James Joyce's "Ulysses,"* ed. Hart and Hayman, p. 148).

27 See Plato, *The Symposium*, trans. Walter Hamilton (Middlesex: Penguin Books, 1975), pp. 58–65. Aristophanes' narrative, of course, deals with both heterosexual and homosexual desire, a complication often ignored in modern interpretations of the tale. Stephen's allusion is not innocent of such interpretation, however. The text's immediate references thereafter to Wilde, the ambiguous sexuality of Stephen's listeners, and Mulligan's final interpretation of Bloom's interest in Stephen as homoerotic (*U*, 9.1210), suggest another aspect of Stephen's earlier anxiety about the "love that dare not speak its name" (*U*, 3.451). Aristophanes' analogies nonetheless hold; whether man becomes a "wife unto himself" by attempted reclamation of androgyny, through homoeroticism, or, as Mulligan suggests, through masturbation, he nonetheless searches for a self free of desire for the other. Richard Brown also notes in passing the relevance of *The Symposium* to this

passage, but emphasizes the confluence of Joyce's interest in androgyny with similar themes in Blake, Lawrence, and the work of late nineteenth and early twentieth-century theorists of sexual sociology, rather than exploring its relationship to Stephen's lecture *per se* (*Joyce and Sexuality* [Cambridge University Press, 1985], pp. 105–06).

28 Ellmann, *Ulysses on the Liffey*, pp. 86, 191.
29 See Robert Greene, *Groats-Worth of Witte* in *The Huth Library Life and Works of Robert Greene*, vol. XIII, ed. Rev. Alexander B. Grosart (London: Hazell, Watson and Viney, 1881–83), p. 145. The disparity between Greene's text and Stephen's quotation was first noted by Robert Martin Adams in *Surface and Symbol: The Consistency of James Joyce's "Ulysses"* (New York: Oxford University Press, 1962), p. 128.
30 Cheryl Herr, for instance, has intriguingly suggested that Molly's speech should be read as a "script," a theatrical "star-turn" rather than an authentic discourse, rooted in theatrical models and performed by an ambiguous voice culturally determined as "an undecidable act(or)/(ress)." See "'Penelope' as Period Piece" (*Novel*, 22: 2, Winter 1989), 130–42.
31 See Jacques Lacan, "The agency of the letter in the unconscious or reason since Freud," in *Ecrits: a Selection* (trans. Alan Sheridan; New York: W. W. Norton and Company, 1977), p. 167. Lacan tends to reduce Joyce's linguistic experimentation to the clinically therapeutic, even as he identifies the valuable territory its practice opens for a critical psychoanalytic discourse: in the English language preface to *The Four Fundamental Concepts of Psycho-Analysis* he writes, "I shall speak of Joyce, who has preoccupied me much this year, only to say that he is the simplest consequence of a refusal – such a mental refusal! – of a psycho-analysis, which, as a result, his work illustrates" (ed. Jacques-Alain Miller, trans. Alan Sheridan [New York: W. W. Norton and Company, 1981], p. ix).
32 James Joyce, *Giacomo Joyce*, in *Poems and Shorter Writings*, ed. Richard Ellmann, A. Walton Litz, and John Whittier-Ferguson (London: Faber and Faber, 1991), p. 240.
33 Gifford with Seidman, *"Ulysses" Annotated*, pp. 32–33.
34 Such is done by Colin MacCabe, who reads Stephen's lecture on Shakespeare politically as a "neurotic problematic" in which Stephen denies historical chance in order to search for fallacious origins. See *James Joyce and the Revolution of the Word* (London: Macmillan Press, 1978), p. 120.
35 Ian Watt, *The Rise of the Novel* (Berkeley and Los Angeles: University of California Press, 1957), p. 296. Vicki Mahaffey

notes, using the same word in a different interpretative context, that the increasing density and obscurity of Joyce's style is "accompanied by an equally marked adulteration of the authorial voice" that marks the culmination of his interest in both "the politics of style and biological metaphors of artistic reproduction" (*Reauthorizing Joyce* [Cambridge University Press, 1988], p. 187).

36 See Tony Tanner, *Adultery in the Novel: Contract and Transgression* (Baltimore: Johns Hopkins University Press, 1979). The nineteenth-century novel is the focus of Tanner's discussion, but he turns his attention in passing to the issue of adultery in *Ulysses*. He suggests that themes of marriage and fidelity are absorbed in *Ulysses* into a pure "exploration of 'linguicity'" (pp. 14–15). Tanner does not explore, however, the problematic nature of that "absorption," failing to qualify whether Joyce's language thematically subsumes issues of adultery, disperses them, or, as he implies, renders them irrelevant. For a provocative interpretation that places adultery at the center of *Ulysses*' narrative see William Empson, "The Ultimate Novel," in *Using Biography* (London: Chatto and Windus/The Hogarth Press, 1984), pp. 217–59.

37 There is a precedent for seeking in the libidinal content of Joyce's work theoretical justifications for his style. Margot Norris has interpreted Joyce's punning in *Finnegans Wake* as a linguistic reflection of that narrative's theme of incest, in which the breakdown of language is homologous with the breakdown of kinship relations enacted by the characters (*The Decentered Universe of "Finnegans Wake"* [Baltimore: Johns Hopkins University Press, 1976], p. 127–29). Colin MacCabe has similarly suggested that the stylistic irregularity of Joyce's language can be understood as a mirror of the "perversity" of the sexual experience of his characters (*Revolution of the Word*, p. 32), while Jean-Michel Rabaté has redefined perversity in terms that relate Joycean stylistic and semiotic practice as "a game of signifiers whose meaning is uncertain," levelling eroticism and textuality into a common analytical vocabulary (*James Joyce, Authorized Reader* [Baltimore: Johns Hopkins University Press, 1991], p. 25).

38 That this is central to the plot of Leopold and Molly Bloom, and particularly Bloom's resignation in the face of the ultimate unknowability of Molly's actions in "Ithaca," needs no comment. Yet the same is exhaustively true elsewhere in the text. In "Circe" Shakespeare's two mangled self-quotations "Iagogo! How my Oldfellow chokit his Thursdaymornun" (*U*, 15.3828–29) (alluding to Othello's strangling of Desdemona) and "Weda seca whokilla farst" (*U*, 15.3853) ("None wed the second but who

kill'd the first," *Hamlet* III.ii.180) reveal adultery as the motivation of drama. Father Conmee considers an historical issue of adultery as a locus for the impossibility of certitudes. He thinks "Who could know the truth?" of whether Mary, countess of Belvedere, committed adultery with her husband's brother (*U*, 10.166). The men in the cabman's shelter in "Aeolus" pronounce upon Parnell's adultery with Kitty O'Shea but hide ignorance and falsehood under the guise of perfect understanding, "laughing immoderately, pretending to understand everything, the why and the wherefore, and in reality not knowing their own minds" (*U*, 16.1530–32). Even Stephen's other self-conscious fictions are haunted by adultery, from the "onehandled adulterer" of Nelson's pillar in the "Parable of the Plums" (*U*, 7.1018) to his thoughts of Paris in "Proteus," which begins with a tableau of multiple and reciprocal betrayal, "Belluomo rises from the bed of his wife's lover's wife" (*U*, 3.211).

39 See Tanner, who suggests that in *Ulysses* "we may say that the old contracts no longer have any force at all" (*Adultery in the Novel*, p. 15), or as the representative of a not atypical American Derrideanism Suzette Henke, who sees in the Gabler edition of *Ulysses* a "lexical play field with infinite possibilities for joyous dissemination" that "opens up a free play of signifiers" implicit in the work itself ("Reconstructing *Ulysses* in a Deconstructive Mode," in *Assessing the 1984 "Ulysses,"* eds. C. George Sandulescu and Clive Hart [Totowa, New Jersey: Barnes and Noble Books, 1986], pp. 88, 90). Karen Lawrence reads the multiple styles of *Ulysses* as successive breaks in the implicit "narrative contracts" between writer and reader, her choice of terminology suggesting the tenacious and lingering presence even of transgressed agreements (*Odyssey of Style*, p. 6).

40 For differing discussions of the narrative norm or "initial style" of the early chapters of *Ulysses* see, among others, Hayman, *Mechanics of Meaning*, pp. 88–93), Lawrence, *Odyssey of Style* (pp. 40–41), Kenner, *Joyce's Voices*, pp. xii–xiii), and Riquelme, *Teller and Tale* (pp. 152–82). Riquelme has noted the relevance of "adultery" as stylistic category in *Ulysses*. While he refers in passing to "a kind of polygamy" in the book's narrative he recuperates its relationship to Stephen's lecture by finding that it helps to illuminate "the epical wanderings in style as the artist's image" (*Teller and Tale*, p. 183). Richard Brown notes that adultery provides *Ulysses* with "the basis of its surest affective appeal," but separates affect implicitly from the book's narrative experimentation (*Joyce and Sexuality*, p. 19).

41 Eugene Jolas, "The Revolution of Language and James Joyce," in *Our Exagmination Round His Factification For Incamination of Work in Progress* (New York: New Directions, 1972), pp. 86–87.
42 See *Inferno*, v, lines 89–96, and *Paradiso*, XXXI, lines 127, 142.

### 3 'THE CRACKED LOOKINGGLASS OF THE MASTER

1 One may agree with both parts of Fredric Jameson's observation that "it would not be wrong, but too simple" to read Joyce's divisions and transformations as reconfirming rather than questioning the psychic unities of the characters from which they spring, a recuperative reading made available by the relative unity of tone of Joyce's styles but denied by Lewis's "expressionism." See Jameson, *Fables of Aggression: Wyndham Lewis, The Modernist as Fascist* (Berkeley: University of California Press, 1979), pp. 57–58.
2 For the former see Kenner, for whom *The Apes* is the production of a "placarded determination not to write like Joyce" (*Wyndham Lewis*, [Norfolk: New Directions Books, 1954], p. 106). For the latter see John Gawsworth, who reads the relationship between Joyce and Lewis according to Lewis's own intellectual schematic: "Latent, under the surface of his latest work *The Apes of God*, it is obvious to us that there lies a quarrel ... It is a quarrel with Joyce, the quarrel of Space and Time" (*Apes, Japes and Hitlerism*, [London: Unicorn Press, 1932], p. 49). Pound, however, recognized *The Apes* as one of a trilogy of "live books" that were "the REAL history of the ERA," "that is the series Ulysses, cummings' EIMI and Lewis's Apes of God." Pound also claimed "I prefer THE APES OF GOD to anything Mr Joyce has written since Molly finished her Mollylogue with her ultimate affirmation." (See *Pound/Joyce: The Letters of Ezra Pound to James Joyce, with Pound's Essays on Joyce*, ed. Forrest Read [New York: New Directions, 1967], pp. 240, 268, 272).
3 Reprinted as frontispiece to *The Apes of God*. Campbell's review had been commissioned and rejected as too laudatory by the *New Statesman*. Lewis published it under the title "A Rejected Review" in *Satire and Fiction*, a separate broadside issued on behalf of *The Apes*.
4 Wyndham Lewis, *Letters*, ed. W. K. Rose (Norfolk: New Directions, 1963), p. 191, letter dated July 30th, 1930 to Richard Aldington. See also his letter ca. August 1940 to Leonard Amster, in which he compares the two parenthetically as though they were in competition: "*The Apes of God* is hardly a novel, though people remember the name of that best. It is a very long book (actually longer than *Ulysses*) ... " (*Letters*, p. 273).

5 See particularly Erich Auerbach, "In The Hôtel de la Mole," in *Mimesis: The Representation of Reality in Western Literature* (Princeton University Press, 1953) pp. 454-92, and Mikhail Bakhtin's discussions of rooms and space in Dostoyevsky in *Problems of Dostoyevsky's Poetics*, ed. and trans. Caryl Emerson, *passim*.

6 For more detailed discussions of Lewis and rooms see John Russell, *Style in Modern British Fiction* (Baltimore: Johns Hopkins University Press, 1978) and Jameson, who allows Lewis's spatial concerns to inflect his metaphors when he notes in his discussion "there exists no ready-made corridor between the sealed chamber of stylistic investigation and that equally unventilated space in which the object of study is reconstituted as narrative structure" (See *Fables of Aggression*, pp. 7, 42-43).

7 One may note, however, that by the time of *Self Condemned* (1954) the room fulfills both roles: it is both protection against World War Two and the enclosure for the bitter dissolution of a marriage, synonymous with its human inhabitants: "He was not looking at a room but at a life... The Room was him, it was them" (*Self Condemned* [Santa Barbara: Black Sparrow Press, 1983], p. 281).

8 Jameson comes to an analogous conclusion about Lewis's rooms, reading them – to appropriate his own terminological appropriations from Deleuze and Guattari – as an aspect of "molar" rather than "molecular" form, an "occasion for a quasi-existential reflection of the narrative upon its own structural limits" (*Fables of Aggression*, p. 42).

9 It is not coincidence that in the contemporaneous and hallucinatory *The Childermass* the Joycean artist Pullman is said to dream of the apotheosis of illusory internality, "of gigantic apparitions inhabiting the dangerous hollows inside the world" (London: John Calder, 1965), p. 17.

10 Kenner, *Wyndham Lewis*, p. 107.

11 See particularly Lewis, *The Art of Being Ruled* (London: Chatto and Windus, 1926), *passim*. For an exemplary political exposition see Georg Lukács, "Reification and the Consciousness of the Proletariat" in *History and Class Consciousness: Studies in Marxist Dialectics*, trans. Rodney Livingstone (Cambridge, Mass.: The MIT Press, 1971, pp. 83-222).

12 See Eve Kosofsky Sedgwick, "Homophobia, Misogyny, and Capital: The Example of *Our Mutual Friend*" in *Between Men: English Literature and Male Homosocial Desire* (New York: Columbia University Press, 1985), pp. 161-79.

13 Beside the reference to Riah, Lewis alludes throughout to the Veneerings: in his discussion of satire Zagreus asks "Or is it that the Veneerings and the Verdurins read about themselves... *and are*

*unabashed*? (*AG*, 255), while the Finnian Shaws' private room has a "veneering" whose lack of initial capital does not hide the Dickensian reference. In the 1927 version of "Inferior Religions" Lewis listed Veneering as a paradigmatic satiric figure, exclusive from the rest of *Our Mutual Friend*, "congealed and frozen into logic, and an exuberant hysterical truth" (*WB*, 150). It is a sign both of Lewis's fictional engagement with Dickens and the corresponding maturation of Lewis's own fictions that in this 1927 version Veneering replaces Sam Weller and Jingle, who were the Dickensian examples in the earlier version of 1917 (*WB*, 316).

14 See Jonathan Swift, Preface to *The Battle of the Books* (in *The Writings of Jonathan Swift*, ed. Robert A. Greenberg and William Bowman Piper [New York: W. W. Norton, Inc., 1973], p. 375) and Oscar Wilde, Preface to *The Picture of Dorian Gray* (Oxford University Press, 1978), p. xxxiii.

15 Pound, for instance, uses Zagreus as a name for Dionysus throughout his nearly contemporary Canto XVII. See *The Cantos of Ezra Pound* (New York: New Directions Books, 1977).

16 The relationship of the Nietzschean to the Dionysiac is implicit elsewhere in Lewis. Pullman relates *The Gay Science* to the Dionysiac experience when he says of the Bailiff: "You know how gay he almost always is it's amazing – it is dionysiac he says" (Lewis, *The Childermass*, p. 79). Lewis himself writes in *Time and Western Man*: "The dynamical – or what Nietzsche called the dionysiac, and which he professed – is a *relation*, a something that *happens*, between two or more opposites, when they meet in their pyrrhic encounters" (*TWM*, 21).

17 Sir James George Frazer, *The Golden Bough: A Study in Magic and Religion, Third Edition. Part V: Spirits of the Corn and of the Wild*, vol. 1 (London: Macmillan and Company, 1919), pp. 12–13.

18 See Wyndham Lewis, *Monstre Gai* (1955) (London: John Calder, 1965), p. 108.

19 For the canonical narrative of Laocoon see Virgil's *Aeneid*, Book II.

20 Lewis was extremely impatient with Chirico's work after 1914. Although admitting Chirico was "the solitary important Italian," Lewis joined most other critics in bewailing his later lapses into neo-classicism: "Giorgio de Chirico has taken to chocolate-boxes – upon which a symbolical charger, more and more, fatigued, languidly prances" ("Super-Nature versus Super-Real" (1938), in *Wyndham Lewis on Art: Collected Writings, 1913–1956*, ed. Walter Michel and C. J. Fox, pp. 306–07). He later particularly condemned Chirico's excessive collusion with the past: "May he yet, fine workman that he is, shake off the spell of the past: which first

21 See Gotthold Lessing, *Laocoon: or The Limits of Poetry and Painting* (1766), trans. William Ross (London: J. Ridgway and Sons, 1836). Further references are to this edition. Although there is no specific evidence that Lewis knew Lessing, it is scarcely possible he did not, given his immersion in aesthetics and German philosophy. Lessing had great intellectual currency at the time, providing, for instance, Stephen Dedalus with a key figure against whom to array his aesthetic argument in *A Portrait of the Artist as a Young Man* (see *P*, 214). A sign of this currency is the fact that even Donovan, an unexceptional fellow student of Stephen's, has read the *Laocoon*, which he finds "idealistic, German, ultraprofound" (*P*, 211).

led him into a high metaphysical region, and now has betrayed him into platitude" (Review for *The Listener*, 12 May 1949, reprinted in *Wyndham Lewis on Art*, pp. 397–98).

22 The centrality of this passage for *The Apes* as a whole may be gauged not only by its appearance in the center of the book, before the massive Lenten Party scenes, but by the fact that it was the first section to appear in print, under the auspices of T. S. Eliot in *The Criterion*. See Lewis, "Mr. Zagreus and the Split-Man," *The Criterion* (2: 6) February 1924, 124–42.
23 Claude Lévi-Strauss, "The Structural Study of Myth" in *Structural Anthropology*, trans. Claire Jacobsen and Brooke Grundfest Schoepf (New York: Basic Books, 1963), pp. 206–31. Lévi-Strauss's own terms, relevant to Lewis's critique of temporality, are that myth partakes of both "reversible time" (*langue*) and "non-reversible time" (*parole*) (p. 209).
24 Frazer, *The Golden Bough*, Part V, p. 2.
25 This is in a sense also implicit in Lévi-Strauss. However imaginatively myth resolves the cultural contradictions reflected in its structure, that resolution must remain *de facto* merely symbolic.
26 See Jameson, *Fables of Aggression*, pp. 102–04. The apparent overriding of political by representational concerns – although only apparently – perhaps explains the marginality of *The Apes of God* to Jameson's argument. As we shall see, however, *The Apes of God* is surprisingly engaged with, although it revises, Jameson's central concerns.
27 There are still intimations of multi-national conflict at the Lenten Party, conceived on a European, rather than a British, scale. The poet who appears throughout the party quoting Boileau is a Finn, while the mysterious trinitarian threesome, "The Unassimilable Three" (*AG*, 357) turn out to be Hungarian reporters (*AG*, 582). In both cases representatives of marginal nationalities and representers themselves, they are a threat to the English center:

the Finn because his satiric verses from the French are all too accurate about his British hosts, the Hungarians because they "look like three friends of Guy Fawkes" (*AG*, 362), and as such are suspected of wishing to blow up England from within.

28 "Starr-Smith" suggests a "maker of stars," which has two opposed and thematically appropriate meanings. Either he is oriented with nature, the maker of stars for whom Zagreus, as an Arghol figure, is the enemy, or he is an artificial crafter of stars, an Arghol himself. In either case he is Zagreus's ambiguous reflection, as a destroying Hanp or as an untrustworthy figure for the authority of artifice—which includes the authority of the Fascist ideas he "seemed *always* to be 'broadcasting'" (*AG*, 482).

29 The magic act in general corresponds to Lewis's statement in *Men Without Art* that his arguments are not about the craft of writing or of painting, but of the "ethical or political status of these performances. It is as though an illusionist came forward and engaged us in argument as to his right to make men vanish ... and the sound reasons that he had for plunging swords into baskets, and bringing them forth dripping with innocent blood" (*MWA*, 11).

30 See, in this context, Lewis's comment at the end of "The Pole," the sketch appended to "Beau Séjour," "All the cast of the *Cherry Orchard* could be massacred easily by a single determined gunman" (*WB*, 73). Even the illusions of an art that deals with the decline of a self-deluding aristocracy are no competition for the real force of social violence whose explicit representation they exclude. Lewis's black vision of the relation between culture and anarchy may also be signaled by Dan's name. When Matthew Arnold discusses the "Hyde Park rioter" in *Culture and Anarchy* he recalls the maxim of Sir Daniel Gooch's mother about the Truss Manufactory: "*Ever remember, my dear Dan, that you should look forward to being some day manager of that concern!*" (Matthew Arnold, *Culture and Anarchy* [London: Smith, Elder and Co., 1875], pp. 58–59).

31 That Melville is closely implicated in Lewis's concerns in this passage is corroborated by *Snooty Baronet* (1932), where the title character explicitly attempts to read *Moby Dick* but encounters "some barrier beneath the surface of the words" (Santa Barbara: Black Sparrow Press, 1984), p. 61.

32 To this degree one may see in Lewis an ambiguous prolepsis of D. A. Miller's argument that "Whenever the novel censures policing power, it has already reinvented it, in *the very practice of novelistic representation*" (*The Novel and the Police* [Berkeley: University of

California Press, 1988]), p. 20. In the case of *The Apes of God* that censure is not necessary, for the police and representation fulfill the same regulatory functions. See also the section of "Vortices and Notes" in *Blast* called "Policeman and Artist," which observes "In England the Policeman is dull" and "It is finer to be an Artist than to be a Policeman!" (*B*1, 137).

33 This is the *British Gazette*, a propaganda sheet published by the government in the absence of commercial newspapers. Its reportage was predictably threatening and biased. See Charles Loch Mowat, *Britain Between the Wars 1918–1940* (University of Chicago Press, 1955), p. 320.

34 See William Ashworth, *An Economic History of England 1870–1939* (London: Methuen and Co., Ltd, 1960), p. 375.

35 According to Ashworth the leaders accomplished none of their objectives and the mineworkers on whose behalf the strike was called "had to accept complete defeat" when they continued their own strike beyond the nine days of the larger action. (See *An Economic History of England 1870–1939*, pp. 375–76). Mowat notes that although the strike was indeed the "great and dramatic event of the mid-twenties" it was "an interruption only" that "marked the end, and not the beginning, of a time of unrest and possible revolution" (See *Britain Between the Wars 1918–1940*, p. 284).

36 Frank Budgen, *James Joyce and the Making of "Ulysses"* (Bloomington and London: Indiana University Press, 1960), p. 228.

37 For Bloom as "slayer" of the suitors, see, among others, Gilbert, *James Joyce's "Ulysses"* ([New York: Vintage Books, 1955], pp. 370–83), Budgen, *James Joyce and the Making of "Ulysses"* (pp. 260–61), Goldberg, *The Classical Temper* (p. 176), and Adaline Glasheen, "Calypso" in Hart and Hayman, *James Joyce's "Ulysses": Critical Essays* ([Berkeley: University of California Press, 1974], p. 60). Dominic Manganiello presents a minority view, noting that "Bloom's opposition to violence also prevents him from 'slaying the suitors' in 'Ithaca'" (*Joyce's Politics* [London: Routledge and Kegan Paul, 1980], p. 99). Lewis was perhaps a yet more astute satiric reader of *Ulysses*, proleptically agreeing with Jennifer Levine that "the task of killing off the suitors is not so much neglected as given over to Molly, who picks them off one by one with dismissive wit in the closing episode" ("*Ulysses*," in Derek Attridge, ed. *The Cambridge Companion to James Joyce* [Cambridge University Press, 1990], p. 133).

## 4 'MINDS OF THE ANTI-COLLABORATORS

1 Adaline Glasheen, *Third Census of "Finnegans Wake"* (Berkeley: University of California Press, 1977), p. 167.
2 Thomas McGreevy, "The Catholic Element in *Work in Progress*," in Samuel Beckett et al., *Our Exagmination Round His Factification for Incamination of Work in Progress* (New York: New Directions, 1972), p. 127. McGreevy refers to *Tales told of Shem and Shaun* (Black Sun Press, August 1929).
3 William Carlos Williams, "A Point for American Criticism," in *Our Exagmination*, p. 184. West was one of Lewis's earliest praisers, and called *Tarr* in an early review "a beautiful and serious work of art" whose Kreisler "reminds us of Dostoevsky" (See West, "'Tarr,'" 1918 review reprinted in *Agenda* [7: 3 and 8: 1 (Autumn – Winter 1969–70)], 67). Joyce himself identified West's book with Lewis. As he wrote to Harriet Shaw Weaver on 20 September 1928, "It is a pity that W. L. did not wait for its publication too as it would probably have much mollified his attack" (*Selected Letters*, ed. Richard Ellmann, p. 337).
4 Marcel Brion, trans. Robert Sage, "The Idea of Time in the Work of James Joyce," in *Our Exagmination*, pp. 26, 31.
5 Robert Sage, "Before *Ulysses* – and After," in *Our Exagmination*, p. 157.
6 See, for instance, David Corbett, "Lewis in *Finnegans Wake*" (*Enemy News* no. 14, 1981, 10–17); William F. Dohmen, "Chilly Spaces: Wyndham Lewis as Ondt" (*James Joyce Quarterly* 11: 4 [Summer 1974], 368–86); Dougald McMillan, "*transition* in the Wake: Friends and the Enemy," in "*transition*": *The History of a Literary Era 1927–1938* (New York: Georges Brazillier, 1976), pp. 204–31; and Dennis Brown, *Intertextual Dynamics within the Literary Group – Joyce, Lewis, Pound and Eliot: The Men of 1914* (New York: St. Martin's Press, 1991), pp. 125–32. The best treatments of Lewis in *Finnegans Wake*, although still concerned primarily with identifications of references and local elucidations, are found in Geoffrey Wagner, "Master Joyce and Windy Nous," in *Wyndham Lewis: A Portrait of the Artist as the Enemy* (New Haven: Yale University Press, 1957), pp. 168–88, and Kenner, "The Enemy as Alter-Ego," in *Dublin's Joyce* (Bloomington: Indiana University Press, 1956), pp. 362–69.
7 Joyce's use of Vico in *Finnegans Wake* has until recently been a largely unexamined truism. He emphasized Vico's cyclical view of history when he wrote to Harriet Shaw Weaver "I would not pay overmuch attention to these theories, beyond using them for all

they are worth" (May 21, 1926, *Letters*, I, p. 241) and Samuel Beckett's essay "Dante...Bruno.Vico..Joyce" (*Our Exagmination*, pp. 3–22) established a model for Joycean criticism by reading Vico in Joyce as largely a matter of cyclical structure. Recently greater attention has been given to the role played in *Finnegans Wake* by Vico's theories of language and social organization. See *Vico and Joyce*, ed. Donald Phillip Verene (Albany: State University of New York Press, 1987) and particularly John Bishop, "Vico's 'Night of Darkness': *The New Science* and *Finnegans Wake*" in *Joyce's Book of the Dark* (Madison: University of Wisconsin Press, 1986), pp. 174–215.

8 "Dante...Bruno.Vico..Joyce," Beckett et al., *Our Exagmination*, pp. 16, 22.

9 Jean-Michel Rabaté, among others, has noted the confluence of "whole" and "hole" in this passage ("Lapsus ex machina," in Derek Attridge and Daniel Ferrer, eds., *Post-Structuralist Joyce: Essays from the French* [Cambridge University Press, 1984], p. 93).

10 All roles suggest HCE's literary affiliations with fallen kings as well as his protest that he is "as much sinned against as sinning" (*FW*, 523.9–10). They furthermore connect him to *Finnegans Wake*'s themes of incest and nihilism, particularly in the references to "nothing" and nature that cluster, as in the play, around references to Shakespeare's Lear: "perhaps there is no true noun in active nature" (*FW*, 523.10–11). For a reading of *King Lear* correlative with Joyce's attention to the submerged theme of father/daughter incest in the play, see Sigmund Freud, "The Theme of the Three Caskets" (in *The Standard Edition of the Complete Psychological Works of Sigmund Freud*, trans. James Strachey [London: Hogarth Press, 1957–74], vol. 12, pp. 289–302). "Laoghaire" is both Irish high king and part of the Irish landscape, the name also belonging to the port of Dun Laoghaire, once Kingstown.

11 Roland McHugh notes in *Annotations to "Finnegans Wake*," revised edition (Baltimore: Johns Hopkins University Press, 1991), that "namar" is Hebrew for "tiger" or "leopard," which suggests the antithetical presence of a figure for absence with a figure of animal potency and strength (p. 374). I have drawn throughout on McHugh's work.

12 See Joyce, *Dubliners* (New York: The Viking Press, 1961), p. 9.

13 Postcard to Harriet Shaw Weaver 16 April 1927, *Letters of James Joyce*, I, ed. Stuart Gilbert (New York: The Viking Press, 1957), p. 251.

14 For the former, see particularly Margot Norris, *The Decentered Universe of "Finnegans Wake"* (Baltimore: Johns Hopkins Uni-

versity Press, 1976) and the essays in *Post-Structuralist Joyce*. There is now ample testimony to the latter. When J. Hillis Miller notes in a defense of literary deconstruction that nihilism and metaphysics fight a "brother battle" in language, "Shem replacing Shaun, and Shaun Shem" it is with the knowledge, as he notes elsewhere, that Derrida was heavily if "rather covertly" influenced by a reading of *Finnegans Wake* in the 1950s (See "The Critic as Host" in Harold Bloom et al., *Deconstruction and Criticism* [New York: Seabury Press, 1979], p. 230) and "From Narrative Theory to Joyce; From Joyce to Narrative Theory" in *The Seventh of Joyce*, ed. Bernard Benstock [Bloomington: Indiana University Press, 1982], p. 4). Derrida has himself admitted "... *l'ensemble de 'La pharmacie de Platon' n'était qu' 'une lecture de Finnegans Wake'*" ("The whole of 'Plato's Pharmacy' is nothing but a reading of *Finnegans Wake*") ("*Deux mots pour Joyce*" in *Ulysse gramophone*, p. 29). Indeed, the single word "soorcelossness," which combines "sourcelessness" and "loss of a source" suggests the central argument of Derrida's seminal essay "Structure, Sign, and Play in the Discourse of the Human Sciences" (see *Writing and Difference*, trans. Alan Bass [University of Chicago Press, 1978], pp. 278–93).

15 The enigma of the father has earlier been presented in terms of clothing in *Ulysses*, where the ghostly king of Stephen's lecture appears "in the vesture of buried Denmark," the "castoff mail of a court buck" (*U*, 9.165, 174–75).

16 One notes in Carlyle, however, a greater willingness to afford significance to the phenomenal surface. Harking to another of Joyce's influences, Sterne, his Teufelsdröckh states "'For indeed, as Walter Shandy often insisted, there is much, nay almost all, in Names... Could I unfold the influence of Names, which are the most important of all Clothings, I were a second greater Trismegistus.'" (See *Sartor Resartus* in "*Sartor Resartus*" and "*On Heroes and Hero Worship*" [London: J. M. Dent and Sons Ltd., 1975], p. 66). Like Joyce, however, Carlyle was concerned with the double nature of the phenomenal sign as both carrier and barrier to meaning: "Of kin to the so incalculable influences of Concealment, and connected with still greater things, is the wondrous agency of *Symbols*. In a Symbol there is concealment and yet revelation: here therefore, by Silence and by Speech acting together, comes a double significance" (*Sartor Resartus*, p. 165).

17 Giambattista Vico, trans. Thomas Goddard Bergin and Max Harold Fisch, *The New Science* (Ithaca: Cornell University Press, 1970), paragraph 448. (Further references are to paragraph numbers of this edition, which will be noted in the text as *NS*).

Vico's prolepsis of the French psychoanalytical positioning of linguistic origin in the paternal prohibition was probably not lost on Joyce, who claimed however "my imagination grows when I read Vico as it doesn't when I read Freud or Jung" (Richard Ellmann, *James Joyce: New and Revised Edition*, p. 693).

18 See Bishop, *Joyce's Book of the Dark*, chapter 7.
19 *Sacra Congregatio de Propaganda Fide*, according to McHugh, is the name of the Vatican's headquarters for missionary work, and therefore the etymological source for the modern sense of "propaganda."
20 See the satiric verse that begins "Let the Brothels of Paris be opened" in *The Complete Poetry and Prose of William Blake*, newly revised edition, ed. David V. Erdman (Berkeley: University of California Press, 1982), p. 499.
21 Besides the well known folk story about earwigs burrowing into the brain through the ear, the insect was also reputed, probably because of its rear pincers, to fight against itself if divided in two. This was a favorite metaphor of Lewis's, appearing at least three times in his work, both before and after the publication of *Finnegans Wake*: "You can divide a person against himself, unless he is very well organized: as the two halves of a severed earwig become estranged and fight with each other when they meet" (*The Art of Being Ruled* [London: Chatto and Windus, 1926], p. 229); "An earwig, or an ant, similarly, cut in half, engages in mortal combat with itself" (*TWM*, 326 [1928]); "The two halves of a severed earwig become estranged and do battle when they meet. So with a 'self,' once it is thoroughly dissociated from the other segments of the individual" (*Rude Assignment: A Narrative of My Career Up-to-date* [London: Hutchinson and Company, 1950], p. 179).
22 See Ludwig Wittgenstein, *Tractatus Logico-Philosophicus*, Proposition 1, "*Die Welt ist alles, was der Fall ist*," "The World is all that is the Case" (London: Routledge and Kegan Paul, 1961), p. 6. Although Joyce never explicitly alludes to Wittgenstein, he was a central presence, beyond the "new Viennese school" of psychoanalysis (*U*, 9.780), in the currents of Austrian thought that Joyce acknowledges as "the wiening courses of this world" (*FW*, 546.31).
23 For a thorough discussion of Freudian dream work in *Finnegans Wake* see Norris, *Decentered Universe*, chapter 5, "Dream and Poetry." There persists controversy over the source or nature of the dream of *Finnegans Wake*, and indeed the number of dreams it may represent, considerations which are ultimately as unfruitful as arguments over many other unresolvable mysteries in Joyce's work. (On this larger subject see Phillip H. Herring, *Joyce's*

*Uncertainty Principle* [Princeton University Press, 1987]). Kenner hedges his bets on the relevance of Freudian analysis to *Finnegans Wake*, insisting on the autonomy of its language while understanding its potential psychic underpinnings: "This is Freudian dream-work, if one likes, but it is also a universe of independent words obeying their chemical affinities with no restraint from things" (*Dublin's Joyce*, p. 303).

24 See Freud, "The Dream Work," chapter VI of *The Interpretation of Dreams* (in *The Standard Edition of the Complete Psychological Works of Sigmund Freud*, vols. 4–5, pp. 277–509).

25 Mahaffey notes that the punning relationship of "son" and "sun" is implicit also in *Ulysses*, particularly in the title of the Circean book "*Was Jesus a Sun Myth?*" (*U*, 15.1579) (*Reauthorizing Joyce*, p. 16). For Joyce's use of heliotrope as motif throughout his work see Norris, "Joyce's Heliotrope" (in *Coping with Joyce*, eds. Morris Beja and Shari Benstock [Columbus: Ohio State University Press, 1989], pp. 3–24). *Finnegans Wake*'s play with heliotrope as figure of representation is implicit behind Derrida's "White Mythology: Metaphor in the Text of Philosophy" (*Margins of Philosophy*, trans. Alan Bass [University of Chicago Press, 1982], pp. 207–71).

26 For Joyce's use of printer's terms throughout *Finnegans Wake*, see John Paul Riquelme, *Teller and Tale in Joyce's Fiction*, chapter 1.

27 Here Joyce wittily blends Lewis with Joseph Collins, ambivalent American critic of *Ulysses*, who noted that Joyce "has been violently rocking the boat of literature" and continues, stretching the metaphor, "his craft has had various names: first 'The Dubliners [sic],' and last 'Ulysses.'" Collins objects to the morality of *Ulysses* and further alludes to Kraft-Ebbing, clinical specialist in perversion (See *The Doctor Looks at Literature: Psychological Studies of Life and Letters* [New York: George H. Doran Company, 1923], pp. 35, 53). See also note 33 below.

28 This is a favorite Lewis expression. In *Blasting and Bombardiering* he writes, referring to *Tarr*, "I started as a novelist and set a small section of the Thames on fire" ([Berkeley: University of California Press, 1967], p. 5). In *Finnegans Wake* the second such reference is followed closely by Shaun's observation that Shem is "as innocent and undesignful as the freshfallen calef" (*FW*, 426.12–13), an allusion to Lewis's 1919 pamphlet *The Caliph's Design: Architects! Where is your Vortex?* (reprinted in *Wyndham Lewis on Art: Collected Writings, 1913–1956*, ed. Walter Michel and C. J. Fox, pp. 129–83).

29 The passage satirizes Lewis's introduction: "I will go over my credentials. I am an artist – if that is a credential. I am a novelist, painter, sculptor, philosopher, draughtsman, critic, politician,

journalist, essayist, pamphleteer, all rolled into one, like one of those portmanteau-men of the Italian Renaissance" (*Blasting and Bombardiering*, p. 3).

30 See *Blasting and Bombardiering*, p. 265–70. Richard Ellmann, who reports Lewis's account, quotes an unpublished letter to Pound in which Joyce implies that the package contained a suit rather than shoes. The associations with footwear in *Finnegans Wake* suggest either that Lewis was accurate or, in keeping with the historiography of *Finnegans Wake*, that Joyce complicates the transmission of historical "fact" by following Lewis's version of events (Ellmann, *James Joyce: New and Revised Edition*, p. 493).

31 There may also be an allusion here to the epigraph, from Guy de Maupassant, that Lewis uses for his *Men Without Art*, implying that the essential self is covered by superficial garb: "I am going to make you a rather original proposal. Supposing we all of us take off our shoes and stockings so that we can see in what condition are our respective feet" (*MWA*, 7).

32 "Professor Jones" equals "Lewis" in the role of pedant insofar as "Jones" and "Lewis" are common Welsh surnames. See the rhomboids and trapezoids that compose Lewis's "Portrait of an Englishwoman," 1913 (plate 146) in Walter Michel, *Wyndham Lewis: Paintings and Drawings* (Berkeley: University of California Press, 1971), also reproduced in *Blast* 1 between the title and the text of *Enemy of the Stars*. (McHugh misidentifies this allusion as referring to Lewis's considerably less experimental "Girl Sewing," 1921 [*Wyndham Lewis: Paintings and Drawings*, plate 461]).

33 As a representative of the satiric forms Lewis called "tyros" (in *Finnegans Wake* the "puir tyron" [*FW*, 163.9] who runs the "tyrondynamon machine" [*FW*, 163.30]), "The Cept" portrays a primitive "beginner." See the cover of *The Tyro*, no. 1, reproduced in *Wyndham Lewis: Painting and Drawings* (plate 451). This passage also satirizes Joseph Collins, who notes in the first chapter of *The Doctor Looks at Literature*, "Psychology and Fiction," that "Recognition of the existence of the two primitive urges, the instincts of self-preservation and of the preservation of the race, is the first step towards appreciation of their reasonable limitations and the extent to which they may be brought into harmony with the requirements of a well-balanced life" (p. 21). The "primitive sept" is also the "first step" towards the "primitive" "urge" and "widerurge" of self and racial preservation. Collins's psychologically naive faith in the simplicity of the "well-balanced life" is given the lie throughout *Finnegans Wake*, not least by his imbrication here with Lewis.

34 That is to say, not simply "theological" or "theosophical" in our search for origins and "disgusted" at our inability to do so, but also disturbed in our "esophagus." For as the transformation of "superficies" into "supperfishies" has already suggested, the phenomenal in *Finnegans Wake*, and particularly the visual, is frequently invoked as food, a matter of Lewisian consumption, "that fat mass you browse on" (*B*2, 91). See particularly Professor Jones's lecture on Burrus and Caseous, in which *Finnegans Wake*'s issues of representation are superimposed by Shaun onto a matrix that includes both regicide (Brutus and Cassius) and dairy products (butter and cheese), Lewis's satiric character the "tyro" leveled with Gr. *tyros*, "cheese" (*FW*, 161–67).

35 See Psalm 115, ll. 5–6 "... *oculos habent, et non videbunt. Aures habent, et non audient*" ("... eyes have they, but they see not: They have ears but they hear not" [trans., King James Version]).

36 The radio or wireless becomes a figure throughout *Finnegans Wake* for the Vichian thunder insofar as it is a paternal transmission of the audible through the atmosphere, from the quiz show of I.vi to the "tolvtubular high fidelity daildialler" (*FW*, 309.14) of II.iii and the "man made static" (*FW*, 309.22) of its "Rowdiose" (*FW*, 324.18) program. As in the absence of the father there is no voice from the heavens, this becomes in modern terms the absence of a daily broadcast – there is "nought a wired from the wordless either" (*FW*, 223.34) ("Not a word from the wireless ether").

37 For more on sight, sound, and the dreaming subject see *Joyce's Book of the Dark, passim*. References to the cinema abound. "Silver on the Screen" (*FW*, 134.10) takes on Godlike status in Shem's epithet "thank Movies" (*FW*, 194.2); *Finnegans Wake* as a whole describes itself as an "allnights newseryreel" (*FW*, 489.35); Shaun as Coemghen is a "Moviefigure on in scenic section" (*FW*, 602.27), a character in "our moving pictures" (*FW*, 565.6). Joyce's interest in cinema is a matter of biographical record – see Ellmann on his part in establishing the first cinema in Dublin and his discussion with Sergei Eisenstein about filming *Ulysses* (*James Joyce*, pp. 301–04, 654). His use of film, and to a lesser extent the "*verbivocovisual*" (*FW*, 341.18) technology of television, suggests the insight reclaimed by later French film theory that the form of the cinematic experience is in and of itself analogous to the dream state, an insight parallel to, and yet separate from those of the Surrealists, who drew on the content and techniques of dreams for their films. See particularly Christian Metz, *Le signifiant imaginaire: psychanalyse et cinéma* (Paris: Union générale d'Éditions, 1977).

38 "Vacticanated" suggests both the Mookse's secondary identity as

Pope Adrian ("vatican") and an echo of the mania over Jimmy's vaccination in *The Apes of God*, another of that novel's motifs of defense against threatened invasion. (See "Pamela Farnham's Tea Party" in *The Apes of God*). By claiming "I am superbly in my supremest poncif!" (*FW*, 154.12–13) Lewis as Mookse not only insists upon his identity as "pontiff" but also reveals the badness of his art. *Poncif*, the French equivalent of *kitsch*, was an insult hurled at the vulgarity of bourgeois taste by the French avant-garde (See Poggioli, *The Theory of the Avant-Garde*, trans. Gerald Fitzgerald, pp. 37, 80).

39 Dounia Bunis Christiani notes that "*ondt*" is Danish for "an evil, a pain." (*Scandanavian Elements of "Finnegans Wake"* [Evanston: Northwestern University Press, 1965, p. 18]).

40 This juxtaposition recalls Lewis's objection in *Time and Western Man* that the interior monologue of Bloom in *Ulysses* imitates the dialogue of Mr. Jingle in Dickens's *Pickwick Papers*. This objection is echoed throughout *Finnegans Wake* where Shaun calls Shem "General Jinglesome" (*FW*, 229.5–6) and "Mr Jinglejoys" (*FW*, 466.18), and where the "tales all tolled" of the schoolroom are said to be "Traduced into jinglish janglage" (*FW*, 275.24, F6), even where Kersse the tailor speaks "norjankeltian" (*FW*, 311.22), an apparently "jangling" form of Norwegian.

41 See Lewis on Tarr meeting Hobson, his own disliked complement – "it was a defeat and *insanitary* to have their bodies shuffling and gesticulating there" (*T*, 12, emphasis mine).

42 This idea appears elsewhere in *Finnegans Wake* as "In the beginning was the gest" (*FW*, 468.5) and earlier in the "Circe" chapter of *Ulysses*, where a drunken Stephen muses upon the Vichian idea that "gesture, not music not odour, would be a universal language" (*U*, 15.105–06).

43 This observation is perhaps implicit (on a Joycean rather than Vichian level) in the title if not the analysis of Jameson's study, *Fables of Aggression*.

44 For historical background on Peter the Painter, see James Joll, *The Anarchists* (Boston: Little, Brown and Company), pp. 176–78. Joyce was interested by the non-violent aspects of anarchism, reading in Bakunin and making Shem "anarchistically respectsful of the liberties of the noninvasive individual" (*FW*, 72.16–17). See Dominic Manganiello, *Joyce's Politics*, chapters 3 and 5.

45 Manganiello, *Joyce's Politics*, p. 122.

46 The reference is to Lewis's fellow-traveling (on "hikler's high-ways" [*FW*, 410.8]) with National Socialism in the 1930s, which he saw as Europe's best hope against Communism (see both *Hitler*

[London: Chatto and Windus, 1931] and his later recantation *The Hitler Cult* [London: Dent, 1939]).
47 See Lewis, *The Childermass* (London: John Calder, 1965), p. 146.
48 This preference is indicated by nomination; ALP is identified as "mother of Shem" but HCE is identified as "father of Shaun" (*FW*, 420.18–19).
49 This axiom is often presented simplistically as the unity of contraries. The clearest statement of the idea occurs toward the end of *Finnegans Wake*, when Muta asks Juva, in what is probably the book's longest continuous passage of standard English, "So that when we shall have acquired unification we shall pass on to diversity and when we shall have passed on to diversity we shall have acquired the instinct of combat and when we shall have acquired the instinct of combat we shall pass back to the spirit of appeasement?" (*FW*, 610.23–27).
50 The Mookse is "our once in only Bragspear" (*FW*, 152.32–33), which plays Adrian's secular name Nicolas Brakespeare. Not coincidentally this issue, which conflates England's secular and religious control over Ireland, is also raised in the most Vichian chapter of *Ulysses*, "Oxen of the Sun," where Dixon refers to the "bull" "sent to our island by farmer Nicholas" "by lord Harry's orders" (*U*, 14.582–83, 617–18), the *laudibiliter* having been received by Henry II.
51 The full title of the first edition of *The New Science* (1725) was *Principles of a New Science concerning the Nature of the Nations, by which are found the Principles of Another System of the Natural Law of the Gentes* (noted by Max Harold Fisch in his introduction to *The New Science*, p. xxi).
52 That is, the "desperate" and "despot" master struggling with the "foeman" of the embryonic feudal class ("feodal" as "fetal") over economic power (the feudal class loses its chains but is without money, "unsheckled"). Actual films cited in *Finnegans Wake* as formal examples of resolution between the visual and audible have similarly strong narratives of revolution and class strife. Eisenstein's *Potemkin* ("Patomkin" [*FW*, 290.F7]), D. W. Griffith's *Birth of a Nation* ("birth of an otion" [*FW*, 309.12]), even the screwball comedy *My Man Godfrey* ("Mind mand gunfree" [*FW*, 387.35]) deal respectively with strike, civil war, and class tension during the American Depression.
53 For the former see the work of the *Tel Quel* group, some of which is represented in *Post-Structuralist Joyce*. Joyce was himself pleased to think that *Finnegans Wake* was prophetic of contemporary political events. He saw in the resistance of the Finns during the

Russians' November 1939 invasion of their country confirmation, as he wrote to Daniel Brody on 10 January 1940, that "the 'Finn again wakes'" (*The Letters of James Joyce*, III, ed. Richard Ellmann, p. 464). After an early enthusiasm, however, Joyce lost faith in organized socialism, which is reflected throughout *Finnegans Wake*.

54 For fuller discussions of allusions to contemporary politics in *Finnegans Wake* see Bernard Benstock, *Joyce-Again's Wake* (Seattle: University of Washington Press, 1965), pp. 42–68 and Manganiello, *Joyce's Politics*, pp. 175–89, 223–34.

55 The Bailiff in *The Childermass* complains in mock-Joycean language about Vico and solipsism in *Work in Progress* ("wirk-on-the-way"): "with Vico the mechanical for guide in the musty labrinths of the latter-days to train him to circle true and make true orbit upon himself" (*The Childermass*, pp. 175–76).

56 The confluence of "millenary" (referring to Vico's thousand-year cycles) and "military" subtly echoes *Finnegans Wake*'s representational conflict of space and time. Taken together they remind one that Shem has earlier been "Wanted for millinary servance" (*FW*, 125.10). By combining battle and historical duration into hat-making ("millinery") Joyce intertwines themes of representation with Carlyle's philosophy of clothes, and specifically invokes the passage in *Sartor Resartus* in which the alternative destruction of time or space is contemplated through the fantastic medium of "Time-annihilating" and "Space-annihilating Hats" (See *Sartor Resartus*, pp. 195–97).

57 Lewis registers his disapproval of a dialectical (which is a temporal) vision of reality by quoting disparagingly from Bosanquet in the introduction of *Time and Western Man*: "*in its basis and meaning reality is a history or an unending dialectical progress*" (*TWM*, xiii). One notes however, that Marx and Vico are not incompatible as visions of social history *per se*. Marx alludes to Vico in *Das Kapital* as a philosophic influence – "Does not the history of the productive organs of man in society, of organs that are the material basis of every particular organization of society, deserve equal attention [as the history of natural technology]? And would not such a history be easier to compile, since, as Vico says, human history differs from natural history in that we have made the former, but not the latter?" (Karl Marx, trans. Ben Fowkes, *Das Kapital*, vol. I [New York: Vintage Books, 1976]), p. 493f.

58 See, for instance, the argument of Georg Lukács in *Realism in Our Time*, trans. John and Necke Mander (New York: Harper and Row, 1964).

59 See Glasheen, *Third Census*, p. 56.

60 This motto appears in progressively more distorted form as "the hearsomeness of the burger felicitates the whole of the polis" (*FW*, 23.15), "the obedience of the citizens elp the ealth of the ole" (*FW*, 76.8–9), "Thine obesity, O civilian, hits the felicitude of our orb" (*FW*, 140.6–7), "the boxomeness of the bedelias makes hobbyhodge happy in his hole" (*FW*, 265.30–266.1–2), "happy burgages abeyance would make homesweetstown hopeygoalucrey" (*FW*, 358.8–9), and "Obeisance so their sitinins is the follicity of this Orp!" (*FW*, 494.21–22).

CONCLUSION

1 Stephen equates homosexuality with incest through Aquinas, who objects that such desire is a hoarding or "avarice of the emotions" (*U*, 9.781), an extreme adherence to unity rather than the multiplicity of normal heterosexuality.
2 Jameson, *Fables of Aggression: Wyndham Lewis, The Modernist as Fascist*, chapter 5.
3 In 1914 Freda Graham slashed five pictures at the National Gallery, earning Lewis's "blessing" in *Blast* (as "Freider Graham" [*B*1, 28]) as a critic of bad art. However, when a hatchet-bearing suffragette destroyed two drawings at the Doré Gallery, where the Vorticists themselves exhibited, Lewis protested: "IN DESTRUCTION, AS IN OTHER THINGS, stick to what you understand ... YOU MIGHT SOME DAY DESTROY A GOOD PICTURE BY ACCIDENT." He continues, however, "WE ADMIRE YOUR ENERGY. YOU AND ARTISTS ARE THE ONLY THINGS (YOU DON'T MIND BEING CALLED THINGS?) LEFT IN ENGLAND WITH A LITTLE LIFE IN THEM" (*B*, 151). See William C. Wees, *Vorticism and the English Avant-Garde* (University of Toronto Press, 1972), p. 19.
4 T. S. Eliot, *Complete Poems and Plays* (London and Boston: Faber and Faber, 1969), p. 59.
5 Wyndham Lewis, *The Lion and the Fox* (London, Grant Richards Ltd., 1927), p. 187, and Friedrich Nietzsche, Preface to the second edition, *The Gay Science*, trans. Walter Kaufmann (New York: Vintage Books, 1974), p. 33.
6 That this is true of Jameson's interest in Lewis is self-evident. Pierre Machery's argument in *A Theory of Literary Production* (trans. Geoffrey Wall [London: Routledge and Kegan Paul, 1978]) on the parodic and deforming nature of literary language shares essential features with Lewis's satiric aesthetic, while the shift in Lewis's treatment of the image between "Bestre" and *The Apes of God* adumbrates the middle pair of what Jean Baudrillard has

described as the "successive phases of the image: – It is the reflection of a basic reality – It masks and perverts a basic reality – It masks the *absence* of a basic reality – It bears no relation to any reality whatever: it is its own pure simulacrum" ("The Precession of Simulacra" in *Simulations*, trans. Paul Foss, Paul Patton, Philip Beitchman [New York: Semiotext(e), 1983], p. 11). That Lewis draws back before Baudrillard's final stage I have shown in my reading of *The Apes of God*, and is also suggested by Lewis's criticism of what he perceives in Joyce: "There is no department that is exempt from the confusions of this strategy – which consists essentially in removing something necessary to life and putting an ideologic simulacrum where it was" (*TWM*, 80).

7 T. E. Hulme, "Humanism and the Religious Attitude" in *Speculations: Essays on Humanism and the Philosophy of Art*, ed. Herbert Read (New York: Harcourt, Brace and Company, Inc., 1924), p. 4. Lewis noted "All the best things Hulme said about the theory of art were said about my art" (Lewis, *Blasting and Bombardiering* [Berkeley: University of California Press, 1967], p. 100).

8 That Lewis was on some level aware of the presence of the ideal in his work is suggested as early as 1922, where he protests too strongly "If you conclude from this that I am treading the road to the platonic heaven, my particular road is deliberately chosen for the immanent satisfactions that may be found by the way" ("Essay on the Objective of Plastic Art in Our Time," in *Wyndham Lewis on Art: Collected Writings, 1913–1956*. ed. Walter Michel and C. J. Fox, p. 208).

9 One sees this biographically in Lewis's late embrace of the Catholic Church, and fictionally in the later turns of *The Human Age*. This surprising move towards Joyce's own rejected absolute was uncannily perceived as early as 1914 by a satirist in *The Egoist*, who noted that although "blighted by the anaemia of abstractions" the "Destiny" of "Mr. W\*\*\*\*\*\* L\*\*\*\*" could be "the Order of Jesus" (John Felton, "Contemporary Caricatures," *The Egoist*, 1: 15 [August 1, 1914], 297).

# Bibliography

Adams, Robert Martin. *Surface and Symbol: The Consistency of James Joyce's "Ulysses."* New York: Oxford University Press, 1962.
Aldington, Richard. "The Influence of Mr. James Joyce." *English Review*, 32, April 1921, 333–41.
Aligheri, Dante. *Inferno*, with trans. and commentary by John D. Sinclair. New York: Oxford University Press, 1978.
  *Paradiso*, with trans. and comment by John D. Sinclair. New York: Oxford University Press, 1977.
*American Dictionary of Printing and Bookmaking.* New York: Howard Lockwood and Co., 1894.
Aristotle. *Metaphysics*, in *Works of Aristotle*, vol. VIII, trans. under the editorship of W. D. Ross. Oxford: Clarendon Press, 1972.
Arnold, Matthew. *Culture and Anarchy*. London: Smith, Elder and Co., 1875.
Ashworth, William. *An Economic History of England 1870–1939*. London: Methuen and Co. Ltd., 1960.
Attridge, Derek, ed. *The Cambridge Companion to James Joyce*. Cambridge University Press, 1990.
Attridge, Derek and Daniel Ferrer, eds. *Post-Structuralist Joyce: Essays from the French*. Cambridge University Press, 1984.
Auerbach, Erich. *Mimesis: The Representation of Reality in Western Literature*. Princeton University Press, 1953.
Ayers, David. *Wyndham Lewis and Western Man*. New York: St. Martin's Press, 1992.
Bakhtin, Mikhail, ed. and trans. Caryl Emerson. *Problems of Dostoevsky's Poetics*. University of Minnesota Press, 1984.
Baudrillard, Jean, trans. Paul Foss, Paul Patton, Philip Beitchman. *Simulations*. New York: Semiotext(e), 1983.
Beckett, Samuel et al. *Our Exagmination Round His Factification for Incamination of Work in Progress*. New York: New Directions Books, 1972.
Beja, Morris and Shari Benstock, eds. *Coping with Joyce*. Columbus: Ohio State University Press, 1989.

Benstock, Bernard. *Joyce-Again's Wake*. Seattle: University of Washington Press, 1965.
Benstock, Bernard, ed. *Critical Essays on James Joyce*. Boston: G. K. Hall and Co., 1985.
*The Seventh of Joyce*. Bloomington: Indiana University Press, 1982.
Bergson, Henri. *Time and Free Will*, trans. F. L. Pogson. London: George Allen and Unwin Ltd, 1950.
Bishop, John. *Joyce's Book of the Dark*. Madison: University of Wisconsin Press, 1986.
Blake, William. *The Complete Poetry and Prose of William Blake*, newly revised edition ed. David V. Erdman. Berkeley: University of California Press, 1982.
Bloom, Harold, et al. *Deconstruction and Criticism*. New York: Seabury Press, 1979.
Brown, Dennis. *Intertextual Dynamics within the Literary Group – Joyce, Lewis, Pound and Eliot: The Men of 1914*. New York: St. Martin's Press, 1991.
Brown, Richard. *Joyce and Sexuality*. Cambridge University Press, 1985.
Budgen, Frank. "Further Recollections of James Joyce." *Partisan Review*, 23: 4 (Fall, 1956), 530–44.
*James Joyce and the Making of "Ulysses."* Bloomington and London: Indiana University Press, 1960.
Campbell, SueEllen. *The Enemy Opposite: The Outlaw Criticism of Wyndham Lewis*. Athens: Ohio University Press, 1988.
Carlyle, Thomas. *"Sartor Resartus" and "On Heroes and Hero Worship."* London: J. M. Dent and Sons Ltd., 1975.
Chapman, Robert T. *Wyndham Lewis: Fictions and Satires*. London: The Vision Press, 1973.
Christiani, Dounia Bunis. *Scandanavian Elements of "Finnegans Wake."* Evanston: Northwestern University Press, 1965.
Collins, Joseph. *The Doctor Looks at Literature: Psychological Studies of Life and Letters*. New York: George H. Doran Company, 1923.
Conrad, Joseph. *Lord Jim*. Middlesex: Penguin Books, 1986.
Corbett, David. "Lewis in *Finnegans Wake*." *Enemy News*, 14, 1981, 10–17.
Cork, Richard. *Vorticism and Abstract Art in the First Machine Age*. Berkeley and Los Angeles: University of California Press, 1976.
Currie, Robert. *Genius: An Ideology in Literature*. London: Chatto and Windus, 1974.
Dasenbrock, Reed Way. *The Literary Vorticism of Ezra Pound and Wyndham Lewis*. Baltimore: Johns Hopkins University Press, 1985.
De Man, Paul. *Blindness and Insight: Essays in the Rhetoric of Contemporary*

*Criticism*, second edition, revised. Minneapolis: University of Minnesota Press, 1981.
Derrida, Jacques. *Dissemination*, trans. Barbara Johnson. University of Chicago Press, 1981.
  *Margins of Philosophy*, trans. Alan Bass. University of Chicago Press, 1982.
  *Ulysses gramophone*. Paris: Éditions Galilée, 1987.
  *Writing and Difference*, trans. Alan Bass. University of Chicago Press, 1978.
Dohmen, William F. "Chilly Spaces: Wyndham Lewis as Ondt." *James Joyce Quarterly*, 11: 4 (Summer 1974), 368–86.
Eilenberg, Susan. *Strange Power of Speech: Wordsworth, Coleridge, and Literary Possession*. New York and Oxford: Oxford University Press, 1992.
Eliot, T. S. *Complete Poems and Plays*. London and Boston: Faber and Faber, 1969.
  "Literature and the American Courts." *The Egoist*, 5: 3 (March 1918), 39.
  "A Note on *Monstre Gai*." *Hudson Review*, 7: 4 (Winter, 1955), 522–26.
  "*Ulysses*, Order and Myth." *Dial*, 75 (November 1923); reprinted in Bernard Benstock, ed. *Critical Essays on James Joyce*, Boston: G. K. Hall and Co., pp. 25–27.
Elliott, Robert C. *The Power of Satire: Magic, Ritual, Art*. Princeton University Press, 1960.
Ellmann, Richard. *The Consciousness of Joyce*. London: Faber and Faber, 1977.
  *James Joyce: New and Revised Edition*. New York: Oxford University Press, 1982.
  *Ulysses on the Liffey*. New York: Oxford University Press, 1972.
Empson, William. *Using Biography*. London: Chatto and Windus/The Hogarth Press, 1984.
Epstein, E. L. "Nestor," in Clive Hart and David Hayman, eds., *James Joyce's "Ulysses": Critical Essays*. Berkeley: University of California Press, 1974, pp. 17–28.
Evenden, Michael. "Inter-Mediate Stages: Reconsidering the Body in 'Closet Drama,'" in Catherine B. Burroughs and Jeffrey David Ehrenreich, eds., *Reading the Social Body*. University of Iowa Press, 1993, pp. 244–69.
Felton, John. "Contemporary Caricatures." *The Egoist*, 1: 15 (August 1, 1914), 297.
Flory, Wendy Stallard. "*Enemy of the Stars*," in Jeffrey Meyers, ed., *Wyndham Lewis: A Revaluation*. London: Athlone Press, 1980, pp. 92–106.

Foshay, Toby Avard. *Wyndham Lewis and the Avant-Garde: The Politics of the Intellect*. Montreal and Kingston: McGill-Queen's University Press, 1992.
Frazer, Sir James George. *The Golden Bough: A Study in Magic and Religion*, Third Edition. Part v: *Spirits of the Corn and of the Wild*, vol. 1. London: Macmillan and Company, 1919.
Freud, Sigmund, trans. James Strachey. *The Interpretation of Dreams*, in *The Standard Edition of the Complete Psychological Works of Sigmund Freud*, vols. 4–5. London: Hogarth Press, 1957–1974.
 "The Theme of the Three Caskets," in *The Standard Edition of the Complete Psychological Works of Sigmund Freud*, vol. 12. London: Hogarth Press, 1957–1974, pp. 289–302.
Gawsworth, John. *Apes, Japes and Hitlerism*. London: Unicorn Press, 1932.
Gifford, Don with Robert J. Seidman, *"Ulysses" Annotated: Notes for James Joyce's "Ulysses,"*, second edition. Berkeley: University of California Press, 1988.
Gilbert, Stuart. *James Joyce's "Ulysses."* New York: Vintage Books, 1955.
Glasheen, Adaline. "Calypso," in Clive Hart and David Hayman, eds., *James Joyce's "Ulysses": Critical Essays*. Berkeley: University of California Press, 1974, pp. 51–70.
 *Third Census of "Finnegans Wake."* Berkeley: University of California Press, 1977.
Goldberg, S. L. *The Classical Temper: A Study of James Joyce's "Ulysses."* London: Chatto and Windus, 1963.
Goldman, Arnold. *The Joyce Paradox: Form and Freedom in His Fiction*. Evanston: Northwestern University Press, 1966.
Gombrich, E. H. *Art and Illusion: A Study in the Psychology of Pictorial Representation*. New York: Pantheon Books, 1960.
Greene, Robert. *Groats-Worth of Witte*, in *The Huth Library Life and Work of Robert Greene*, Vol. XIII, ed. Rev. Alexander B. Grosart. London: Hazell, Watson and Viney, 1881–83.
Hart, Clive. *A Concordance to "Finnegans Wake."* Minneapolis: University of Minnesota Press, 1963.
 *Structure and Motif in "Finnegans Wake."* Chicago: Northwestern University Press, 1962.
Hart, Clive and David Hayman, eds. *James Joyce's "Ulysses": Critical Essays*, Berkeley: University of California Press, 1974.
Hayman, David. *"Ulysses": The Mechanics of Meaning*, revised and expanded edition. Madison: University of Wisconsin Press, 1982.
Henke, Suzette. "Reconstructing *Ulysses* in a Deconstructive Mode," in *Assessing the 1984 "Ulysses,"* eds. C. George Sandulescu and

Clive Hart. Totowa, New Jersey: Barnes and Noble Books, 1986, pp. 86–91.
Herr, Cheryl. *Joyce's Anatomy of Culture*. Urbana and Chicago: University of Illinois Press, 1986.
"'Penelope' as Period Piece." *Novel*, 22: 2, Winter 1989, 130–42.
Herring, Phillip H. *Joyce's Uncertainty Principle*. Princeton University Press, 1987.
Hulme, T. E. *Speculations: Essays on Humanism and the Philosophy of Art*, ed. Herbert Read. New York: Harcourt, Brace and Company, Inc., 1924.
Jameson, Fredric. *Fables of Aggression: Wyndham Lewis, The Modernist as Fascist*. Berkeley: University of California Press, 1979.
*The Prison-House of Language: A Critical Account of Structuralism and Russian Formalism*. Princeton University Press, 1972.
Joll, James. *The Anarchists*. Boston: Little, Brown and Company, 1964.
Joyce, James. *Dubliners*. New York: The Viking Press, 1961.
*Finnegans Wake*. New York: The Viking Press, 1939.
*The Letters of James Joyce, I*, ed. Stuart Gilbert. New York: The Viking Press, 1957.
*The Letters of James Joyce, II and III*, ed. Richard Ellmann. New York: The Viking Press, 1966.
*Poems and Shorter Writings*, ed. Richard Ellmann, A. Walton Litz, and John Whittier-Ferguson. London: Faber and Faber, 1991.
*A Portrait of the Artist as a Young Man*. New York: The Viking Press, 1975.
*Selected Letters*, ed. Richard Ellmann. New York: Viking Press, 1966.
*Stephen Hero*. New York: New Directions, 1963.
*Ulysses: The Corrected Text*, ed. Hans Walter Gabler. New York: Random House, 1986.
Kain, Richard M. *Fabulous Voyager: James Joyce's "Ulysses."* The University of Chicago Press, 1947.
Kellogg, Robert. "Scylla and Charybdis," in Clive Hart and David Hayman, eds., *James Joyce's "Ulysses": Critical Essays*. Berkeley: University of California Press, 1974, pp. 147–79.
Kenner, Hugh. *Dublin's Joyce*. Bloomington: Indiana University Press, 1956.
*Joyce's Voices*. Berkeley: University of California Press, 1978.
*The Pound Era*. Berkeley and Los Angeles: University of California Press, 1971.
*Wyndham Lewis*. Norfolk: New Directions Books, 1954.
Kinnimont, Tom. "Max Stirner and the Enemy of the Stars." *Lewisletter* no. 1, December 1974, 5–6.
Lacan, Jacques. *Ecrits: A Selection*, trans. Alan Sheridan. New York: W. W. Norton and Company, 1977.

*The Four Fundamental Concepts of Psycho-Analysis*, ed. Jacques-Alain Miller, trans. Alan Sheridan. New York: W. W. Norton and Company, 1978.
Law, Jules David. "Joyce's 'Delicate Siamese' Equation: The Dialectic of Home in *Ulysses*." *PMLA*, 102: 2, March 1987, 197–205.
Lawrence, D. H. *Women in Love*. Middlesex: Penguin Books, 1976.
Lawrence, Karen. *The Odyssey of Style in "Ulysses."* Princeton University Press, 1981.
Leavis, F. R. "Two Cultures? The Significance of Lord Snow," in *Nor Shall My Sword: Discourses On Pluralism, Compassion, and Social Hope*. London: Chatto and Windus, 1972, pp. 41–74.
Lernout, Geert. *The French Joyce*. Ann Arbor: University of Michigan Press, 1990.
Lessing, Gotthold. *Laocoon: or The Limits of Poetry and Painting*, trans. William Ross. London: J. Ridgway and Sons, 1836.
Levenson, Michael. *A Genealogy of Modernism*. Cambridge University Press, 1984.
*Modernism and the Fate of Individuality: Character and Novelistic Form from Conrad to Woolf*. Cambridge University Press, 1991.
Levin, Harry. *James Joyce: A Critical Introduction*. Revised and augmented edition. New York: New Directions, 1960; originally published 1941.
Levine, Jennifer. "*Ulysses*," in Derek Attridge, ed. *The Cambridge Companion to James Joyce*. Cambridge University Press, 1990, pp. 131–59.
Lévi-Strauss, Claude, trans. Claire Jacobsen and Brooke Grundfest Schoepf. *Structural Anthropology*. New York: Basic Books, 1963.
Lewis, Wyndham. *The Apes of God*. Santa Barbara: Black Sparrow Press, 1981.
*The Art of Being Ruled*. London: Chatto and Windus, 1926.
*The Art of Being Ruled*, critical edition, ed. Reed Way Dasenbrock. Santa Barbara: Black Sparrow Press, 1989.
*Blast*, ed. Wyndham Lewis. no. 1, June 1914; no. 2, July 1915. Reprinted Santa Barbara: Black Sparrow Press, 1981.
*Blasting and Bombardiering*. Berkeley: University of California Press, 1967.
*The Childermass*. London: John Calder, 1965.
*Collected Poems and Plays*, ed. Alan Munton. Manchester: Carcanet New Press, 1979.
*The Complete Wild Body*, ed. Bernard Lafourcade. Santa Barbara: Black Sparrow Press, 1982.
*Hitler*. London: Chatto and Windus, 1931.

*The Hitler Cult*. London: Dent, 1939.
*The Letters of Wyndham Lewis*, ed. W. K. Rose. Norfolk: New Directions, 1963.
*The Lion and the Fox*. London: Grant Richards Ltd., 1927.
*Men Without Art*. London: Cassell and Company Ltd., 1934.
*Monstre Gai*. London: John Calder, 1965.
"Mr. Zagreus and the Split-Man." *The Criterion*, 2: no. 6, February 1924, 124–42.
*Mrs. Dukes' Million*. Toronto: The Coach House Press, 1977.
*Paleface: The Philosophy of the Melting Pot*. London: Chatto and Windus, 1929.
*Rude Assignment: A Narrative of My Career Up-to-date*. London: Hutchinson and Company, 1950.
*Self Condemned*. Santa Barbara: Black Sparrow Press, 1983.
*Snooty Baronet*. Santa Barbara: Black Sparrow Press, 1984.
*Tarr* (1928 Version). Middlesex: Penguin Books, 1982.
*Time and Western Man*. New York: Harcourt, Brace and Company, 1928.
*The Tyro*, ed. Wyndham Lewis. London: The Egoist Press, no. 1, 1921; no. 2, 1922.
*Wyndham Lewis on Art: Collected Writings, 1913–1956*, ed. Walter Michel and C. J. Fox. London: Thames and Hudson, 1969.
Lukács, Georg. *History and Class Consciousness: Studies in Marxist Dialectics*, trans. Rodney Livingstone. Cambridge, Mass.: The MIT Press, 1971.
*Realism in Our Time*, trans. John and Necke Mander. New York: Harper and Row, 1964.
MacCabe, Colin. *James Joyce and the Revolution of the Word*. London: Macmillan Press, 1978.
Machery, Pierre, trans. Geoffrey Wall. *A Theory of Literary Production*. London: Routledge and Kegan Paul, 1978.
Mahaffey, Vicki. *Reauthorizing Joyce*. Cambridge University Press, 1988.
Manganiello, Dominic. *Joyce's Politics*. London: Routledge and Kegan Paul, 1980.
Marx, Karl. trans. Ben Fowkes. *Das Kapital*, vol. 1. New York: Vintage Books, 1976.
Materer, Timothy. *Vortex: Pound, Eliot, and Lewis*. Ithaca: Cornell University Press, 1979.
*Wyndham Lewis the Novelist*. Detroit: Wayne State University Press, 1976.
McHugh, Roland. *Annotations to "Finnegans Wake,"* revised edition. Baltimore: Johns Hopkins University Press, 1991.

McMillan, Dougald. *"transition": The History of a Literary Era 1927–1938.* New York: George Braziller, 1976.
Metz, Christian. *Le signifiant imaginaire: psychanalyse et cinéma.* Paris: Union générale d'Éditions, 1977.
Meyers, Jeffrey, ed. *Wyndham Lewis: A Revaluation.* London: Athlone Press, 1980.
Michel, Walter. *Wyndham Lewis: Paintings and Drawings.* Berkeley: University of California Press, 1971.
Miller, D. A. *The Novel and the Police.* Berkeley: University of California Press, 1988.
Mowat, Charles Loch. *Britain Between the Wars 1918–1940.* University of Chicago Press, 1955.
Nietzsche, Friedrich. *The Gay Science,* trans. Walter Kaufmann. New York: Vintage Books, 1974.
Noon, William T. *Joyce and Aquinas.* New Haven: Yale University Press, 1957.
Normand, Tom. *Wyndham Lewis the Artist: Holding the Mirror up to Politics.* Cambridge University Press, 1992.
Norris, Margot. *The Decentered Universe of "Finnegans Wake."* Baltimore: Johns Hopkins University Press, 1976.
"Joyce's Heliotrope," in *Coping with Joyce,* eds. Morris Beja and Shari Benstock. Columbus: Ohio State University Press, 1989, pp. 3–24.
*Joyce's Web: The Social Unraveling of Modernism.* Austin: University of Texas Press, 1992.
O'Connell, Daniel. *The Opposition Critics: The Antisymbolist Reaction in the Modern Period* (De Proprietatibus Litterarrum, Series Minor, 14). The Hague and Paris: Mouton, 1974.
Plato, trans. Walter Hamilton. *The Symposium.* Middlesex: Penguin Books, 1975.
Poe, Edgar Allan. *Poetry and Tales.* New York: Library of America, 1984.
Poggioli, Renato. *The Theory of the Avant-Garde,* trans. Gerald Fitzgerald. Cambridge: The Belknap Press of Harvard University Press, 1968.
Porteus, Hugh Gordon. *Wyndham Lewis: A Discursive Exposition.* London: Desmond Harmsworth, 1932.
Pound, Ezra. *The Cantos of Ezra Pound.* New York: New Directions, 1977.
*Gaudier-Brzeska.* New York: New Directions, 1970.
*The Literary Essays of Ezra Pound,* ed. T. S. Eliot. New York: New Directions, 1968.
*Pound/Joyce: The Letters of Ezra Pound to James Joyce, with Pound's*

*Essays on Joyce*. ed. Forrest Read. New York: New Directions, 1967.

"Wyndham Lewis." *The Egoist*, 1: 12 (June 15, 1914), 233–34.

Rabaté, Jean-Michel. *James Joyce, Authorized Reader*. Baltimore: Johns Hopkins University Press, 1991.

"Lapsus ex machina," in Derek Attridge and Daniel Ferrer, eds., *Post-Structuralist Joyce: Essays from the French*. Cambridge University Press, 1984.

Rank, Otto. *The Double*, trans. and ed. Harry Tucker, Jr. Chapel Hill: University of North Carolina Press, 1971.

Restuccia, Frances L. *Joyce and the Law of the Father*. New Haven: Yale University Press, 1989.

Richardson, Alan. *A Mental Theater: Poetic Drama and Consciousness in the Romantic Age*. University Park: Pennsylvania State University Press, 1988.

Riquelme, John Paul. *Teller and Tale in Joyce's Fiction: Oscillating Perspectives*. Baltimore: Johns Hopkins University Press, 1983.

Ruskin, John. *The Stones of Venice*, vol. 2. Boston: Dana Estes and Company, undated.

Russell, John. *Style in Modern British Fiction*. Baltimore: Johns Hopkins University Press, 1978.

Said, Edward W. *The World, The Text, and the Critic*. Cambridge, Mass.: Harvard University Press, 1983.

Sandulescu, C. George and Clive Hart, eds. *Assessing the 1984 "Ulysses."* Totowa, New Jersey: Barnes and Noble Books, 1986.

Schenker, Daniel. *Wyndham Lewis: Religion and Modernism*. Tuscaloosa and London: The University of Alabama Press, 1992.

Schutte, William. *Joyce and Shakespeare: A Study in the Meaning of "Ulysses."* New Haven: Yale University Press, 1957.

Sedgwick, Eve Kosofsky. *Between Men: English Literature and Male Homosocial Desire*. New York: Columbia University Press, 1985.

Sharp, Cecil J. and Herbert C. Macilwaine. *The Morris Book, with A Description of Dances as Performed by the Morris Men of England*, Part 1. London: Novello and Company, Ltd., 1912.

Sherry, Vincent. *Ezra Pound, Wyndham Lewis, and Radical Modernism*. New York and Oxford: Oxford University Press, 1993.

Spoo, Robert E. "'Nestor' and the Nightmare of History: The Presence of the Great War in *Ulysses*." *Twentieth Century Literature*. 32: 2, Summer 1986, 137–54.

Stirner, Max. *The Ego and His Own*, trans. Steven T. Byington, ed. John Caroll. London: Jonathan Cape, 1971.

Swift, Jonathan. *The Writings of Jonathan Swift*, ed. Robert A. Greenberg and William Bowman Piper. New York: W. W. Norton, Inc., 1973.

Symons, Julian. *Makers of the New: The Revolution in Literature, 1912–1939*. New York: Random House, 1987.
Synge, John Millington. *The Playboy of the Western World*. New York, Random House, 1935.
Tanner, Tony. *Adultery in the Novel: Contract and Transgression*. Baltimore: Johns Hopkins University Press, 1979.
Theoharis, Theoharis Constantine. *Joyce's "Ulysses": An Anatomy of the Soul*. Chapel Hill: University of North Carolina Press, 1988.
Trilling, Lionel. "The Leavis-Snow Controversy," in *Beyond Culture: Essays on Literature and Learning*. New York: Viking Press, 1965, pp. 145–77.
Verene, Donald Phillip, ed. *Vico and Joyce*. Albany: State University of New York Press, 1987.
Vico, Giambattista, trans. Thomas Goddard Bergin and Max Harold Fisch. *The New Science*. Ithaca: Cornell University Press, 1970.
Wagner, Geoffrey. *Wyndham Lewis: A Portrait of the Artist as The Enemy*. New Haven: Yale University Press, 1957.
Watt, Ian. *The Rise of the Novel*. Berkeley and Los Angeles: University of California Press, 1957.
Wees, William C. *Vorticism and the English Avant-Garde*. University of Toronto Press, 1972.
West, Rebecca. "'Tarr,'" Reprinted *Agenda*, 7: 3 – 8: 1 (Autumn–Winter 1969–70), 67–69.
Wilde, Oscar. *The Picture of Dorian Gray*. Oxford University Press, 1978.
Wittgenstein, Ludwig. *Tractatus Logico-Philosophicus*, with English trans. D. F. Pears and B. F. McGuiness. London: Routledge and Kegan Paul, 1961.
Yeats, William Butler. *The Collected Poems of W. B. Yeats*. New York: Macmillan Publishing Co., Inc., 1979.

# Index

Adams, Robert Martin, 221n.29
Adonis, 102
Adrian IV, Pope, 189
Adultery, 101, 111–12, 149, 150, 158, 187, 200
 and dialectic, 107–11
 and language, 106–07
 and style, 107–10
 and uncertainty, 222n.38
Aeschylus, 60
Aesop, 182
Aldington, Richard, 9, 115
Alienation, economic, see also 43
 reification
Allegory, 66, 171, 182
Aquinas, St. Thomas, 240n.4
 *Summa Theologiae*, 69, 217n.4
Aristotle and Aristotelianism, 6–7, 69, 86, 87, 88, 91, 92, 93, 166, 176
 *Metaphysics*, 6
Arius, 6
Arnold, Matthew: *Culture and Anarchy*, 228n.30
Artaud, Antonin, 48
Arthur Press, The, 195
Ashworth, William, 229n.34–35
Attridge, Derek, 13
Auerbach, Erich, 225n.5
Authoritarianism, 6, 190, 199, 203
Authority, 19, 23, 118, 133, 180, 188, 194, 198, 204
 challenge to, 136–37, 182
 decentering of, 126
 and falsehood, 131
 linguistic, 163
 paternal, 159, 167
 and representation, 19, 147, 172, 204
Authorship, 19–20, 186–88

Averroes, 84
Ayers, David, 211n.24

Bakhtin, Mikhail, 225n.5
Bakunin, Mikhail, 237n.44
Balla, Giacomo, 32
Balzac, Honoré de, 16, 119
Baudelaire, Charles, 28, 195
 *Les Fleurs du Mal*, 204
Baudrillard, Jean, 241n.6
Beckett, Samuel, 151, 165
 "Dante...Bruno. Vico...Joyce," 156
Beddoes, Thomas Lovell, 59
Benda, Julien, 47
Benstock, Bernard, 239n.54
Bentham, Jeremy, 184
Bergson, Henri, 2, 12, 44–46, 47, 64, 137
Berg, Alban: *Lyric Suite*, 130
Berkeley, Bishop, 41
Bishop, John, 164, 177, 231n.7
Blake, William, 78, 164, 165
Boccioni, Umberto, 32
Bomberg, David, 34
Boucicault, Dion: *Arrah-na-Pogue*, 184
Brion, Marcel, 154
*British Gazette*, 229n.33
Brown, Dennis, 212n.36, 230n.6
Brown, Richard, 220n.27, 223n.40
Bruno, Giordano, 6–7, 155, 160, 175, 179, 188
Budgen, Frank, 3, 9–12, 218n.10, 229n.37
Bürger, Peter, 210n.22
Byron, Lord: *Manfred*, 60

Campbell, Roy, 115
Campbell, SueEllen, 209n.16
Capitalism and modes of production, 43

# Index

Carlyle, Thomas: *Sartor Resartus*, 162–63, 166, 172, 178, 192, 232n.16, 239n.56
Cervantes, Saavedra, Miguel de: *Don Quixote*, 180
Chapman, Robert T., 210n.23
Chirico, Giorgio de, 130–31, 144, 226n.20
Christiani, Dounia Bunis, 237n.39
Church, Catholic, 68, 70–71, 75, 78, 87, 164
Classicism, 7, 9, 42, 47
Coleridge, Samuel Taylor, 19, 37, 98
Collins, Joseph, 234n.27, 235n.33
Communism, 190–91, 237n.46
Conrad, Joseph, 202, 204
    *Lord Jim*, 18
    *Under Western Eyes*, 202
Constable, John, 213n.9
Corbett, David, 230n.6
Corday, Charlotte, 201
Cork, Richard, 213n.10
Council of Trent, 78
*Criterion, The*, 227n.22
Criticism, Marxist, 193, 205
Cubism, 11, 30, 31
Currie, Robert, 213n.4

Daniel, Arnaut, 204
Dante, 66–69, 112, 158, 159, 179, 204
    *Inferno*, 66, 89, 112, 179
    Letter to Can Grande, 66
    *Paradiso*, 66–67, 112
Dasenbrock, Reed Way, 34, 36, 211n.25, 212n.39, 215n.22, 215n.24
Deconstruction, 161 see also Post-structuralism
Defoe, Daniel, 22
De Man, Paul, 17
De Maupassant, Guy, 235n.31
Derrida, Jacques, 18, 69, 217n.5, 232n.14, 234n.25
Desire, 47, 100–04, 113
    and fragmentation, 58, 61–62
    and history, 203
    and kinesis, 57
    for knowledge, 52
    and narrative, 109–11
    rejection of, 49, 52
    for satiation, 63
    and selfhood, 101–02
    and social forces, 200, 202–03
    for synthesis, 68
    and temporality, 57, 139
    and violence, 58
    for wholeness, 100
    and writing, 105–07
Dialectic, 35, 68, 86, 98, 189, 190
    and adultery, 107–11
    and the father, 194
    and mimesis, 176–77
    and politics, 97
    rejection of, 192–93, 194
    and synthesis, 68, 87, 97–8, 113
    two meanings of, 97, 98–99
    and the Vortex, 192, 194
Dickens, Charles, 125–26
    *Our Mutual Friend*, 124, 125, 226n.13
    *The Pickwick Papers*, 12, 237n.40
Dionysus, 129
Dohmen, William F., 230n.6
*Doppelgänger*, 150, 195 see also Doubles
Dostoyevsky, Fyodor, 10, 119
Doubles, Gothic, 61–62 see also *Doppelgänger*
Dream work, 166, 168, 233n.23

Earwig, 165, 233n.21
Easter Rising (1916), 140, 143, 184
Economics, 190, 192
    and character, 125
Egoism, 51–54, 57–59, 60–62
*Egoist, The*, 8, 195, 241n.9
    see also *The New Freewoman*
Eilenberg, Susan, 19
Eisenstein, Sergei, 236n.37, 238n.52
Eliot, T. S., 4, 9, 16, 19, 170, 208n.2, 227n.22
    and impersonality, 3
    and myth, 136
    and Ezra Pound, 204
    "*Ulysses*, Order and Myth," 9
    *The Waste Land*, 204
Ellmann, Richard, 90–91, 92, 100, 211n.27, 219n.17, 236n.37
Empson, William, 222n.36
Epistemology, 136, 166
Epstein, E. L., 218n.8
Eroticism, see Sexuality
Evenden, Michael, 216n.36
Expressionism, 32
Externality, 118, 120–21, 123
    and aesthetics, 29–30

capitulation to, 58–59, 62
fear of, 138, 139, 141
opposition to, 32, 36, 47, 51–53, 60–61, 120
and selfhood, 40–41
and the will, 39, 45
versus internality, 119–20, 122–23, 130–31

Fables, 155, 177–81, 181–82, 186–90
and myth, 181–82
and politics, 182–87
Fascism, 141, 184, 190, 191
Felton, John, 241n.9
Ferrer, Daniel, 13
Flory, Wendy Stallard, 215n.24
Ford, Ford Madox, 55, 204
Formalism, Russian, 23
Forster, E. M., 149
Foshay, Toby Avard, 216n.27
Frazer, Sir James George: *The Golden Bough*, 130, 136–37, 143–44
Freud, Sigmund, 159, 166–67, 168, 231n.10, 233n.17
 *Civilization and its Discontents*, 58
 "The Dream Work," 234n.24
 "The Theme of the Three Caskets," 231n.10
 *Totem and Taboo*, 96
Fry, Roger, 214n.20
Futurism, 11, 30, 32, 36, 42
Futurism, Russian, 48

Gaddis, William, 205
Gaudier-Brzeska, Henri, 35
Gawsworth, John, 224n.2
General Post Office, Dublin, 184
General Strike (1926), 143–49
Genest, Saint, 126
Gestapo, 191
Gifford, Don, 219n.15
Gilbert, Stuart, 9, 86, 90, 220n.26, 229n.37
Glasheen, Adaline, 153, 229n.37, 239n.59
Gnomon, as narrative symbol, 160–61
Goldberg, S. L., 90, 229n.37
Goldman, Arnold, 208n.8, 210n.22
Gombrich, E. H., 213n.9
Graham, Freda, 240n.3
Greene, Robert: *Groats-Worth of Witte*, 102–03

Griffith, Arthur, 201
Griffith, D. W., 238n.52
Grimm, Brothers, 181

Hart, Clive, 219n.20, 220n.23
Hayman, David, 91, 223n.40
Hegel, Georg, 17, 59, 60, 97, 98, 99, 190
Henke, Suzette, 223n.39
Herr, Cheryl, 211n.27, 221n.30
Herring, Phillip H., 233n.23
History, contemporary, 183, 184, 191, 199–200, 201
and desire, 203
as dream, 193
and imperialism, 139
and language, 181–82, 185, 192
and memory, 156
and narrative, 159
processes of, 4
and space, 139
subsumption of, 199
transmission of, 83–84
and vision, 184
Hoffmann, E. T. A., 213n.4
Homer, 86, 88
Homosexuality and homoeroticism, 125, 138, 200, 220n.27
Hulme, T. E., 42, 44, 205
Hyde, Douglas, 85–86, 95–96, 105
Hyde Park, 143, 147

Imagism, 35
Impressionism, 32
Incest, 200
Interior monologue, 117, 168
Irish Civil War (1922), 202

Jameson, Fredric, 13–14, 15, 16, 28, 137, 141, 200–01, 212n.39, 215n.24, 224n.1, 225n.6, 225n.8, 227n.26, 237n.43, 240n.6
Jolas, Eugene, 110–11
Joll, James, 237n.44
Joyce, James, aesthetics of, 3, 6–7, 17–18, 19–20, 113–15
and collaboration, 18, 204
criticism on, 9–13, 206
and Dante, 66–67, 112, 204
and history, 199–200
and individuality, 200
and modernism, 2–3, 7–8, 15–16, 19, 23, 203, 206–07

and opposition, 4, 6-7, 17-18,
    205-06
parodied by Lewis, 8
pattern of career, 7-8
and philosophic structure, 21-23
and politics, 15-16, 19, 115, 189-95,
    202-03
reaction to criticism, 3
and violence, 199
Works: *Chamber Music*, 169
*Dubliners*, 7, 20, 231n.12
    "The Dead," 203
    "A Painful Case," 77
    "The Sisters," 160-61
*Exiles*, 13
*Finnegans Wake*, aesthetics in, 156,
    168, 170-71, 173, 182, 183, 187
    audibility and the ear in, 171,
        174-77, 177-78, 180
    cinema in, 177, 236n.37, 238n.52
    contemporary history in, 190-91,
        199-200
    and "The Dead," 203
    father and dialectic in, 194
    father as origin in, 158-59, 162,
        163-65, 175, 177
    father and repression in, 185-86,
        194
    father versus sons in, 167, 199
    footwear in, 170, 235n.30
    forgery in, 188
    the Letter in, 157, 161, 166, 169,
        170, 171, 172, 173, 181, 196
    Lewis in, 3, 8, 18, 22-23, 153-56,
        167-70, 171-73, 177-81, 183-85,
        186-88, 191-97
    metaphysics in, 156, 165, 172, 176,
        178-79, 189, 190
    metonymy and metaphor in, 166
    philosophic relation to *Ulysses*, 163
    photography in, 173-74
    radio in, 236n.36
    reading in, 187, 190
    status as dream, 166, 177
    totalitarianism in, 184-85, 190-91,
        194
    troping in, 157, 166-67, 170-71,
        176-77, 180, 186, 192-93, 194,
        196
    visuality and the eye in, 168,
        171-72, 174-77, 177-81, 183, 184
*Giacomo Joyce*, 105

*A Portrait of the Artist as a Young Man*,
    8, 10, 12, 19, 67, 71, 72, 74, 93, 95,
    114, 143, 174, 195, 202, 208n.8,
    227n.21
*Stephen Hero*, 7, 96, 220n.25
*Ulysses*, adultery and language in,
    107-10, 187
    and *The Apes of God*, 8, 22, 115-17,
        133-35, 148-52, 156, 198
    conflicting interpretations of, 13,
        90-93, 205-06
    critical defenses of, 9-13
    Dante and, 66-68, 112
    dialectic and, 189, 190
    exclusion in, 68, 71-73, 81-82, 89,
        94-96
    father and son in, 93-94, 95-96,
        101, 103
    figurations of attack in, 72-73
    and gender, 104
    and history, 77-78, 82-84, 200, 203
    lecture on Shakespeare in, 68, 86,
        87, 90-104, 104-05, 107, 109-11,
        113-14, 158, 161, 199
    Lewis's criticisms of, 2-3, 156, 168
    and myth, 136
    national identity and language in,
        72, 76-77
    national identity and representation
        in, 83
    performance in, 114-15
    referentiality in, 18, 113-14, 163,
        166
    schemata to, 21, 86
    style versus content in, 16
    Chapters in: "Aeolus," 112,
        223n.38
    "Circe," 20, 65, 73, 82, 97, 103,
        133, 148, 219n.14, 222n.38,
        237n.42
    "Cyclops," 11, 133-35
    "Ithaca," 6, 65, 107, 108, 110,
        222n.38
    "Nestor," 73, 79, 105
    "Oxen of the Sun," 111, 162-63,
        238n.50
    "Penelope," 108, 110
    "Proteus," 80, 100, 105, 176,
        223n.38
    "Scylla and Charybdis," 21, 69,
        86-104, 109-10, 111
    "Telemachus," 77, 110

Jung, Carl, 233n.17

Kain, Richard M., 12
Kandinsky, Vasilly, 32
Kant, Immanuel, 41
Keats, John, 42
Kellogg, Robert, 91, 220n.26
Kenner, Hugh, 12–13, 91, 124, 137, 210n.24, 223n.40, 224n.2 230n.6, 234n.23
Kettle, Thomas, 184
Kinnimont, Tom, 51

Lacan, Jacques, 18, 221n.31
  and metonymy, 105
Laocoon, 130–31, 144
Lawrence, D. H., 16
  *Women in Love*, 18
Lawrence, Karen, 219n.12, 223n.40
Law, Jules David, 218n.6
Leavis, F. R., 20
Le Fanu, Sheridan, 86
Lernout, Geert, 218n.5
Lessing: *Laocoon*, 131–32, 227n.21
Levenson, Michael, 211n.25, 215n.26
Levin, Harry, 12
Levine, Jennifer, 229n.37
Lévi-Strauss, Claude, 136, 227n.25
Lewis, Wyndham, and authoritarianism, 16, 199
  and collaboration, 18, 204
  and Joseph Conrad, 202
  criticism about, 13–14, 16–17
  effect on Joycean criticism, 9–13
  in *Finnegans Wake*, 3, 8, 18, 22–23, 153–56, 167–70, 171–73, 177–81, 183–85, 186–88, 191–97
  and history, 199–200
  and ideological analysis, 14–15, 16–17
  and individuality, 200
  and Marxist criticism, 205
  and modernism, 2, 203–04, 206–07
  and opposition, 2, 5, 7, 17–18, 205
  pattern of career, 7–8
  and philosophic structure, 20–23
  and politics, 14–15, 16–17, 19, 115, 199–200, 200–01
  and post-modernism, 206
  and primitivism, 172
  and style, 20
  and violence, 199
  Paintings and drawings: "Anti-War Design," 216n.34
    "The Duc de Joyeux Sings," 11
    "Plan of War," 216n.31
    "Portrait of an Englishwoman," 172, 235n.32
    "Slow Attack," 216n.31
    "Timon of Athens," 216n.34
    "Two Soldiers," 216n.34
  Works: "The 1956 Retrospective at the Tate Gallery," 214n.11
    "An Analysis of the Mind of James Joyce," 9
    *The Apes of God*, declared unreadability of, 22
      desire in, 200
      fear of vaccination in, 237n.38
      gossip in, 147
      history and, 141–44, 147–48, 151, 193
      metonymy in, 133
      myth in, 128–37, 138, 141
      national identity in, 138, 141
      performance and, 122–23, 126
      philosophic relation to *Blast*, 121, 133, 163, 200
      police in, 146–47
      and politics, 18, 138–44, 147–50, 151–52
      publication of, 195
      repression in, 125–26, 143
      as response to Roger Fry, 214n.20
      rooms in, 118–23, 127, 139, 143, 149
      and satiric language, 11, 169, 210n.20
      and *Ulysses*, 8, 22, 115–17, 133–35, 148–52, 156
      xenophobia in, 139–40
    *The Art of Being Ruled*, 43, 47, 225n.11, 233n.21
    *Blast*, 14, 15, 21, 43, 113–14, 166, 168, 169, 213n.4, 229n.32, 236n.34
      abstraction in, 30, 32, 33, 34–36, 39, 40, 55–56
      aesthetics in, 28, 29–42, 45–48
      block typography of, 172, 184
      failure of transcendence in, 57, 61–62
      Joyce blessed in, 18
      naturalism in, 30–34, 37–41, 44, 45–46
      philosophic relation to *The Apes of God*, 121, 133, 163, 200

# Index

politics in, 200–01, 240n.3
position of *Enemy of the Stars* in, 48–49, 54–56, 57
referentiality in, 18
relation to audience, 55
transcendence in, 38, 39–40, 49
*Blasting and Bombardiering*, 170, 234n.28, 234n.29, 235n.30, 241n.7
*The Caliph's Design: Architects! Where is your Vortex?*, 178, 234n.28
"Cantleman's Spring Mate," 208n.2, 215n.23
*The Childermass*, 8, 14, 15, 115, 141, 185, 191, 225n.9, 226n.16, 239n.55
*Collected Poems and Plays*, 215n.25, 217n.38
*Count Your Dead: They are Alive!*, 216n.34
*The Enemy*, 9
*Enemy of the Stars*, and the creative self, 21, 54–55, 127, 198–99
 and dramatic form, 29, 48, 55, 57, 59–60
 dream in, 51, 53, 60–61, 118
 as performance, 114
 position within *Blast*, 48–49, 54–56, 57
 and Romanticism, 21, 29, 59
 and style, 20, 55–57, 132
 temporality and desire equated in, 57, 139
 and Vorticism, 48–49, 54–56, 57–58
"Essay on the Objective of Plastic Art in Our Time," 31, 213n.8, 241n.8
*Hitler*, 237n.46
*The Hitler Cult*, 238n.46
*The Human Age*, 14, 241n.9
*The Lion and the Fox*, 217n.36, 240n.5
*The Man of the World*, 169
*Men Without Art*, 15, 57, 136, 151, 210n.20, 213n.4, 228n.29, 235n.31
*Monstre Gai*, 130
"Mr. Zagreus and the Split-Man," 227n.22
*Mrs. Dukes' Million*, 27–28, 118
*Paleface: The Philosophy of the Melting Pot*, 208n.3
"Prevalent Design," 1, 214n.15
*The Revenge for Love*, 14
"A Review of Contemporary Art," 36
*Rude Assignment: A Narrative of My Career Up-to-date*, 29, 57, 233n.21
*Self Condemned*, 216n.29, 225n.7

*Snooty Baronet*, 228n.31
"Super-Nature versus Super-Real," 212n.38, 216n.32, 226n.20
*Tarr*, 8, 10, 11, 14, 15, 19, 28, 37, 43, 57, 118–19, 122, 123, 141, 183, 195, 214n.14, 237n.41
*Time and Western Man*, 2, 6, 8, 9, 12, 13, 28, 43, 122, 153, 155, 168, 200, 202, 209n.13, 210n.19, 212n.36, 226n.16, 233n.21, 237n.40, 239n.57, 241n.6
*The Tyro*, 18, 27, 235n.33
"Tyros and Portraits," 213n.7
*The Wild Body*, 8, 25–27, 118–19, 122
 "Beau Séjour," 27, 118–19
 "Bestre," 25–27, 29, 62–64, 113–14, 122, 171, 195, 196
 "Inferior Religions," 226n.13
 "The Pole," 228n.30
 "A Soldier of Humour," 26–27
 "Some Innkeepers and Bestre," 27, 62
Linati, Carlo, 219n.17
Lukács, Georg, 2, 16, 125, 225n.11, 239n.58
Lyotard, Jean-François, 201

MacCabe, Colin, 211n.27, 221n.34, 222n.37
Machery, Pierre, 240n.6
Machiavelli, Niccolò, 217n.36
Macilwaine, Herbert C., 219n.13
Mahaffey, Vicki, 210n.22, 212n.35, 221n.35, 234n.25
Maimonides, Moses, 84
Mallarmé, Stéphane, 88
Manganiello, Dominic, 184, 211n.27, 229n.37, 237n.45, 239n.54
Marinetti, Filippo Tommaso, 6
Marriage, 99–101, 149–50, 158, 192, 203
 and language, 109–12
Marx, Karl, 125, 192–93
 *Das Kapital*, 239n.57
Marxism, 141, 190–91
Materer, Timothy, 209n.11, 210n.23, 213n.10
McGreevy, Thomas, 153, 230n.2
McHugh, Roland, 231n.11, 233n.19
McMillan, Dougald, 230n.6
Melville, Herman, 46, 144
 *Moby Dick*, 228n.31

Meredith, George, 85
Metz, Christian, 236n.37
Miller, D. A., 228n.32
Miller, J. Hillis, 232n.14
Modernism, 2, 4, 8–9, 19, 20–21, 23, 35, 203–05
  and flux, 11
  Marxist criticism of, 2, 193
  and myth, 136–37
  and politics, 14–17, 19, 149–50, 198–203
Morris-dance, 83, 219n.13
Mowat, Charles Loch, 229n.33
Munton, Alan, 215n.26

Narcissus, 46, 47, 58
Nashe, Thomas, 12, 169
National allegory, 141, 227n.27
Nationalism, 7, 183–84, 186, 189
National Socialism, 191, 237n.46
*New Freewoman, The*, 195
  see also *The Egoist*
Nietzsche, Friedrich, 37, 39, 129, 159, 204, 206
  *The Gay Science*, 29, 226n.16
Noon, William T., 69, 90
Normand, Tom, 211n.29
Norris, Margot, 210n.22, 211n.27, 218n.10, 222n.37, 231n.14, 233n.23, 234n.25
*Nouveau roman*, 205

O'Connell, Daniel, 214n.16
Oedipus, 159
*Our Exagmination Round His Factification for Incamination of Work in Progress*, 9, 153, 154

Palestrina, Giovanni Pierluigi da: *Missa Papae Marcelli*, 78
Parnell, Charles Stewart, 203
Pearse, Patrick, 184, 185
Peter the Painter, 183
Phaedrus, *Fables*, 182
Picasso, Pablo, 2, 32
Plato, 69, 86–87, 91, 100, 119
  *The Symposium*, 100
Platonism, 32, 87–89, 111, 127, 166
  and Aristotelianism, 91–92
  and language, 107
  and mysticism, 98
  and myth, 136
  and narrative, 158

Poe, Edgar Allan, 24–29, 62
  and Vorticism, 27–28
  "The Philosophy of Composition," 28
  "The System of Doctor Tarr and Professor Fether," 28
  "The Tell-Tale Heart," 24–25, 27, 28, 62
Poggioli, Renato, 217n.40, 237n.38
Politics, 69, 138–44, 148–49, 156, 199–200
  and aesthetics, 15–17, 19, 186, 196–97
  and allegory, 182
  and dialectic, 97
  and fables, 182–86
  and the individual, 7, 42–43
  Joyce and, 15–16, 19, 115, 189–95, 202–03
  and language, 19, 71–72, 73–74, 76–77, 79, 82, 145–46, 151, 206
  Lewis and, 14–15, 16–17, 19, 115, 199–200, 200–01
  and modernism, 14–17, 19, 149–50, 198–203
  and narrative, 115
  and ontology, 137–38
  and representation, 4, 128, 141–43, 183, 189–95
  and space, 139
  and violence, 140, 143–44, 148, 199–200
  and Vorticism, 201
  and writing, 88, 189–90
Porteus, Hugh, 7
Post-modernism, 206
Post-structuralism, 4, 13, 16–17, 171 see also Deconstruction
Pound, Ezra, 4, 8, 14, 16, 27, 35, 170, 204, 224n.2
  *The Cantos*, 226n.15
  *Gaudier-Brzeska*, 214n.13
Printing terms, 46, 168
Proust, Marcel, 2, 138
Psychoanalysis, 14, 62, 185
Pynchon, Thomas, 205

Quodlibet, as musical form, 196

Rabaté, John-Michel, 222n.37
Rank, Otto, 61
Reification, 125
Representation, and authority, 19, 147, 172, 204
  and consciousness, 41

as control, 145–46
and exile, 84
Joyce's and Lewis's theories of, 21–22, 113, 170–71, 180–81, 204–06
and myth, 130–33, 135–37
and narrative, 157
and noumenality, 150
and opposition, 1–5
in painting, 29–35
and politics, 4, 128, 141–43, 183, 189–95
and repetition, 103
and satire, 12–13
and sensory impressions, 44
troping as, 166–67
and violence, 119
Restuccia, Frances L., 212n.35
Revolution, 151, 199
Richardson, Alan, 59–60, 216n.35
Richardson, Samuel, 22
Riquelme, John Paul, 212n.35, 215n.21, 223n.40, 234n.26
Roberts, William, 34
Rodin, Auguste, 11
Romance and Romanticism, and Bergson, 43–44
capitulation to, 47, 61–62, 199
rejection of, 27, 31, 41–42, 49
and temporality, 44
and Vorticism, 21, 60, 61–62
Ruskin, John, 8
"The Nature of Gothic," 43
Russell, John, 225n.6

Sage, Robert, 154
Said, Edward W., 16, 218n.6
Sartre, Jean Paul, 126, 191
Satire, 12–13, 19, 20, 116, 128, 149–50, 204
equated with fiction, 11–12, 204
of myth, 136–37
"non-moral," 150
Saussure, Ferdinand de, 69, 136
Schenker, Daniel, 211n.24, 215n.24
Schoenberg, Arnold: *Pierrot Lunaire*, 130
Schutte, William, 92
Science, as improper justification for art, 31, 173
Script, see Writing
Sedgwick, Eve Kosofsky, 125
Seidman, Robert J., 219n.15
Selfhood, and art, 5, 7, 17, 29, 39–41, 42–48, 108–109

and desire, 102
and externality, 40–41
and fragmentation, 18, 25, 44, 45–48, 57–59, 77, 84–86, 98, 100–01, 103–04, 105–06
and language, 68–69, 71–72, 87–88, 92, 104
misrepresentation of, 63
and modernity, 3
and power, 95–96
rejection of, 53–54, 62
theories of, 49–54. 61–62
and Vorticism, 39–41, 48, 61–62
and wholeness, 2, 91, 92–93, 100–01, 102–03
Sexuality, 58, 100–103, 111, 126, 139, 200
and language, 187
and politics, 202–03
and repetition, 101, 103
and writing, 104–07, 111
Shakespeare, Characters: Alcibiades, 195
Coriolanus, 217n.36
Hamlet, 93–96, 107, 187
Timon of Athens, 217n.36
Plays and poems: *Cymbeline*, 111
*Hamlet*, 89, 90, 93–96, 101, 107, 223n.38
*King Lear*, 231n.10
*The Merchant of Venice*, 100, 142
*Othello*, 111
*Timon of Athens*, 195, 217n.36
"Venus and Adonis," 101
*The Winter's Tale*, 111
see also James Joyce, Works: *Ulysses*
Sharp, Cecil J., 219n.13
Sherry, Vincent, 211n.25, 211n.29, 213n.39
Siege of Sidney Street, 183
Socialism, 43, 239n.53
Society of Authors, 195
Sophocles, 60, 158, 159
Space, as aesthetic category, 2, 4, 11, 131–32, 172–73, 180, 187
fictional, 126
and history, 139
internal versus external, 119–23
transgression of, 126–29
Speech, see Voice
Spoo, Robert E., 218n.8
Squaring the circle, 65–67, 68, 109, 161
and the Vortex, 113

Stein, Gertrude, 22
Stirner, Max, 51–53, 60, 199
　*Der Einzige und Sein Eigentum*, 51–52
Stoker, Bram, 86
Surrealism and Surrealists, 18, 56, 236n.37
Swift, Jonathan, 12, 155
　*The Battle of the Books*, 128
Symons, Julian, 209n.11
Synge, John Millington, 19

Tanner, Tony, 222n.36, 223n.39
*Tel Quel*, 238n.53
Teleologies, 77, 193, 199
Temporality, see Time
Theoharis, Theoharis Constantine, 208n.6
Theology, 66, 68, 78, 93, 94, 99
Theosophy, 87, 90
Thoth, 111, 128, 187
Time, as aesthetic category, 1–3, 28, 42, 43–44, 48, 179, 200
　and desire, 57, 139
　and Joyce, 11, 153–54
Transcendental philosophy, 172
*transition*, 191
Trilling, Lionel, 15

Vampires and vampirism, 85, 105, 144
Vico, Giambattista, *The New Science*:
　cycles in, 156, 160
　and fables, 181–82
　and the formation of states, 191–93
　and language, 159, 163–65, 171, 175, 181–82, 188, 191–92
　and Marx, 239n.57
Victorianism, 28, 42, 46, 151
Violence, and desire, 58
　and metaphor, 38
　and modernity, 151–52
　and noumenality, 150
　and politics, 140, 143–44, 148, 199–200
　and representation, 119
　room as enclosure of, 120
　and sexuality, 58, 118–19
　and the will, 39
Virgil, 66, 81
　*The Aeneid*, 132

Voice, 79, 83, 92–94, 171–72
　of the father, 164–65
　and lending, 104
　and myth, 181–82
　and politics, 186
　and singularity, 190
　and writing, 18, 69, 79–86, 88–90, 91, 92–93, 95–96, 171
Vortex, 34–35, 38, 40, 55, 196
　and dialectic, 192, 194
　and the squaring of the circle, 113
Vorticism, 35–37, 127, 172
　and abstraction, 32–33
　Bergson and, 45
　and *Enemy of the Stars*, 48–49, 54–56, 57–58
　and Poe, 27–28
　and politics, 201
　and Romanticism, 21, 60, 61–62
　and selfhood, 39–41, 48, 61–62
　and style, 21, 55–56, 59–60, 117, 132
　and the will, 39, 42

Wagner, Geoffrey, 230n.6
Watt, Ian, 108
Wees, William C., 213n.10, 240n.3
Wellington Monument, 203
West, Rebecca, 10, 55, 154, 230n.3
Wilde, Oscar, 220n.27, 226n.14
Williams, William Carlos, 154
Wittgenstein, Ludwig: *Tractatus Logico-Philosophicus*, 165, 233n.22
Wordsworth, William, 19, 59
Writing, as clothing, 162
　and politics, 88, 189–90
　and sexuality, 104–07, 111
　and speech, 18, 69, 79–86, 88–90, 91, 92–93, 95–96, 171
　as vandalism, 172

Xenophobia, within the British Isles, 139–40

Yeats, William Butler, 16, 76
　"Who Goes With Fergus?," 84–85

Zagreus, as version of Dionysus, 129–30, 143–44

Plea
finis
b